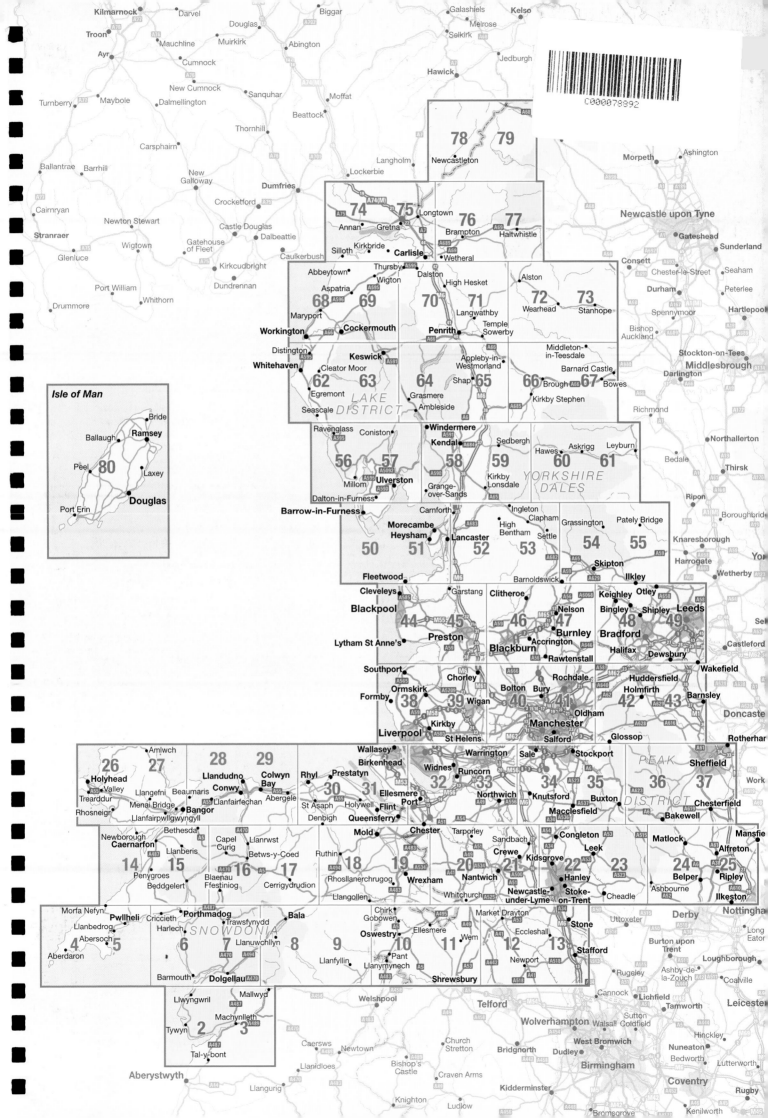

Outdoors

Nature reserves & conservation areas

For outdoor activities, see *Sports*

Cheetham Park/Eastwood RSPB *near Stalybridge, Greater Manchester* A nature reserve adjoining one of the oldest RSPB reserves in the country. ☎01270 610180 **41 E8**

Formby Squirrel Reserve★ *Formby, Merseyside* A nature reserve owned by the National Trust and home to one of the last thriving colonies of red squirrels in the UK. Pine woodland and dune walks available. ☎01704 878591 **38 D2**

Gelt Woods *near Brampton, Cumbria* A RSPB reserve forming a superb walking site and containing a rock with an inscription carved by a Roman soldier in the 3rd century. **65 B8**

Healey Dell Nature Reserve *Rochdale, Greater Manchester* A beauty spot and wildlife sanctuary with dramatic waterfalls that powered ancient mills, a nature trail on a disused 1800s railway line and 100ft viaduct, and a visitor centre with an exhibition on the industrial heritage of the reserve. ☎01706 350459 **41 B6**

Hilbre Island Nature Reserve★ *Wirral, Merseyside* A reserve comprising three tidal islands at the mouth of the Dee Estuary, boasting seals, wading and migratory birds, and a famous dinosaur footprint. Advance permits required; tide times must be checked before setting out. ☎0151 648 4371 **31 B5**

Hodbarrow Lagoon RSPB Reserve *Haverigg, Cumbria* A site formed by the flooding of an iron ore mine, home to more than 100 bird species and containing slag banks that provide breeding ground for terns. There's also a hide, two lighthouse towers and the walls of a windmill. ☎0191 281 3366 **56 E4**

Leighton Moss Nature Reserve *near Silverdale, Lancashire* An RSPB reserve with reed beds providing a habitat for rare species such as the bittern. Demonstrations and guided rambles offered. ☎01524 701601 **58 E3**

Marshall's Arm *Hartford, Cheshire* Vale Royal's first nature reserve, located on an old meander of the River Weaver, with open water, reedbeds, woodland and meadows providing habitats for birds and wildflowers. **33 E7**

Marshside RSPB Reserve *Southport, Merseyside* An important site for wintering waterfowl, with two birdwatching hides. ☎01704 533333 **38 A3**

Marton Mere Reserve *Blackpool* A habitat for breeding and wintering birds, with various rare species. Guided walks and nature rambles are available. ☎01253 830805 **44 C3**

Mere Sands Wood *Holmeswood Road, Rufford, Lancashire* A Lancashire Wildlife Trust reserve with seven hides for viewing wildfowl, waders and other wildlife. ☎01704 821809 **39 A6**

Morfa Madryn Reserve *Llanfairfechan, Conwy* A bird reserve with views of the high-tide oystercatcher roost on the shingle spit at Glan y Môr Elias. **28 D3**

Pickering's Pasture *Halebank, Widnes, Halton* A reserve on a former salt marsh and reclaimed refuse tip, with acres of wildflower meadows commanding views across the Mersey with its wintering wildfowl and waders. There's a hide to watch birds on Hale Marshes, a Site of Special Scientific Interest. ☎0151 425 4706 **32 C5**

Risley Moss Local Nature Reserve *Ordnance Avenue, Birchwood, Cheshire* A reserve with paths through woodland and meadows, an Observation Tower with views of one of the UK's last mosslands, a Woodland Hide, natural sculptures and Ranger-led events. ☎01925 824339 **33 A8**

RSPB Conwy Nature Reserve *Llandudno Junction, Conwy* A feeding and roosting site for ducks, geese and wading birds, with short nature trails, a visitor centre, binocular hire and hides. ☎01492 584091 **29 D6**

St Annes Nature Reserve *North Promenade, St. Anne's, Lancashire* The UK's best surviving example of a sand dune habitat. ☎01253 724141 **44 E3**

St Bees Head RSPB Reserve *St. Bees, Cumbria* A RSPB reserve on the only designated Heritage Coast between Wales and Scotland, the site of England's only breeding black guillemots. **62 D2**

WWT Martin Mere *Burscough, Lancashire* A huge Wildfowl and Wetlands Trust site with thousands of wild birds in their natural habitat. In winter, ducks, geese and swans form spectacular feeding flocks on the flooded wetlands. ☎01704 895181 **39 B5**

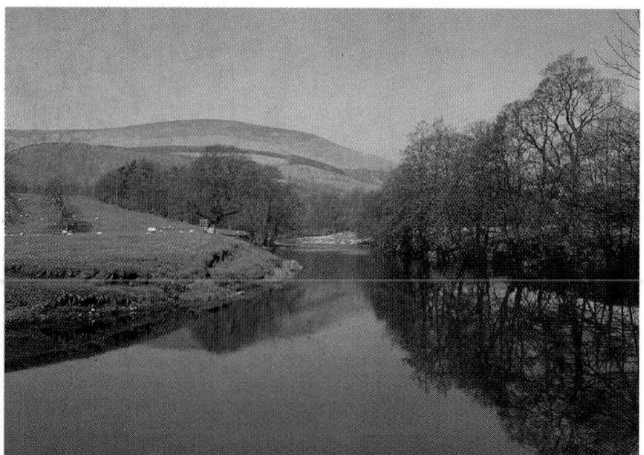

River Hodder, Whitewell, Ribble Valley

Country & forest parks

Arrowe Country Park *Arrowe Park Road, Upton, Merseyside* Four hundred acres of parkland, including orienteering areas, woodland trails, a lake, an adventure playground and a golf course. ☎0151 678 4200 **31 B7**

Beacon Country Park *Skelmersdale, Lancashire* A 300-acre park on the slopes of Ashurst Beacon above Skelmersdale, with woodland walks and spectacular views. Activities include horseriding, orienteering, kite-flying and golf, and there are exhibitions and displays. ☎01695 622794 **39 C6**

Black Rocks Country Park *Cromford, Derbyshire* A wind- and rain-sculpted gritstone outcrop with rock-climbing, forest trails, an orienteering course and a visitor centre. ☎01629 540696 **24 C3**

Blackleach Country Park *Hill Top Road, off Bolton Road, Walkden, Greater Manchester* A 100-acre greenbelt on the site of a former chemical works, with wildlife, nature walks, fishing on the reservoir, and a visitor centre. ☎0161 790 7746 **40 D3**

Clifton Country Park *Clifton House Road, Salford, Greater Manchester* An 80-acre countryside park with a wet-earth colliery, woodland, wetland, ponds, a fishing lake, pathways, a sensory garden, an arboretum, a working farm with shire horses and a visitor centre. ☎0161 793 4219 **41 E5**

Cuerden Valley Park *Chorley, Lancashire* A 600-acre park along the River Lostock valley, with woods, grasslands, ponds, a river, a lake, part of which is fenced off as a nature reserve, and the remains of the lower Kem Mill bleach and print works. **39 A8**

Eastham Country Park *Eastham, Merseyside* A Victorian pleasure garden turned beauty spot on the banks of the Mersey. ☎0906 680 6886 **32 C2**

Etherow Country Park *Compstall, Greater Manchester* One of Britain's first country parks, established in 1968 around an old cotton mill, covering 240 acres, and forming the starting point of the Goyt Way, a 10-mile footpath to Whaley Bridge. Its nature reserve is a designated Site of Special Scientific Interest. ☎0161 427 6937 **35 A6**

Fell Foot Park *Newby Bridge, Cumbria* A park on the shores of Lake Windermere, with magnificent scenery. ☎015395 31273 **57 C8**

Great Orme Country Park★ *Llandudno, Conwy* A limestone headland designated a Special Area of Conservation, Site of Special Scientific Interest and Heritage Coast, containing some famous Kashmiri goats and the Great Orme Bronze Age Copper Mines. The refurbished Visitor Centre has interactive displays and a live camera link to a seabird colony. ☎01492 874151 **28 C5**

Greenfield Valley Heritage and Country Park *Holywell, Flintshire* A park containing St Winefride's Well (see *Religious buildings*), the ruins of the 12th-century Basingwerk Abbey and various mill buildings (many of them scheduled ancient monuments), a reconstructed Victorian school, farmhouses, five lakes, and woodland walks. There's also a farm museum and a museum about naturalist and explorer Thomas Pennant. ☎01352 714172 **31 D5**

Greenwood Forest Park★ *Y Felinheli (Port Dinorwic), Gwynedd* A family attraction with a 70m Great Green Run, the longest slide in Wales, longbow shooting, log sawing, peacock feeding, a Forest Theatre, mini tractors, stiltwalking, and woodland crafts and sculptures. The visitor centre has displays on ancient forests and modern conservation. ☎01248 670076 **27 F7**

Gwydyr Forest Park *Betws-y-Coed, Conwy* A forest park ranging across eastern Snowdonia's hills, with more than 20 miles of trails through mountain forest, plus riding, canoeing and mountain biking. ☎01492 640578 **16 C3**

Halewood Park *Okell Drive, Halewood, Halton* A mature birchwood and oak woodland set up on the site of an old railway junction, with footpaths, cycle tracks and bridleways. Part of the Trans-Pennine Trail and the Mersey Forest. ☎0151 488 6151 **32 B4**

Hollingworth Lake Country Park *Rakewood Road, Littleborough, Greater Manchester* The gateway to the open moorlands of the South Pennines, with a lake (with fishing, watersports and a pleasure launch), a bird hide, footpaths and trails, and regular guided walks, cycle trips and outdoor activities. ☎01706 373421 **41 A7**

Holyhead Breakwater Country Park *Holyhead, Isle of Anglesey* A disused quarry with a large seabird population, nature trails and a visitor centre. **26 C2**

Kilnsey Park *Kilnsey, North Yorkshire* Situated beneath Kilnsey Crag in the Yorkshire Dales, a 'countryside experience' with a squirrel trail, a nature trail, a freshwater aquarium, fly-fishing lakes and fishing pools for children. ☎01756 752150 **54 B3**

Lever Park *Rivington Lane, Horwich, Greater Manchester* A country park within the West Pennine moors, with a reservoir, arboretum and pinetum, plus the remains of Lord Leverhulme's Japanese terraced gardens, two cruck barns, the ruined replica of Liverpool Castle and Rivington Pike, an ancient beacon. ☎01204 691549 **40 B1**

Little Budworth Country Park *Little Budworth, Cheshire* Lowland heathland, a remnant of the ancient hunting forest of Mara and Mondrum, with purple heather, green woodpeckers and a Heathland Trail. ☎01606 593133 **20 A4**

Loggerheads Country Park *Denbighshire* Woodland trails and guided walks (an Industrial Trail tracing the history of leadmining in the park, a Nature Trail, and the Squirrel Nuttley children's trail), plus a Countryside Centre with displays. ☎01352 810586 **18 B4**

Moel Famau Country Park★ *Ruthin, Denbighshire* One of Wales' biggest country parks, covering about 2000 acres of uplands and containing the remains of three hillforts dating from 500BC to 43AD and a seven-mile stretch of the Offa's Dyke Trail, and providing a home to many bird of prey species. **18 C3**

Moses Gate Country Park *Rock Hall, Hall Lane, Bolton, Greater Manchester* Walking trails (part of the Kingfisher Way, an 11-mile trail through the Croal Irwell Valley, crosses the park), picnic areas, boating and a bird hide. ☎01204 334343 **40 C3**

Outwood Forest Park *Radcliffe, Greater Manchester* A former colliery now composed of woodland and a sculpture park, with views of the West Pennine moors. Traversed by the Outwood Trail, a three-mile route for walkers, cyclists and horseriders along a former railway. ☎0161 761 1438 **40 C4**

Padarn Country Park *Llanberis, Gwynedd* Nature, woodland and industrial trails, the Welsh Slate Museum, craft workshops, a watersports centre, Cwm Derwen Woodland Centre with its audio-visual displays, and an adventure playground. ☎01286 872014 **15 B7**

Prestwich Forest Park *Bury, Greater Manchester* A large park in the Irwell Valley, part of which is a Local Nature Reserve, containing the Philips and Drinkwater parks, the ancient woodlands of Mere Clough and Prestwich Clough, and the reclaimed land of Waterdale. **40 B4**

Reddish Vale Country Park *Stockport, Greater Manchester* A former industrial site with an impressive railway viaduct, a reservoir, a visitor centre next to the old mill lodges of a calico printing works, which provide a habitat for wildlife and stopoff point for migrating wildfowl, a butterfly park, and cycling and walking trails. ☎0161 477 5637 **35 A5**

Rivacre Valley Country Park *Ellesmere Port, Cheshire* More than 400 acres of woodland and wildflower meadows following the course of Rivacre Brook, with a self-guided nature trail and a ranger centre. ☎0151 357 1991 **32 D3**

River Lune Millennium Park★ *Salt Ayre, Lancaster, Lancashire* A park stretching 10 miles along the riverbank and including a sculpture trail, the modern Millennium Bridge alongside historic St George's Quay, the newly reopened Gray's Seat viewpoint (recommended by Wordsworth and painted by Turner), and cyclepaths and footpaths. ☎01524 328178 **51 C8**

Sankey Valley Country Park *St Helens, Merseyside* A park linking St Helens town centre to Spike Island at Widnes, via Warrington, with footpaths, a Site of Special Scientific Interest, fishing areas, a visitor centre (Blackbrook Road) and some of St Helen's most important historical landmarks. ☎01744 739252 **39 F8**

Stadt Moers Park *Pottery Lane, Whiston, Merseyside* A reclaimed landfill site forming part of the Mersey Forest and including nature reserves, wildflower meadows, a large pond, formal parkland and a visitor centre. Named after Knowsley's twin town of Moers in Germany. **32 A4**

Talkin Tarn Country Park *near Brampton, Cumbria* A 120-acre farmland and mature woodland site with a 65-acre glacial lake fed by underground streams, with windsurfing, canoeing, rowing and fishing facilities. There's also a permanent orienteering course and mountain bike hire. ☎016977 3129 **65 B8**

Ty Mawr Country Park *Cae Gwilym Lane, Cefn-mawr, Wrexham* A wildlife-rich, organically farmed country park on the banks of the Dee, with hay meadows, animal feeding sessions, a play area, a visitor centre and panoramic views. ☎01978 822780 **19 F6**

Whinlatter Forest Park *Keswick, Cumbria* England's only mountain forest, with 14 miles of roads suitable for walkers and cyclists, footpaths (including junior trails) and a forest playground. The visitor centre at Braithwaite has a working model of forest life and a walk-through badger sett. ☎01768 778469 **63 B8**

Wirral Country Park★ *Station Road, Thurstaston, Merseyside* Britain's first country park, created from an old train line to the coast in 1973 and including the Dee Estuary, one of the North West's last surviving wildernesses, and the sheltered inland 12-mile Wirral Way footpath. Summer activities include smugglers' trails, scavenger hunts and cruises to see seals. ☎0151 648 4371 **31 C6**

Wyre Estuary Country Park and Wyreside Ecology Centre★ *River Road, Stanah, Lancashire* An award-winning country park with outstanding disabled access and estuary and riverside views, based around the Ecology Centre. ☎01253 857890 **44 B4**

National Parks and AONBs

Anglesey AONB *Isle of Anglesey* An AONB taking in almost the entire Anglesey coastline, from steep limestone cliffs and sandy beaches in the east to rolling sand dunes in the south-west. **26 C4**

Forest of Bowland AONB *Lancashire* A spectacular biking area comprising the Forest of Bowland and Pendle Hill, with 11 routes for different abilities. **52 E4**

Lake District National Park★★ *Cumbria* A picturesque area of mountains, valleys and glacial lakes (15, including Conistion, Derwentwater, Ullswater and Windermere) that once inspired the Romantic poets, a National Park since the 1950s. The main towns are Ambleside, Keswick and Windermere. **63 C7**

Nidderdale AONB *Pateley Bridge, North Yorkshire* A wildlife-rich area ranging from high fells, upland reservoirs and heather moorland in Upper Nidderdale to farmed landscapes in the north and east, with eroded limestone caves and gorges below ground. ☎01423 711147 **55 B7**

North Pennines AONB *Cumbria* An unspoilt and remote area of high, wild moorland, green dales, rivers and waterfalls, the second-largest of the 41 AONBs in the country. **72 C5**

Peak District National Park★★ *Derbyshire and Staffordshire* A 555 square mile national park, Britain's first, situated at the southern end of the Pennines, covering covers parts of six counties, and roughly divided into the high, wild Dark Peak and the limestone White Peak with its craggy dales. ☎01629 816200 **36 B2**

Snowdonia National Park★★ *Gwynedd* The second largest National Park in the country, covering most of the county of Gwynedd and containing the Snowdonia mountain ranges and Cambrian Coast. ☎01766 770274 **15 E7**

Solway Coast AONB *Cumbria* An AONB with a new discovery centre (Liddell Street, Silloth-on-Solway) about the geography of the Solway Coast, including displays about how Romans, Vikings and medieval monks developed the area. ☎016973 33055 **68 C4**

Yorkshire Dales National Park★★ *North Yorkshire and Cumbria* A huge upland area designated a National Park in 1954, with visitor centres (exhibitions and tourist information) in Sedbergh (015396 20125), Reeth (01748 884059), Hawes (01969 667450), Grassington (01756 752748), Malham (01729 830363) and Aysgarth Falls (01969 663424). ☎015396 20125 **59 C8**

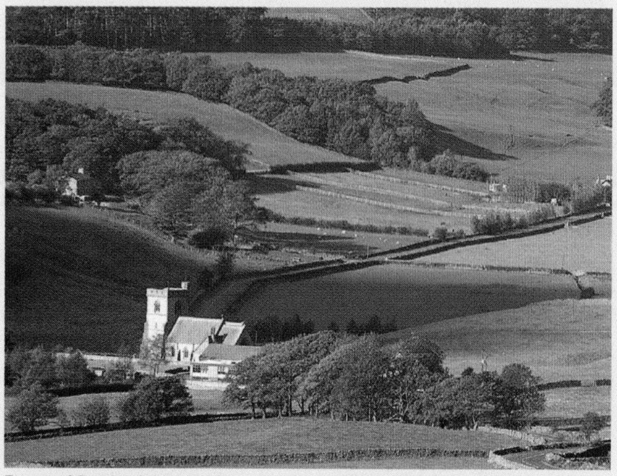

Forest of Bowland, Lancashire

Caves, caverns & potholes

Blue John Cavern *near Castleton, Derbyshire* Part natural cavern, part mine-workings, with natural chambers, fossils, and stalactites and stalagmites. ☎01433 620638 **36 C3**

Eldon Hole *Peak Forest, Derbyshire* The deepest pothole in the area, at almost 200ft, first descended in 1780 and now regularly explored by potholers. **36 D2**

Gaping Gill and Ingleborough Show Cave★ *Clapham, North Yorkshire* A spectacular site where Fell Beck drops from the moor into Britain's largest cavern, into which visitors can descend by bosun's chair at selected times of year. The floodlit show cave at the system's outlet has stalactites and stalagmites up to 350 million years old. ☎015242 51242 **53 A7**

How Stean Gorge *Lofthouse, North Yorkshire* An 80ft limestone ravine with narrow paths and footbridges, containing Tom Taylor's Cave complete with dripping stalactite. ☎04123 755666 **61 F8**

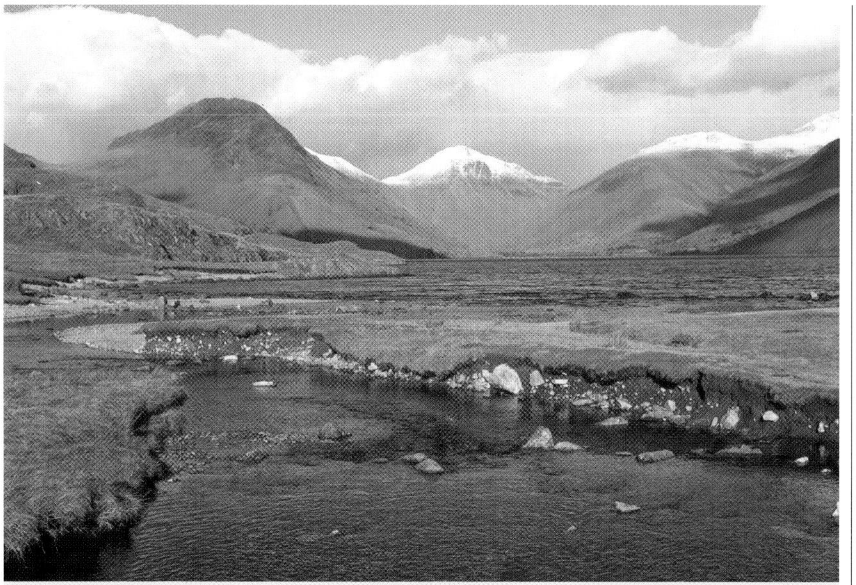
The Lakes, Cumbria

Peak Cavern★ *near Castleton, Derbyshire* The only entirely natural cavern of the four Castleton caverns and the least commercialised, with an entrance that was wide enough to accommodate several small cottages. Beyond the 200ft Great Cave is the Orchestral Chamber, where village maidens sang distinguished visitors such as Queen Victoria. 01433 620285 **36 C3**

Poole's Cavern *near Buxton, Derbyshire* Part of the Wye system, with some impressive formations, including the 'Flitch of Bacon' stalactite and the 'Poached Egg Chamber', with formations coloured by minerals leached out of lime-tips on the hillside above. **35 E8**

Speedwell Cavern *Winnats Pass, near Castleton, Derbyshire* A mine with several natural chambers and an underground canal, the most popular of the four Castleton caverns. 01433 620512 **36 C3**

Stump Cross Caverns *Greenhow Hill, North Yorkshire* A half-million-year-old cave with stalactites and stalagmites, a video presentation and a visitor centre with a display of animal remains. 01756 752780 **55 C6**

Thor's Cave *near Wetton, Staffordshire* A spectacular cave forming one of the oldest sites of human activity in the Peak District, with evidence of occupation dating back 10,000 years. **23 C8**

Treak Cliff Cavern *near Castleton, Derbyshire* One of the four Castleton caverns, a former mine with impressive stalactites and stalagmites and fine natural formations such as the Frozen Waterfall. 01433 620571 **36 C3**

White Scar Cave *Ingleton, North Yorkshire* A huge Ice Age cavern forming Britain's longest show cave, with underground waterfalls and stalactites. Guided tours. 01524 241244 **53 A5**

Other natural features

Aberffraw Heritage Coast *Aberffraw, Isle of Anglesey* A coastline with sand dunes up to 30 feet high, on the site of a silted-up estuary. The Llys Llewelyn Countryside Heritage Centre in Aberffraw has displays on local history and wildlife. 01407 840845 **26 F4**

Aira Force Waterfall *near Penrith, Cumbria* A spectacular National Trust owned waterfall that was popular with Victorians, located in the ancient Gowbarrow deer park, a good walking spot. 01768 482067 **71 E5**

Alderley Edge *Macclesfield, Cheshire* A National Trust property with a wooded sandstone escarpment commanding views across the Cheshire Plain, remains of old copper mines and a historic beacon. 01625 584412 **35 E5**

Ashworth Valley *Bury New Road, between Bury and Rochdale, Greater Manchester* Deciduous woodland with a range of wildlife habitats and remnants of the industrial heritage, including mill ruins testifying to the importance of the area in the Industrial Revolution. 01706 350459 **40 B4 to 41 B6**

Aysgarth Force★ *North Yorkshire* One of the Yorkshire Dales' most popular attractions, an area of woodland with three dramatic waterfalls, which featured in 'Robin Hood, Prince of Thieves'. 01969 663424 **61 C6**

Bala Lake (Llyn Tegid) *Bala, Gwynedd* The largest natural body of water in Wales, at four miles in length and up to a mile wide, popular for watersports. Among its many species of fish is the very rare gwyniad, and there are steam trains along its southern shore. **8 A3**

Bardsey Island *Gwynedd* A small island and wildlife sanctuary about 1.5miles off the eastern tip of the Llyn peninsula, also known as Enlli. It also has the remains of St Mary's Augustinian abbey and some farmhouses listed as Ancient Monuments. 01758 730740 **4 D2**

Beacon Fell *Preston, Lancashire* Moorland, heather, sculptures, a viewing point over to the Great Orme at Llandudno, and a visitor centre hosting special events. 01995 640557 **45 E7**

Beeley Moor *Beeley, Derbyshire* A wild moor area dotted with hut circles and tumuli dating from a large Bronze Age community, including Hob Hurst's House, an unusual square tumulus and scheduled National Monument. **37 F5**

Bidston Hill *Birkenhead, Merseyside* Paths through heath and bracken, a windmill, a lighthouse with views across the peninsula, an observatory, stone carvings, crofters' cottages, including Tam O'Shanter Cottage (see *Animal attractions*), and Flaybrick Memorial Gardens (see *Parks & gardens*). **31 B8**

Brandlehow Wood *Derwentwater, Keswick, Cumbria* The former Brandlehow estate, the National Trust's first purchase in 1902; oak trees and a commemorative stone placed here by Princess Louise at the opening ceremony can still be seen. 017687 72645 **63 B8**

Buckden Pike and Cross *North Yorkshire* A summit with fine views down Langstrothdale and a cross with a bronze fox's head commemorating the death of five Polish crewmembers of an RAF aircraft that crashed here in WWII. **61 E5**

Ceiriog Valley *Wrexham* An unspoilt valley described by Lloyd George as 'a little bit of heaven on earth', once home to poets John 'Ceiriog' Hughes, Huw Morus and Rev. Robert Ellis. Crossed by the Offa's Dyke path and other footpaths and bridleways, including the former Glyn Valley Tramway. **19 D7**

Conwy Falls (Rhaeadr y Graig Lwyd) *Penmachno, Conwy* A waterfall providing a habitat for ducks, otters and crested newts, set in 9.5 acres of ancient woodland with 32 species of birds, polecats and more. 01690 710696 **16 D3**

Delamere Forest *Delamere, Cheshire* A massive conifer plantation, part of the Mersey Forest and an ancestor of the Norman hunting forests of Mara and Mondrem. There are well-marked trails, including the 20-mile Delamere Way, cycle tracks, picnic sites and a visitor centre at Linmere. **33 F6**

Dovedale★ *Staffordshire* One of the most famous Peak District areas, with scenic attractions such as the beautiful River Dove, immortalised in 'The Compleat Angler', and Beresford Dale. **35 F7**

Eden Valley *Cumbria* A little-known gem with miles of footpaths along the River Eden, which is bordered by sandstone walls, caves, gorges, fords and contemporary sculptures by local artists. **66 E3 to 75 E8**

Friars Crag *Derwentwater, Keswick, Cumbria* A promontory jutting into Derwentwater about half a mile from the boat landing stages, belonging to the National Trust. Ruskin described the view from here as one of the three most beautiful in Europe; there is a memorial to him here, dating from 1900. 017687 72645 **63 B8**

Glan y Môr Elias *Traeth Lafan, Llanfairfechan, Conwy* A saltmarsh attracting all manner of birdlife, particularly roosting seabirds. **28 D3**

Heights of Abraham *Matlock Bath, Derbyshire* A beech-covered hilltop popular as a site for short walks, accessed via a cable car, and home to the Rutland Cavern and Great Masson Cavern, part natural caves and part lead mines. **24 C3**

Holcombe Moor *Bury, Greater Manchester* Windswept Pennine moorland, home to the Peel Tower commanding views as far as North Wales and to a footpath leading to the 'Pilgrims Cross' on the ancient Stanlaw-Whalley Abbey route. 0161 253 5899 **40 B4**

Ladybower and the Derwent Dams *Edale, Derbyshire* A flooded valley caused by the building of three dams in the first half of the 20th century, now a tourist attraction and popular area for walking, cycling and fishing, with a visitor centre. 01433 650953 **36 B3**

Lindow Common *Wilmslow, Cheshire* One of Cheshire's only surviving lowland heathlands and a Site of Special Scientific Interest, containing Black Lake, a haven for aquatic life and birds. It was in a nearby peat bog that 'Lindow Man' was discovered. 01625 504509 **34 C3**

Lodore Falls *Derwentwater, Keswick, Cumbria* A waterfall formed by the beck from Watendlath Tarn cascading over boulders for about 100 feet; a Victorian tourist attraction and the subject of a famous onomatopoeic poem by poet laureate Robert Southey. 017687 72645 **63 B8**

Malham Cove and Gordale Scar *near Malham, North Yorkshire* A famous beauty spot consisting of two limestone features formed by the freezing and melting of glaciers thousands of years ago. **54 C2**

Mam Tor *near Castleton, Derbyshire* A National Trust viewpoint dubbed the 'shivering mountain' (it is comprised of shale and crumbling rock), with the fortifications of an Iron Age fort and a tumulus that probably dates from the Bronze Age. A popular location for hanggliding and paragliding. **36 C3**

Spike Island *Mersey Road, Halton* The birthplace of the British chemical industry, now consisting of grassland, woodland, watersides and a visitor centre and hosting the annual Halton Show. The rail lines have been replaced by footpaths, including parts of the Mersey Way and Trans-Pennine Trail. 0151 420 3707 **33 C5**

Stanage Edge *Derbyshire* The biggest and most impressive of the Peak District's gritstone edges, at 3.5 miles, crossed by the Long Causeway, an old Roman road, and currently boasting more than 800 recorded rock climbs. **36 B4**

Stanton Moor★ *Derbyshire* A stunningly sited moor overlooking the Derwent and Wye valleys, the eastern edge of which is owned by the National Trust and contains a gritstone tower commemorating the first Great Reform Act of 1832. The moor contains at least 70 Bronze Age barrows, plus stone circles, ancient enclosures and standing stones. **24 B2**

Swallow Falls *Betws-y-Coed, Conwy* A series of dramatic waterfalls, considered one of the prettiest spots in North Wales. 01690 420486 **16 C3**

The Cloud *Congleton, Cheshire* A distinctively shaped heather-covered hill between the Peak District and the Cheshire Plain, popular with walkers and also known as 'Red Rock Fault'. **22 B3**

The Howgills *Cumbria* A popular walking area with smooth rounded fells, limestone terraces, charming villages and views over the North Pennines, eastern fells of the Lake District and Yorkshire Dales. **59 B7**

The Roaches *Staffordshire* A gritstone escarpment marking the south-western edge of the Peak District, popular with walkers and rock-climbers (classic routes include the Valkyrie, Sloth and Swan). The rocks of the Lower Tier contain Rock Cottage, a primitive gamekeeper's residence converted into a climbing hut. **23 B5**

Upper Goyt Valley *Derbyshire* A famous beauty spot and walking area, with excellent views, Errwood reservoir with its sailing club and picnic area, and the ruins of Errwood Hall, plus the family's shrine and chapel. **35 D7**

Wastwater★ *Wasdale Head, Cumbria* Europe's deepest lake (260ft), surrounded by Scafell Pike (England's highest mountain), Red Pike, Kirk Fell and Great Gable. At its Wasdale Head end is St Olaf's, one of the smallest churches in the country. **63 E6**

Parks & gardens

See also *Houses & gardens*

Acorn Bank Garden *Temple Sowerby, Cumbria* A National Trust garden with a walled garden containing 250 species of culinary and medicinal herbs and a watermill. 01768 361893 **71 F7**

Avenham Park *Preston, Lancashire* Traditional Victorian parkland designed by Edward Milner, with a famous Japanese rock garden and host to events such as Easter Egg Rolling, the Preston Mela and Caribbean Carnival. **45 E7**

Birkenhead Park★ *Conway Street, Birkenhead, Merseyside* Britain's first public park and the model for New York's Central Park, designed by Sir Joseph Paxton (of London's Crystal Palace fame) and featuring two lakes, a boathouse, a Swiss bridge and listed Gothic-style buildings. 0151 670 0695 **31 B8**

Bodnant Gardens★ *near Llandudno, Conwy* Late-19th-century gardens with views across to the Snowdonian mountains, divided into a series of Italianate terraces and the Deep Dell, traversed by the River Hiraethlyn. 01492 650460 **28 C5**

Botanic Gardens *Churchtown, Merseyside* A small botanic garden with a museum with local history and Victoriana displays, including dolls, plus a programme of talks. 01704 27547 **38 A4**

Cholmondeley Castle Gardens *Malpas, Cheshire* Romantically landscaped gardens containing a private chapel and picnic area, and home to various rare farm breeds. 01829 720383 **20 E2**

Constable Burton Hall Gardens *Constable Burton, Leyburn, North Yorkshire* The romantic terrace garden of John Carr House (closed to the public), in 18th-century parkland with garden trails and woodland walks. 01677 450428 **61 B8**

Court Hey Park and National Wildflower Centre *Knowsley, Merseyside* A Victorian park within 35 acres of parkland, with an innovative centre with displays about wildflowers and their cultivation and conservation. The location for the free annual Knowsley flower show. 0151 737 1819 **39 E5**

Dunge Valley Hidden Gardens *Kettleshulme, Whaley Bridge, Derbyshire* A Pennine Hills garden set up to resemble a Himalayan valley, with rhododendrons, azaleas, magnolias, acers and blue poppies, and streams, waterfalls, ponds, bridges and bog gardens. 01663 733787 **35 C7**

Flaybrick Memorial Gardens *Tollemache Road, Bidston Hill, Birkenhead, Merseyside* The former Flaybrick Cemetery, with mature trees used as the starting point for the development of an arboretum that includes ornamental cherries and giant redwoods. Guided tree walks are offered. 0151 653 9332 **31 B8**

Fletcher Moss Botanical Gardens and Parsonage Gardens *Wilmslow Road, Didsbury, Greater Manchester* A small botanical garden based around a rock garden with rare plants, pools and waterfalls. The building with the cafe where the RSPB began; the high-walled Parsonage Gardens boast roses, rare trees, an orchid house and a pet cemetery. 0161 434 1877 **34 A3**

Happy Valley Park *Llandudno, Conwy* A Victorian park with a restored 1890 camera obscura, an artificial ski slope and toboggan run, a tea pavilion and an entertainment centre. **28 C5**

Hare Hill Garden *Over Alderley, near Macclesfield, Cheshire* A National Trust garden with a pergola, a walled garden, rhododendrons and azaleas, and parkland. 01625 828981 **35 E5**

Heaton Park *Prestwich, Greater Manchester* Europe's biggest municipal park, once the estate of the Earls of Wilton and containing their 18th-century neo-classical house, a farm, gardens, a golf course and a boating lake. 0161 773 1231 **41 D5**

Henblas Park *Isle of Anglesey* A family park with falconry displays, pony rides, tractor tours, farm animals and lamb feeding, sheepdog displays, a dragon train ride, a pet corner, face painting, crazy golf and more. 01407 840440 **27 E5**

Millcroft Tea Gardens *Rood Lane, Norden, Greater Manchester* A garden with Victoria tearooms displaying photos and artefacts depicting local history, plus the biggest collection of monkey puzzle trees in northern England. A stopping off point on the Rochdale Way. **41 B6**

Ness Botanic Gardens *University of Liverpool, Neston, Cheshire* Rock and water gardens, spectacular azalea and rhododendron collections, views over the Dee Estuary, and a tearoom and adventure playground. 0151 353 0123 **31 D7**

Parcevall Hall Gardens *Skyreholme, near Skipton, North Yorkshire* Sixteen-acre hillside and woodland gardens with pools, streams, an old orchard, and rock gardens and terraces, plus views of Simon's Seat and Wharfedale. 01756 720311 **54 E3**

Stapeley Water Gardens *Nantwich, Cheshire* A water garden containing the National Collection of Water Lilies and the Palms Tropical Oasis, boasting a koi pool, a 'zoo room' with a cottontop tamarin monkey family, water dragons and a baby Caiman crocodile, and a stingray pool. 01270 623868 **21 D6**

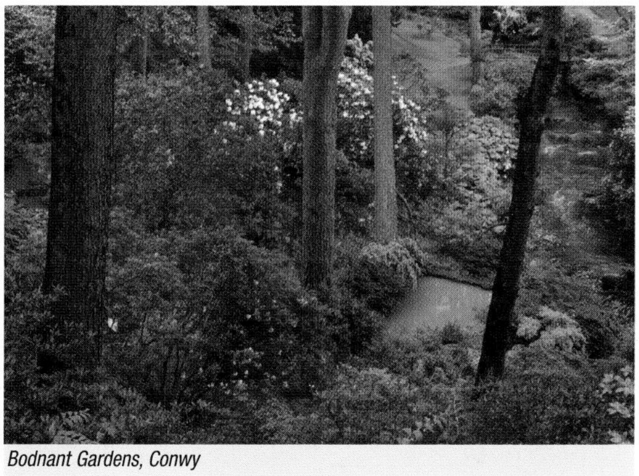
Bodnant Gardens, Conwy

Where telephone numbers have not been provided, visitors are advised to contact the local tourist information centre for further details.

Useful websites include:
www.visitnorthwest.com
www.visitpeakdistrict.com
www.visitcumbria.com
www.visitwales.com
www.cheshire.gov.uk

Walking, cycling & riding trails

For more information on the following selected trails, contact the Ramblers Association (020 7339 8500/www.ramblersorg.uk) or the nearest tourist information office. For mountain biking, bike hire and pony trekking, see *Sports*.

Allerdale Ramble *Seathwaite, Cumbria* A walk taking in mountain scenery (including an ascent of Skiddaw) and a flat coastal section along the Solway Firth, starting at Seathwaite in the Lakeland fells and ending at Grune Point just north of Silloth. ☏017687 72645 **63 D7**

Blackpool Countryside Experience *Blackpool* A series of nature walks starting at Stanley Park and passing through woodland gardens. ☏01253 478428 **44 C3**

Border Reivers Trail★ *Cumbria* A discovery trail about the bandits operating at the western Scotland-England border in the 14th-17th centuries; the 'In search of the Border Reivers' leaflet is available from tourist information points. Among places of interest are pele towers designed to withstand short sieges. **75 E7**

Cheshire Cycleway *Ellesmere Port and Neston, Cheshire* A newly extended 176-mile cycleway through some of Cheshire's finest countryside. **32 F2**

Cheshire Ring Canal Walk *Cheshire* A 97-mile section of connecting waterways, including the Macclesfield Canal, with a towpath walk, taking in various towns and villages, some wonderful scenery, and numerous pubs. ☏01625 504507 **35 B6**

Clywedog Trail *Wrexham* A nine-mile trail exploring the industrial heritage of Wrexham, starting at Minera Lead Mines (see *Factories, Mills and Mines*) and taking in Nant Mill, Bersham Ironworks and Heritage Centre and the Erddig estate on its way to the town of Wrexham. ☏01978 752772 **19 D7**

Coast to Coast Walk *St Bees, Cumbria* A famous 190-mile walk spanning northern England from St Bees (where walkers traditionally wet their boots in the Irish Sea) to Robin's Hood Bay on the east coast, crossing the Pennines and North Yorkshire Moors. **62 D2**

Cumbria Coastal Way *Cumbria* A 124-mile walk along the Cumbrian coastline, from Milnthorpe to Carlisle via the Duddon Estuary, St Bees Head and the Solway Coast AONB, with superb birdlife. ☏01900 813738 **58 D4 to 75 E8**

Cumbria Cycle Way★ *Ulverston, Cumbria* A new 72-mile route around the edge of the county, starting in Ulverston, passing through Coniston, Elterwater, Grasmere, Keswick, Threlkeld, Skiddaw and Bassenthwaite, and ending at Carlisle. Terrains ranges from country lanes to rugged off-road trails. ☏01768 773216 **57 E6**

Cumbria Way *Ulverston, Cumbria* A popular 70-mile trail between Ulverston and Carlisle in the north, keeping mostly to valleys and with the opportunity to take in lots of heritage sites. ☏01229 587120 **57 E6**

Dales Way *North Yorkshire and Cumbria* An 83-mile walk through some of northern England's best scenery, starting at Ilkley in the Yorkshire Dales and finishing at the shores of Windermere in the Lake District. **55 F6 to 57 A8**

Gritstone Trail *Macclesfield, Cheshire* An 18.5-mile signposted walk from Lyme Park to the Staffordshire border, over rugged upland country, pastureland and wooded river valleys, with a visitor centre, orienteering and magnificent views. ☏01625 614279 **35 E5**

Hadrian's Wall Path★ *Cumbria* A new 81-mile path that opened in May 2003, running along the frontier of the Roman Empire from the Solway Firth to the mouth of the River Tyne. ☏0191 269 1600 **74 D4 to 77 B9**

High Peak Trail *Cromford, Derbyshire* A cycleway coverted from the defunct Cromford and High Peak Railway from Parsley Hay to Cromford, with several relatively steep inclines and sharp curves. Cycle hire available at Middleton Top (01629 823204). **24 C3**

Ingleton Waterfalls Walk★ *Ingleton, North Yorkshire* A famous 4.5-mile walk through stunning waterfall scenery and ancient oak woodland, much of which has been designated a Site of Special Scientific Interest. ☏015242 41930 **53 A5**

Irwell Sculpture Trail★ *Bury, Greater Manchester* The biggest public art project in the North, with 30 sculptures celebrating the area's heritage and landscape along a 30-mile footpath from Salford Quays through Bury and up to the the Pennine source of the Irwell north of Bacup in Lancashire. ☏0161 253 5111 **40 B4**

Keswick Railway Footpath *Keswick, Cumbria* A four-mile scenic footpath through the Greta Gorge, with is impressive bridges and information plaques about the railway's history, the River Greta, the local bobbin industry and the natural history of the area. **63 B8**

Lôn Las Cymru Cycle Trail *Gwynedd and Isle of Anglesey* A challenging 175-mile trail, the northern section of which passes through Snowdonia National Park and takes in the quiet lanes of Anglesey. **6 A3 to 26 C2**

Longendale Trail *Hadfield, Derbyshire* A cycle trail covering about 12 miles from Hadfield station to the Woodhead tunnel entrance, affording views across the Longendale Valley and its reservoirs up to Black Hill. Bike hire available at Longendale Valley Cycles in Hadfield (01457 854672). **42 E2**

Lunesdale Walk *Carnforth, Lancashire* A 38-mile figure-of-eight walk taking in a variety of Lune Valley scenery, including part of the Forest of Bowland (see *National Parks and AONBs*). ☏01524 32878 **52 A1**

Marin Trails★ *Betws-y-Coed, Conwy* Marked mountain biking trails from the centre of Betws-y-Coed, linking challenging climbs and fire-road descents winding past waterfalls, lakes, mountain vistas and river valleys in the Gwydyr forest. ☏01492 640578 **16 C3**

Middlewood Way *Macclesfield, Cheshire* A reclaimed railway line forming an 11-mile 'greenway' for walkers, cyclists and horse riders, from Macclesfield to Marple on the Peak District National Park fringe. ☏01625 573998 **35 E5**

Midshires Way *Stockport, Greater Manchester* A 225-mile footpath and bridleway route starting at Stockport and running across middle England between the Pennines and the Chilterns, via historic estates, farmland and the Peak District National Park. **35 A5**

North Wales Path *Prestatyn, Denbighshire* A path following the coast and lower mountain slopes between Prestatyn and Bangor. ☏01492 575200 **30 C3**

Nunnery Walks *near Kirkoswald, Cumbria* Walks from the Nunnery, a hotel in a 1715 building by Christopher Aglionby on the site of a Benedictine nunnery, through ancient woodland down to the River Eden and Eden gorge. **71 C6**

Offa's Dyke Path★ *Prestatyn, Denbighshire* A 176-mile path from Prestatyn to Sedbury Cliffs near Chepstow, roughly following the line of an ancient dyke built by Offa, King of Mercia, about 1200 years ago and offering a wide variety of countryside. ☏01547 528753 **30 C3**

Oldham Way Circular Walk *Oldham, Greater Manchester* A trail starting and finishing at the spectacular Dove Stone reservoir, easily accessible from the village of Greenfield, with excellent views from the war memorial on 'Pots and Pans' and a vast area of open-access moorland to the east. **41 D7**

Pendle Witches Trail★ *Pendle, Lancashire* The 45-mile route travelled by the Pendle witches to where they were convicted at Lancaster Castle, beginning at the Pendle Heritage Centre and passing through the scenic Ribble Valley. ☏01282 661702 **47 C6 to 51 C8**

Pennine Bridleway★ *Rochdale, Greater Manchester* An important new national trail for walkers, cyclists and horseriders – the only one of its kind in the north of England – that runs through parts of Rochdale. ☏01706 864604 **41 B6**

Pennine Way★ *Derbyshire* A popular 430-mile footpath from Derbyshire to the Scottish border; the Peak District section, beginning at Edale, takes in all the major gritstone peaks of the area. **36 B2 to 79 A8**

Ribble Way *Lancashire* A 70-mile footpath along the Ribble from its source at Ribblehead to the estuary at Preston, through limestone gorge, open moorland and tidal marsh and including the Ribble Valley Sculpture Trail with pieces by local people and commissioned artists. ☏01200 443071 **60 E1 to 45 E7**

Ridding Wood Sculpture Trail *Grizedale Forest Park Centre, Hawkshead, Cumbria* An all-ability two-mile trail through oak woodland and the once-formal gardens of Grizedale Hall, with 20 sculptures, many interactive. Seven other walking trails in the Grizedale Forest contain a total of 90 sculptures. ☏01229 860010 **57 A7**

Sandstone Trail *Cheshire* A 32-mile trail that runs for almost half its length through Vale Royal; some of the best scenery is on the route marked between Frodsham and Tarporley. **33 D5 to 20 F3**

Sea to Sea (C2C) Cycle Route *Workington/Whitehaven, Cumbria* A challenging 140-mile cycleway starting on the Cumbrian coast and ending at the North Sea at Newcastle or Sunderland. ☏0117 929 0888 **68 F2 or 62 C2 to 73 D7**

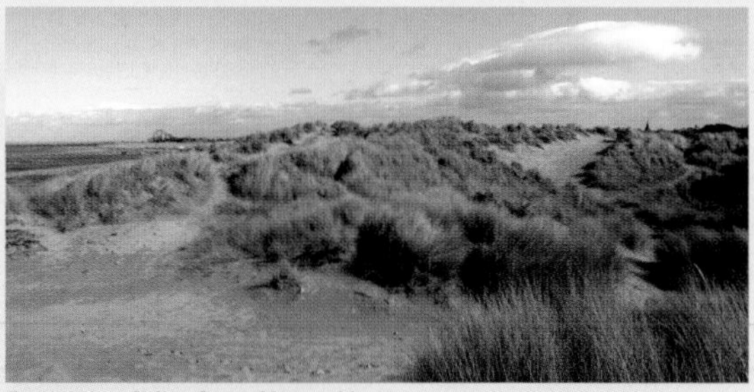

Sand dunes, Sefton Coast, Merseyside

Sefton Coastal Footpath *Southport to Crosby, Merseyside* A 21-mile path across dunes, farmland and pine woods, with wonderful views of the sea and wide beaches, and nature trails allowing glimpses of rare wildlife such as natterjack toads. **38 A3 to 38 E3**

Tameside Trail *Greater Manchester* A 40-mile circular trail covering recognised areas of beauty and interest, including the Tame Valley and numerous country parks. **41 E6**

Three Peaks Walk *Horton in Ribblesdale, North Yorkshire* An arduous walk taking in three 2200ft mountains (Pen-y-ghent, Ingleborough and Whernside) in a day. Walkers clock out and in at the Pen-y-ghent Cafe. **53 A8**

Upper Derwent Valley Trails *Derbyshire* A popular area with mountain bikers and other cyclists, with old railway lines and a circuit of the Derwent and Howden reservoirs. Cycle hire available at Fairholmes, near Hagg Side (01433 651261). **36 B3**

West Cumbria Cycle Network *Cumbria* A string of meandering cycle paths through interesting towns and scenic countryside. **69 E5 to 62 C4**

West Park *Macclesfield, Cheshire* An 1854 park with a museum and art gallery (see *Local History* Macclesfield Silk Museums), ornamental gardens a woodland walk, a picnic area, an aviary, a playground and play castle, and three pre-Norman cross-shafts (a National Monument). ☏01625 500203 **35 E5**

Williamson Park *Lancaster, Lancashire* A 54-acre park on a disused quarry site overlooking Lancaster, Morecambe Bay and the Lakeland fells, with woodland walkways, an Edwardian tropical butterfly house and the landmark folly of Ashton Memorial with its viewing gallery and exhibition space. ☏01524 33318 **51 C8**

Boat trips

See also *Museums & galleries*: TRANSPORT and *Sport*: WATERSPORTS

Keswick Launches *on Derwentwater, Keswick, Cumbria* A fleet of launches from traditional to modern, operating on serene Derwentwater. ☏017687 72263 **63 B8**

Pennine Boat Trips *Waterside Court, Coach Street, Skipton, North Yorkshire* Cruises on the 'Dalesman' on an attractive stretch of the Leeds and Liverpool Canal through the the Pennines and Yorkshire Dales, with skipper commentary. ☏01756 790829 **54 E3**

Queen Victoria *Conwy Quay, Conwy* River-bus trips to the Conwy Valley or around the estuary to see Puffin Island, Anglesey and the Great Orme. ☏01492 592830 **28 D5**

Ullswater Steamers *on Ullswater, Glenridding, Cumbria* The 19th-century steamers that sail Lake Ullswater between Glenridding, Pooley Bridge and Howtown. ☏01768 482229 **64 C2**

Windermere Lake Cruises *Lakeside, Cumbria* Daily trips by steamers and launches between Ambleside, Bowness and Lakeside on England's longest lake. ☏015395 31188 **57 C8**

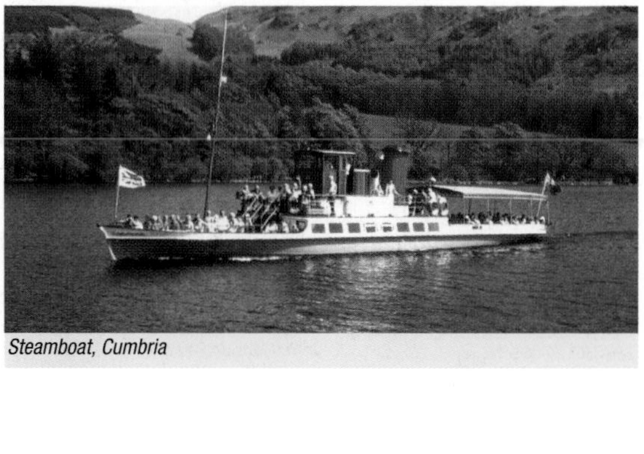

Steamboat, Cumbria

Animal attractions

See also *Nature reserves and conservation areas*

Alpaca Centre *Snuff Mill Lane, Stainton, Cumbria* A working farm where alpacas are bred, reared and sold. ☏01768 891440 **58 C4**

Anglesey Sea Zoo *Brynsiencyn, Isle of Anglesey* Award-winning displays of marine life from the surrounding waters. ☏01248 430411 **27 F6**

Animal World and Butterfly House *Moss Bank Park, Moss Bank Way, Bolton, Greater Manchester* Everything from farm animals to chipmunks and wildfowl to exotic birds, plus a tropical environment with butterflies, moths, insects, spiders, reptiles and plants. The park also has a play area, rock garden, old English garden, tennis courts and more. ☏01204 334050 **40 C3**

Aquarium of the Lakes★ *Lakeside, Cumbria* An award-winning freshwater aquarium with Britain's biggest collection of freshwater fish, a simulated lake bed, and otters and ducks. ☏015395 30153 **57 C8**

Blackpool Zoo Park *East Park Drive, Blackpool, Blackpool* A 32-acre zoo with more than 400 animals and including a Gorilla Mountain and dolphin 'Swimulator'. ☏01253 830830 **44 C3**

Blue Planet Aquarium★ *Cheshire Oaks, Ellesmere Port, Cheshire* The UK's largest aquarium, with interactive displays and themed areas, including an 'aquatheatre' including one of the world's longest underwater 'safari tunnels' housing more than 20 sharks. ☏0151 357 8800 **32 D3**

Bodafon Farm Park *Llandudno, Conwy* A working farm with rare farm breeds, aviaries with owls and tropical birds, a heritage trail and miniature farm tractors. ☏01492 549060 **28 C5**

Bolton Aquarium *Le Mans Crescent, Bolton, Greater Manchester* An aquarium adjoining

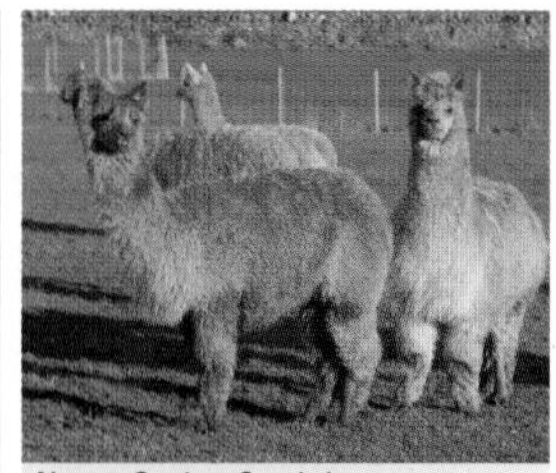

Alpaca Centre, Cumbria

Bolton Museum and Art Gallery, with a breeding programme for endangered species. ☏01204 332211 **40 C3**

Bowland Wild Boar Park *Chipping, Lancashire* A scenic wooded park in the Ribble Valley, with wild boar, longhorn cows and deer. ☏01995 61554 **46 B1**

Chester Zoo★ *Upton-by-Chester, Chester, Cheshire* The UK's most-visited zoo, famous for its conservation work, large paddocks and gardens. Highlights include the Chimpanzee Forest, 'Zoofari' monorail and National Elephant Centre with two baby elephants. ☏01244 380280 **32 F2**

Conwy Butterfly Jungle *Bodlondeb Park, Conwy, Conwy* A 2000 sq ft jungle garden with freeflying tropical butterflies and rainforest surround-sound, plus other 'mini-beasts'. ☏01492 593149 **28 D5**

Cumberland Bird of Prey Centre *Sandhill, Thurstonfield, Cumbria* Daily displays by hawks, falcons, owls, buzzards and unusual species such as black vultures and Falkland Island caracaras, plus a Hawk Lawn, bow perches, avaries and woodland. ☏01228 576889 **75 E6**

Eden Ostrich World *Langwathby, Cumbria* A open-air farm where visitors can feed a variety of animals and see ostrich chicks hatch in summer. ☏01768 881771 **71 E6**

Ewe-Phoria *Llangwm, Conwy* An 'agri theatre' with sheepdog and shearing demonstrations, a ram parade and a children's play area. ☏01490 460369 **17 F7**

Farmworld *Rhosllanerchrugog, Wrexham* A working dairy farm with an adventure park, 'cuddle corner', lamb-feeding sessions, tractor tours, milking demonstrations and pony rides. ☏01978 840697 **19 E7**

Gayle Lane, Hawes, Yorkshire Dales *North Yorkshire* A working dairy where visitors can see Wensleydale cheese being produced, with a small museum about its history. ☏01969 667664 **60 C3**

Hazel Brow Farm Visitor Centre *Low Row Village, Richmond, South Yorkshire* An award-winning attraction with guided tours, walks, demonstrations, craft activities and a farm shop. ☏01748 886224 **37 B8**

Highgate Farm and Animal Trail *Morland, Cumbria* An attraction aimed at young children, with sheep races, pony rides, lamb, hen and duck feeding, and egg collecting, plus pygmy goats, llamas and deer. ☏01931 714347 **65 B7**

International League for the Protection of Horses Centre *Penny Farm, Blackpool* A horse recovery and rehabilitation centre with a visitor centre. ☏01253 766983 **44 C3**

Island Heritage *Pott Hall Farm, Healey, North Yorkshire* A working farm with living examples of the some of Britain's earliest domesticated sheep, a display of traditional spinning wheels and weaving looms and the opportunity to watch lambs being born and sheep sheared. ☏01765 689651 **61 E8**

Keswick Sheep Dog Demonstrations *Greta Bank Field, Brundholme Road, Keswick, Cumbria* Displays of dogs being trained to handle sheep. ☏017687 79603 **63 B8**

Knowsley Safari Park *Prescot, Merseyside* The historic parkland surrounding Knowsley Hall, ancestral home of the Earls of Derby, now home to big-game animals. The winner of various animal husbandry awards. ☏0151 430 9009 **32 A4**

Lake District Coast Aquarium *South Quay, Maryport, Cumbria* An aquarium in the renovated Maryport harbour, with displays on aquatic life in British waters, particularly Cumbria's seas and coasts, including a mockup of Maryport's harbour wall and a ray pool where gentle stroking is allowed. ☏01900 817760 **68 D3**

Lakeland Bird of Prey Centre *Lowther, Cumbria* Flying demonstrations and the chance to learn about conservation work. ☏01931 712746 **65 B5**

Lakeland Sheep and Wool Centre *Egremont Road, Cockermouth, Cumbria* A working farm with a daily show about sheeprearing, also containing the CUMWEST Visitor Centre providing information on the area. ☏01900 822673 **69 E5**

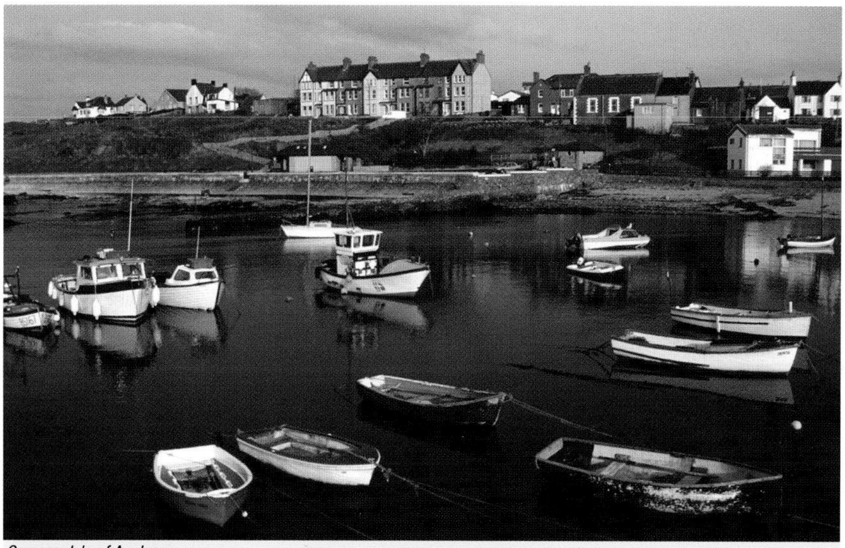

Cemaes, Isle of Anglesey

Pili Palas *Menai Bridge, Isle of Anglesey* A tropical environment with butterflies, exotic plants, birds, snakes and lizards. ☎01248 716518 **27 E8**

Rhyl Sea Life Centre *East Parade, Rhyl, Denbighshire* An aquarium with Wales' only walkthough underwater tunnel, the Ocean Falls Cascade, the Sea at Night, with catfish and octopuses, and the Shark Encounter. ☎01745 344660 **30 C2**

RSPB Discovery Centre★ *Fairhaven Lake, Lytham St Anne's, Lancashire* Interactive displays, illustrated talks and activities, including guided walks to see birds on the Ribble Estuary, the UK's foremost site for migratory birds. ☎01253 796292 **44 E3**

Sea Life Centre *Promenade, Blackpool* One of the biggest marine collections in Europe, with a tropical shark display. ☎01253 622445 **44 C3**

Seacombe Aquarium *Seacombe Ferry Terminal, Wallasey, Merseyside* Displays of lifeforms in the Mersey and surrounding seas, including sharks and octopuses. ☎0151 630 1030 **31 A7**

South Lakes Wild Animal Park★ *Crossgates, Dalton-in-Furness, Cumbria* A tiger conservation centre offering walking safaris. Other residents include kangaroos, emus and parrots. ☎01229 466086 **57 F5**

Southport Zoo and Conservation Trust *Princes Park, Merseyside* A family-run zoo in landscaped gardens, including a schoolroom and Natural History museum, a Pets Corner Barn, a Reptile House, a Parrot House and a picnic area. ☎01704 548894 **32 B2**

Tam O'Shanter Urban Farm *Boundary Road, Bidston, Merseyside* A former crofter's cottage running animal petting sessions, slide talks, nature walks and children's craft activities. ☎0151 653 9332 **31 A7**

Thornby Moor Dairy *Crofton Hall, Thursby, Cumbria* A working dairy in the old piggery at Crofton Hall, which dates from 1390; visitors can observe the cheesemaking process and taste the produce. ☎016973 45555 **70 A1**

Trotters and Friends Animal Farm *Bassenthwaite, Cumbria* A farm with rabbits and exotic animals, birds and reptiles, plus a play centre and picnic areas. ☎017687 76239 **69 E7**

Welsh Mountain Zoo *Colwyn Bay, Conwy* A conservation zoo in beautiful gardens above Colwyn Bay, with hundreds of animal and plant species from around the world. ☎01492 532938 **29 D7**

Windmill Animal Farm *Red Cat Lane, Burscough, Lancashire* A working farm with a renovated windmill, unusual breeds, a Children's Pet Area and an indoor activity centre with slides and a ball pool. ☎01704 892282 **39 B5**

Beaches & resorts

Aberdaron★ *Gwynedd* An old fishing village with whitewashed houses, at the mouth of the river Daron, spanned by a 17-century stone bridge. There are heritage trails and a popular beach, and about 1.5 miles away Porthor Beach has sand that whistles when walked on. **4 C3**

Aberdyfi (Aberdovey) *Gwynedd* A pretty little harbour resort within Snowdonia National Park, with award-winning beaches and an estuary with views of Cardigan Bay. Popular with watersports fans and golfers. **2 D3**

Abersoch *Gwynedd* A busy coastal resort and important sailing and surfing centre on Cardigan Bay, with the sandy beaches of Porth Fawr, Porth Bach and Porth Ceiriad. **5 C6**

Allonby *Cumbria* An attractive Solway Coast village with an award-winning shingle and sand beach hosting windsurfing tournaments, a Quaker Reading Room, and famous free-roaming ponies on the greens where weavers used to lay out their cloths. Part of the Cumbria Coastal Way (see *Walking, cycling & riding trails*). **68 C4**

Barkby Beach, Central Beach and Ffrith Beach *near Prestatyn, Denbighshire* Three sandy beaches joined by a four-mile promenade that has been incorporated into the National Cycle Network and has spectacular views of Snowdonia, Anglesey and the Wirral. The award-winning Central marks the start of the Offa's Dyke Trail (see *Walking, cycling & riding trails*). **30 C3**

Barrow-in-Furness *Cumbria* A historic Victorian town with fine beaches and coastal walks, a ruined red-sandstone abbey dating back to 1123, once the country's second wealthiest, and the Dock Museum (see *Museums and Heritage Centres*). **50 A3**

Cable Bay *near Rhosneigr, Isle of Anglesey* Anglesey's best beach, set in a picturesque cove with clean water and excellent sand. **26 E3**

Cemaes *Isle of Anglesey* The most northerly village on Anglesey, situated in an AONB and part of the 18-mile North Anglesey Heritage Coast, with a natural harbour that housed ancient settlements, a popular sheltered sandy beach and a Llanbadrig Church with its Muslim features (see *Religious buildings*). **26 A4**

Criccieth *Gwynedd* An attractive resort on the shores of Cardigan Bay, with the remains of a 1239 stone castle (see *Castles*), a Lloyd George Museum (see *Local History*), a central green that was part of the medieval common, and sandy beaches drawing watersports enthusiasts. **6 A2**

Fleetwood *Lancashire* A busy seaside resort and port with a traditional pier, a promenade, a marina, a famous market, a lighthouse and the UK's only original main-street tramway. **51 F5**

Grange-over-Sands *Cumbria* A peaceful, elegant Edwardian seaside resort with a mild climate, dubbed 'Lakeland's Riviera'. **58 E2**

Hoylake *Merseyside* A busy seaside town with sandy beaches and a promenade where you can buy seafood from incoming fishermen; home to the Royal Liverpool Golf Club (see *Sports*). **31 B6**

LLanbedrog *Gwynedd* A village best known for its for its sheltered sandy beach beneath a heather-covered, pine-fringed headland, owned by the National Trust. Nearby is Mynydd Tir y Cwmwd mountain, with panoramic views, and Tremfan Hall, once home to scholar John Gwenogfryn Evans. **5 B6**

Llandudno *Conwy* A Victorian seaside resort with a host of attractions, including a promenade, a pier (see *Family attractions*), two beaches and a cable car to the summit of the Great Orme headland (see *Outdoors: Country & forest parks*). **28 D5**

Lytham *Lancashire* A seaside town with a landmark windmill (see **Local History**), a famous green, old fishermens' cottages, traditional shops, a new heritage centre and gallery (2 Henry Street), a hall (see *Houses & gardens*), an Old Lifeboat House (see *Local history*) and wonderful views to the Welsh mountains. **44 E4**

New Brighton *Merseyside* A seaside resort with a three-mile coastal promenade dating back to the 1830s, affording unparalleled views across Liverpool Bay, a Sailing School (see *Sports*), the Fort Perch Rock built in 1827 to defend the Mersey, a lighthouse, fun rides, bowls and the like. **38 F3**

Parkgate *near Neston, Cheshire* A once-bustling port from which sailing ships left for Ireland, with views across the Dee Estuary towards the Welsh Hills and a marsh providing some of the most spectacular bird-watching in the North West. Famous for its home-made ice cream and shrimps. **31 D7**

Porth Dinllaen *Gwynedd* An old fishing hamlet with a rich maritime history, a lifeboat station and a spectacularly sited golf course on the headland. The surrounding land was recently purchased by the National Trust. **14 F1**

Porthmadog *Gwynedd* A harbour town on the Glaslyn Estuary, with a seafaring past, numerous craft shops and a beach, Black-rock Sands, on its outskirts. The Ffestiniog Railway (see *Transport*) starts here, TE Lawrence (of Arabia) lived nearby and the poet Shelley visited often. **6 A3**

Pwllheli *Gwynedd* A characterful coastal market town with narrow streets, a historic harbour, a Blue Flag beach, Hafan Pwllheli Marina (see *Watersports*), Plas Glyn y Weddw Art Gallery (see *Art and crafts*) and Pennarth Fawr, a medieval stone house with a wooden interior. **5 A7**

Ravenglass *Cumbria* A fishing town between the Lake District Mountains and the sea, once an important Roman naval base in the 2nd century and containing the remains of their Glannaventa bath house, as well as Muncaster Castle, Gardens and World Owl Trust (see *Castles*) and Muncaster Water Mill (see *Local History*). **56 A2**

Rhosneigr *Isle of Anglesey* A popular resort with award-winning beaches: Traeth Crigyll (Town Beach), a magnet for windsurfers and sailors; and Broad Beach, a venue for canoeing, surfing and walking. **26 E3**

St Bees★ *Cumbria* A coastal village near an RSPB reserve (see *Nature reserves & conservation areas*), with a links boasting panoramic views, a mile-long beach with tidal rock pools and wave-sculpted rock formations, and the 12th-century church of St Mary and St Bega (see *Religious buildings*). The starting point for the Coast to Coast Walk (see *Walking, cycling & riding trails*). **62 D2**

Silloth *Cumbria* A charming planned Victorian town on the shores of the Solway Firth, with cobbled streets, views of Scotland, and the award-winning West Beach. The surrounding coast is an AONB (see *National Parks and AONBs*). **74 F2**

Southport *Merseyside* A large seaside town with a restored iron pier (see *Family attractions*), a Blue Flag beach with donkey rides, a new seawall, a miniature railway (see *Transport*), an award-winning promenade famous for its floral displays, and more. **38 A3**

West Kirby *Merseyside* A bustling seaside town with miles of award-winning beaches and promenades and splendid views of North Wales. The starting point for day trips to Hilbre Islands Nature Reserve (see *Nature reserves & conservation areas*). **31 B6**

Towns & villages

See also *Outdoors:* BEACHES & RESORTS

Alston *Cumbria* England's highest market town, with Pennine views, a huge water-wheel and cobbled lanes filled with antique shops and craft workshops. An activity centre for walks and other outdoor pursuits. **72 B2**
Local history & industry Nenthead Mines Heritage Centre
Transport The HUB Exhibition • South Tynedale Railway

Appleby-in-Westmorland *Cumbria* A picturesque market town with cloisters designed by Sir Robert Smirke in 1811, St Anne's Hospital (almhouses built for poor widows by Lady Anne Clifford, who restored neglected estates, castles and churches in the area) and the Church of St Lawrence, with Anne's tomb and one of the UK's oldest surviving organs. **65 B8**
Art & crafts Courtyard Gallery
Buildings Appleby Castle

Ashford in the Water *Derbyshire* A sleepy little village that used to be a major crossing point on the Wye, with the 17th-century Sheepwash Bridge (with a pen next to it to wash sheep) and a church with a 14th-century tower and font. **36 F3**

Askrigg *North Yorkshire* A pretty village where the famous Wensleydale cheese is made, used as a location in 'All Creatures Great and Small'. Features include a market cross and an old iron bull baiting ring. **60 B4**
Religious buildings St Oswald's Church

Austwick *North Yorkshire* A village surrounded by some of the best limestone scenery in the Yorkshire Dales National Park, with three well-preserved clapper bridges and a restored sheep wash dub. **53 B7**

Bainbridge *North Yorkshire* A picturesque Yorkshire Dales village with a series of greens, one of which has some medieval stocks, and a restored millrace. **60 B4**

Bakewell *Derbyshire* An ancient town in the heart of the Peak District National Park, dating back to Saxon times and with a market going back to at least 1300. The famous Bakewell pudding (the origin of the Bakewell tart) comes from here. **36 F4**
Buildings Bakewell Church • Chatsworth House
Local history & industry Old House Museum

Bangor-is-y-coed (Bangor-on-Dee) *Bangor-is-y-coed, Wrexham* A picturesque village accessed via a part-medieval, part-17th-century bridge (a scheduled Ancient Monument), once the site of an important monastery and now home to a country race-course. **19 F7**

Beddgelert★ *Gwynedd* An award-winning mountain village at the confluence of the Glaslyn and Colwyn rivers, where Alfred Bestall wrote Rupert the Bear stories and Prince Llywelyn had a cottage (visitors can see the grave of Gelert, the dog left by Llywelyn to guard his child). **15 E7**
Local history & industry Sygun Copper Mine

Betws-y-coed★ *Conwy* The main village of the Snowdonia National Park and North Wales' most popular inland resort, with many craft and outdoor activity shops. Popular in Victorian times as an artists' colony. **16 C3**
Country & forest parks Gwydyr Forest Park
Other natural features Swallow Falls
Walking, cycling & riding trails Marin Trails

Bostock Green *Cheshire* A town with a church tower claimed as the centre of Cheshire to 'within three barleycorns', a picturesque late-Victorian model village and a hall built in 1775 and remodelled in the 1870s. **33 F8**

Brampton *Cumbria* A small sandstone town with an octagonal Moot Hall built in 1817 and, just to the east, a 135ft motte with a statue of the 7th earl of Carlisle. **65 B8**
Outdoors Gelt Woods • Talkin Tarn Country Park
Religious buildings Lanercost Priory • St Martin's Church

Broughton in Furness *Cumbria* An unspoilt village in the foothills of the Lake District Fells, once home to Branwell Bronte, immortalised in poetry by Wordsworth and now popular with walkers. **57 C5**
Activity centres Kepplewray Centre

Burnsall *North Yorkshire* One of the Yorkshire Dales' most attractive villages, boasting possibly the most photographed stone bridge in the area and surrounded by hillsides covered with ancient cultivation terraces or 'lynchets'. **54 C4**

Buxton *Derbyshire* An important town just outside the National Park boundary, famous for its warm springs on which the Romans built baths, with splendid buildings dating from its heyday as a fashionable spa, including The Crescent and the Opera House. **35 E8**
Local history & industry Buxton Museum and Art Gallery

Caldbeck *Cumbria* A traditional fell village with old corn, wool, paper and bobbin mills dating from the 17th and 18th centuries, a paper mill, a brewery and a duck pond in an old clay dubs. **70 D1**
Local history & industry Priests Mill
Religious buildings St Kentigern's Church

Capel Curig *Conwy* A rugged mountain village at the heart of Snowdonia National Park, a mecca for climbers and walkers. **16 C2**
Climbing and Caving Plas-y-Brenin National Mountain Centre
Houses & gardens The Ugly House

Castleton *Derbyshire* A popular and picturesque village overlooked by Mam Tor, with a surviving section of the Norman town ditch and interesting geological features, such as Winnats Pass and four nearby caverns (see *Caves, caverns & potholes*). **36 C3**

Chipping *Lancashire* A village in a conservation area, with stone-built cottages, a 17th-century school, some old almshouses and inns, and a traditional cheese-maker. **46 B1**
Animal sttractions Bowland Wild Boar Park

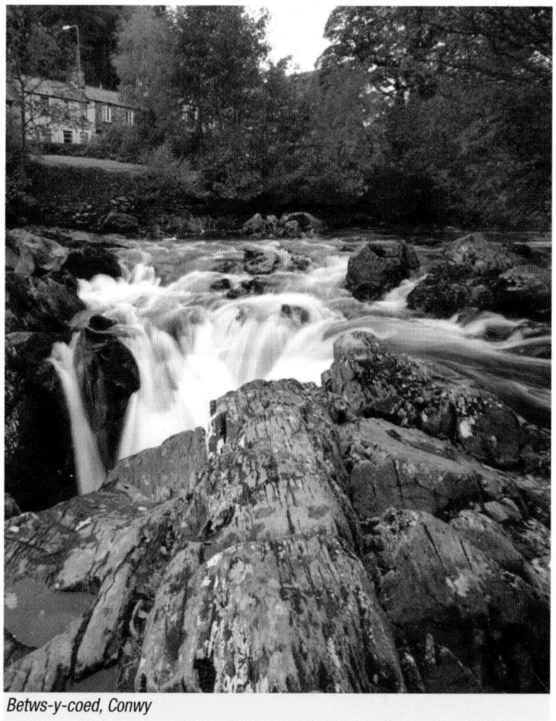

Betws-y-coed, Conwy

Church Minshull *Cheshire* A picturebook-pretty village with attractive half-timbered houses, including a 17th-century miller's house, and an old mill on the site of one mentioned in the Domesday Book. 21 B6

Clapham *North Yorkshire* A pretty village with a beck running through the centre, situated at the foot of Ingleborough, one of the Yorkshire Dales' Three Peaks. There's a restored market cross dating back to 1203 and an early 16th-century Old Manor House. 53 B6
Religious buildings St James' Church

Conwy ✶ *Conwy* One of the best-preserved walled towns in Europe, containing the 'smallest house in Britain' (6ft x 10ft). Nearby Gwydir Forest and Coed y Brenin Forest are good for walks. 28 D5
Art & crafts Royal Cambrian Academy
Buildings Aberconwy House • Conwy Castle • Plas Mawr
Museums Teapot World
Local history & industry Conwy Mussel Museum
Outdoors Conwy Butterfly Jungle • Queen Victoria Boat Trips
Transport Conwy Suspension Bridge

Corwen *Denbighshire* A quaint market town in the Vale of Edeyrnion, at the foot of the Berwyn Mountains, often described as the 'crossroads of North Wales' because it forms a good base for touring. Overlooked by Caer Drewyn, an Iron Age hill fort. 18 F2
Religious buildings Llangar Church • Rug Chapel

Daresbury ✶ *Halton* The village where Lewis Carroll spent his first ten years (he was born in nearby Newton-by-Daresbury in 1832); 'Alice in Wonderland' references include a model of the Mad Hatter on top of the village school. 33 C6
Religious buildings All Saints Church

Denbigh *Denbighshire* An old market town with steep streets, two ruined churches, the early-14th-century church of St Hilary's, a Carmelite friary, the remnants of town walls and an ancient market. 18 A1
Buildings Denbigh Castle • Leicester's Church

Dent *Cumbria* A handsome Yorkshire Dales village with unusual cobbled streets, whitewashed cottages and a speciality brewery. Parts of the much-restored St Andrew's Church date back to the 12th century. 59 C8

Dobcross *Greater Manchester* One of the most attractive Pennine villages, with weavers' cottages, clothiers' and merchants' houses and an unspoilt square. 42 C1

Downham *Lancashire* One of the prettiest villages in Lancashire, with stone-built cottages around a green, a brook and a church with a 15th-century tower. Linked with Lancashire witches such as Old Mother Demdike. 46 B4

Dunsop Bridge *Newton, Lancashire* A photogenic village declared by Ordnance Survey the official 'centre of the kingdom'. In 1992 Sir Ranolph Fiennes unveiled the 100,000th payphone in the country on its riverside green. 53 E5

Eyam *Derbyshire* A well-preserved village with fine old buildings, some bearing plaques explaining their role in the Plague drama of 1665. There is also a mound containing the shaft of Glebe Lead Mine, a former silk mill, remnants of one of the areas's earliest public water supplies (1588), and some natural potholes. 36 D4
Religious buildings Eyam Church

Eyam, Derbyshire

Fairfield Moravian Settlement *around Fairfield Square, Droylsden, Greater Manchester* A well-preserved settlement dating back to 1785, with cobbled streets and a church with a graveyard in which married couples shared the same grave, with single men and women on either side. 41 E6

Foolow *Derbyshire* A picturesque former lead-mining village with 17th-century houses grouped around a village green, where there is a cross with a medieval shaft and a bull-baiting ring, and a duckpond. 36 D3

Grassington *North Yorkshire* A pretty, popular little town in a stunning setting, with a cobbled square, former miners' cottages and Lea Green, a scheduled Ancient Monument consisting of prehistoric and medieval field systems and other archaeological features. 54 C4
Local history & industry Upper Wharfedale Folk Museum

Great Budworth *Cheshire* A lovely village largely created by a Victorian landowner and local architect by incorporating remnants of its Tudor half-timbered houses into modern homes. By the church wall are some restored stocks and remains of the shackles from a whipping post. 33 D8
Religious buildings Great Budworth Church

Grindon *Staffordshire* A charming village above the Manifold Valley, formerly a staging post along the packhorse route from Ecton Hill copper mine, with a rare 'Rindle' stone by the church. 23 D7

Hartington *Derbyshire* A busy tourist centre granted a market charter in 1203, with a central green and duckpond, and Nuttall's Creamery producing Stilton and Buxton Blue cheese. 23 B8

Hathersage ✶ *Derbyshire* An historical village linked with Robin Hood and the Brontes (it doubled as 'Norton' in 'Jane Eyre'), containing Camp Green earthwork (probably Danish in origin) and several old mills, and surrounded by moorland, gritstone edges, spectacular tors and Carl Wark hill fort. 36 C4

Holywell *Flintshire* A quaint, slow-paced historic town with more than 60 listed buildings and specialist shops. 31 D5
Country & forest parks Greenfield Valley Heritage and Country Park
Religious buildings St Winefride's Well

Hornby *Lancashire* A beautiful Lune Valley village that grew prosperous from its coaching trade in the 18th century, with some fine Georgian buildings and a riverside castle (not open to the public). 52 B3

Ilam *Staffordshire* A pretty, historic village dating back to Saxon times, moved here from its position near Ilam Hall by Jesse Watts-Russell in the 1820s and rebuilt in his 'Alpine style'. 23 D8
Religious buildings Ilam Church

Keld *North Yorkshire* A tiny village, the highest in Swaledale, with old lead mining buildings, the newly restored ruins of Crackpot Hall, an imposing 18th-century farmhouse and some attractive 'forces' (waterfalls) nearby. 67 F5

Kirkby Lonsdale *Cumbria* A beautifully sited and unspoilt market town in the idyllic Lune Valley, described by Ruskin as 'naturally divine'. 59 E6

Kirkoswald *Cumbria* A picturesque large village with a cobbled former market place, some fine Georgian buildings, the two-storied 'College', built in 1450 as a pele tower and converted into a college for priests, and a ruined castle (not open to the public). 71 C6
Religious buildings St Oswald's Church
Walking, cycling & riding trails Nunnery Walks

Knutsford *Cheshire* A charming town with literary connections (Elizabeth Gaskell is buried in the Brook Street Unitarian Church), fine buildings and specialist shops, and a moor with wetland/marsh habitat and extensive reed beds. 34 D2
Houses & gardens Peover Hall and Gardens • Tabley House • Tatton Park

Langthwaite *North Yorkshire* An idyllic spot once famous for its lead industry, used as a location in 'All Creatures Great and Small' and surrounded by internationally important birdlife-rich high moorland with purple heather and blanket bog. 67 F8

Last Drop Village *Hospital Road, Bromley Cross, Bolton, Greater Manchester* A picturesque 'village' converted from 18th-century farm buildings, with an antiquarian bookseller, craft toy shop, bakery, tearoom, pub and hotel. Hosts antiques fairs. ☏01204 591131 40 C3

Little Budworth *Cheshire* A pretty village boasting two watermills with lakes where watercress was harvested in Victorian times and sold from donkey carts, almshouses presented by Lady Egerton and an old pinfold. 20 A4
Country & forest parks Little Budworth Country Park
Motorsports Oulton Park
Religious buildings Little Budworth Church

Littleborough *Greater Manchester* A thriving former weaving town in the Pennines, with a conservation area including the old Falcon Inn and the circular Wheatsheaf building, reminders of the town's role as a trade crossroads. 41 A7
Country & forest parks Hollingworth Lake Country Park
Historic buildings Littleborough Coach House and Heritage Centre

Llanfairpwllgwyngyllgogerychwyrndrob-wllllantysiliogogogoch *Isle of Anglesey* The town with perhaps the world's most-photographed railway-station sign. Also the Marquis of Anglesey's Column dating back to 1816 and panoramic views of Anglesey and Snowdonia. 27 E7

Llangollen ✶ *Denbighshire* A small town dating back to the 7th century, with the famous Dee Bridge (a scheduled Ancient Monument), some old mill sluice gates and the remains of a weir. 18 F5
Buildings Castell Dinas Bran • Plas Newydd • Valle Crucis Abbey
Family attractions Llangollen Exhibition Centre • Victorian School of the 3 R's and Heritage Centre
Transport Llangollen Motor Museum • Llangollen Railway

Lymm *Cheshire* A charming village with a late medieval cross, the 17th-century Dane Bank House and Lymm Hall, 18th-century buildings associated with the Manchester Ship Canal, and a stream and a dam. 33 B8

Portmeirion, Gwynedd

Macclesfield *Cheshire* The area's main town, long associated with the silk industry and among the UK's 30 most wealthy towns. A medieval town, it has cobbled streets and many quaint old buildings, including the former Hovis Mill. 35 E5
Buildings Adlington Hall • Gawsworth Hall
Local history & industry Macclesfield Silk Museums
Outdoors Alderley Edge • Gritstone Trail • Middlewood Way • West Park

Malham *North Yorkshire* An attractive and popular little village which affords access to some of the country's best limestone scenery. It contains a Dales clapper bridge and a pinfold, and nearby is the romantically set waterfall of Janet's Foss. 54 C2
Other natural features Malham Cove and Gordale Scar
Sport Yorkshire Dales Trekking Centre

Malpas *Cheshire* A pleasant small town with a character typical of this part of England containing many charming old buildings, including a 17th-century tithe barn. 20 E2
Outdoors Parks & gardens Cholmondeley Castle Gardens

Matlock and Matlock Bath *Matlock, Derbyshire* A former spa resort just outside the Peak District National Park, divided into Matlock with its orderly Victorian stone houses and the more frivolous tourist centre of Matlock Bath. 24 B4
Local history & industry Mining Museum • Temple Mine
Outdoors Heights of Abraham
Transport Red House Stables Working Carriage Museum

Milldale *Staffordshire* An unspoilt hamlet with a National Trust information barn for walkers, the remains of three mills and a restored sheepwash. Linked to Dovedale by the picturesque Viator ('Traveller') Bridge. 23 D8

Monyash *Derbyshire* A popular but unspoilt village around a green, with a village cross dating from 1340, and old Quaker meeting house and cemetery, ancient farms and narrow fields that were enclosures of medieval strips. 23 A9

Muker *North Yorkshire* A Viking-origin village in a remote, unspoilt area, surrounded by protected flower-rich hay meadows and 'buttertubs' (deep potholes used to store butter). Nearby is high, single-span Ivelet Bridge, one of the finest Swale bridges. 60 A4

Northwich *Cheshire* A town that grew wealthy from salt mining, now a conservation area with timber-framed shops and other buildings; the Weaver Heritage Trail and Northwich Town Trail retrace its history. 33 E8
Local history & industry Salt Museum

Ormskirk *Lancashire* A prosperous market town with Viking roots, surrounded by farms and market gardens. The historic Charter Market – one of the UK's oldest and most traditional street markets – dates back to 1286. 38 C5
Religious buildings St Peter and St Paul Church

Port Sunlight ✶ *Merseyside* A Victorian garden village founded by soap magnate William Hesketh Leverhulme to share his profits with his factory workers and pursue his interest in housing reform. There's a heritage centre and self-guided trails. ☏0151 644 6466 32 C1
Art & crafts Lady Lever Art Gallery

Portmeirion ✶✶ *near Porthmadog, Gwynedd* An Italianate village created by architect Sir Clough Williams-Ellis from 1925 to 1975 and made famous by the cult 1960s show 'The Prisoner'. ☏01766 770000 6 A3

Rheged *Redhills, Cumbria* The 'Village in the Hills', named after Cumbria's Celtic Kingdom, with an IMAX cinema in Europe's largest earth-covered building, a tourist information centre, craft demonstrations and specialist shops, and the new Helly Hansen National Mountaineering Exhibition. ☏01768 868000 71 F5

Rhiw *Gwynedd* One of the highest villages on the Llyn peninsula, with some of the best views in Wales and much evidence of early settlement, including dolmens, early field patterns and the site of a Stone Age axehead 'factory'. 4 C4
Houses & gardens Plas yn Rhiw

Ruthin *Denbighshire* A picturesque hilltop town with half-timbered buildings and medieval street; King Arthur is reputed to have had a love rival executed at the 'Maen Huail' stone in front of Exmewe Hall. 18 C3
Art & crafts Ruthin Craft Centre Gallery
Country & forest parks Moel Famau Country Park
Local history & industry Old Gaol

St Asaph *Denbighshire* An prominent town, with the 16th-century Bishops Palace, two old deaneries, some 1680 almshouses and the 1840 workhouse where HM Stanley of 'Doctor Livingstone, I presume' fame spent his early years. 30 E2
Religious buildings St Asaph Cathedral

St Asaph Cathedral

Malpas, Cheshire

Sedbergh *Cumbria* An historic market town beneath the Howgill Fells, with a 1675 Quaker meeting house, a peaceful Victorian park, the remnants of a Norman earthwork motte and bailey castle, a wooden spinning gallery and a conservation area including a medieval shop. **59 B7**

Singleton *Lancashire* A conservation area dubbed the 'model village of the Fylde', with a Grade II listed church and one of the UK's few remaining half-timbered fire stations. It was remodelled as an estate village by a Preston cotton magnate in the late 19th century. **44 D3**

Slaidburn *Lancashire* An attractive grey-stone village in the moorland area of the Forest of Bowland, with The Hark to Bounty Inn containing the Halmote Courtroom, thought to have been used by Cromwell and still employed in the 1930s, plus a village pottery. **53 E6**
Religious buildings St Andrew's Church

Summerseat *Greater Manchester* A former mill village, part of which is a conservation area, boasting the preserved millworker's red-bricked terraced houses. Crossed by the East Lancashire Steam Railway (see *Transport*) and situated beside Irwell Gorge beauty spot. **40 B4**

Thornton Hough *Merseyside* A traditional village set amidst pastures and woodland, with an ancient green where cricket matches are played, a manor house, a Norman-style church and a working smithy. **31 C8**

Tissington *Derbyshire* A charming village and access point to the Tissington Trail, dominated by the 1609 hall of the FitzHerbert family and containing five wells, many fine early-19th-century buildings and an avenue of lime trees. **24 D1**

Trefriw *Conwy* A village skirted by an ancient Roman road, with the still-operational Trefriw Wells, a spa used by the Romans. A one-time river port and then a tourist centre, it retains some large Victorian houses that began life as boarding houses, and also boasts a wool mill. **16 B3**

Ulverston *Cumbria* A Georgian market town full of specialist shops, cobbled streets and winding ginnels, best known as the birthplace of Stan Laurel, and home to Britain's shortest, widest and deepest canal. **57 E6**
Museums Laurel and Hardy Museum
Religious buildings Conishead Priory
Walking, cycling & riding trails Cumbria Cycle Way • Cumbria Way

Uppermill *Greater Manchester* The largest of the Saddleworth villages, with an impressive viaduct and some late-18th-century woollen mills. **42 C1**
Local history & industry Saddleworth Museum

Waddington *Lancashire* The frequent winner of the 'Best Kept Village in Lancashire' award, largely thanks to its brook and Coronation Gardens. The almshouses constructed in the 1700s were rebuilt around the green. **46 B3**

Wardle *Greater Manchester* An old weaving hamlet and former staging post on the Long Causeway (a packhorse road over the moors), with a spectacular setting and a conservation area based around its square and old chapel. **41 A7**

Watendlath★ *Cumbria* A National Trust owned hamlet 847 feet above sea level, with a tarn surrounded by fells in a classic 'hanging valley'. There's a packhorse bridge, two famous viewpoints (Ashness Bridge and Surprise View) and a tearoom. ☎017687 72645 **63 C8**

Whalley *Lancashire* A pretty village full of old cottages, Tudor and Georgian buildings, and shops and galleries. The first 'Roses' cricket match between Lancashire and Yorkshire was held here. **46 C3**
Religious buildings Whalley Church • Whalley Abbey

Whitegate *Cheshire* One of the area's prettiest villages, with thatched cottages and a green, said to have got its name from the gate of the white monks of Vale Royal Abbey. **33 F7**

Wincle *Cheshire* One of area's most picturesque villages, situated on the banks of the River Dane and a favourite place among walkers, with fine views of moorland, woodland and drystone-walled pastureland. **22 A5**

Winster *Derbyshire* One of the Peak District's oldest and most attractive villages, once the centre of the local lead mining industry. Among its impressive buildings are Winster Hall, Dower House and the 16th- and 17th-century Market Hall, owned by the National Trust. **24 B2**

Worsley★ *Greater Manchester* A village with timbered housing, idyllic scenery and industrial heritage in the form of the underground canals at The Delphone, making it a potential World Heritage site. Other interesting sights include the Alphabet Bridge, 17th-century Nail Maker's shop, grand Court House and 18th-century dry docks. **40 D3**
Religious buildings St Mark's Church

Wray *Lancashire* A delightful village with a number of 17th-century yeomen's cottages, once a textile centre with silk mills, tanners and basket-makers. **52 B4**

Wrea Green *Lancashire* An archetypal English country village with Lancashire's biggest village green, once the site of cockfighting, now used for cricket matches. **44 D5**

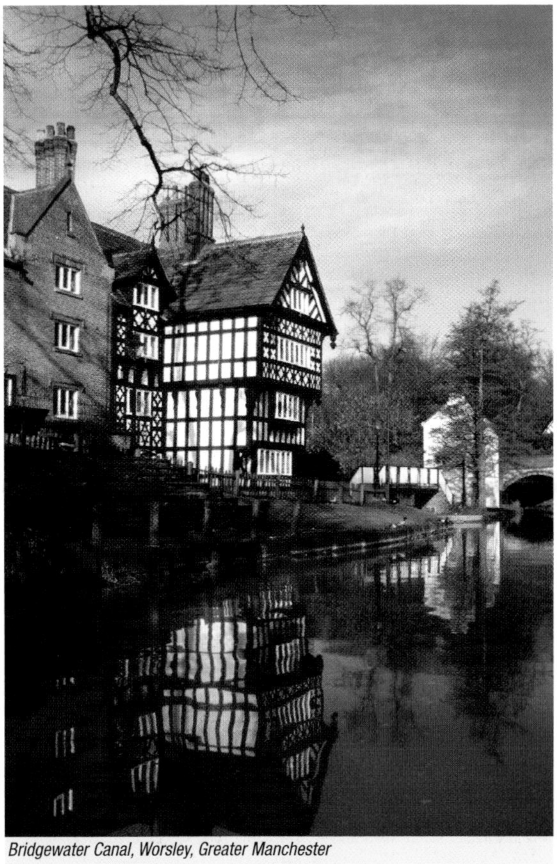

Bridgewater Canal, Worsley, Greater Manchester

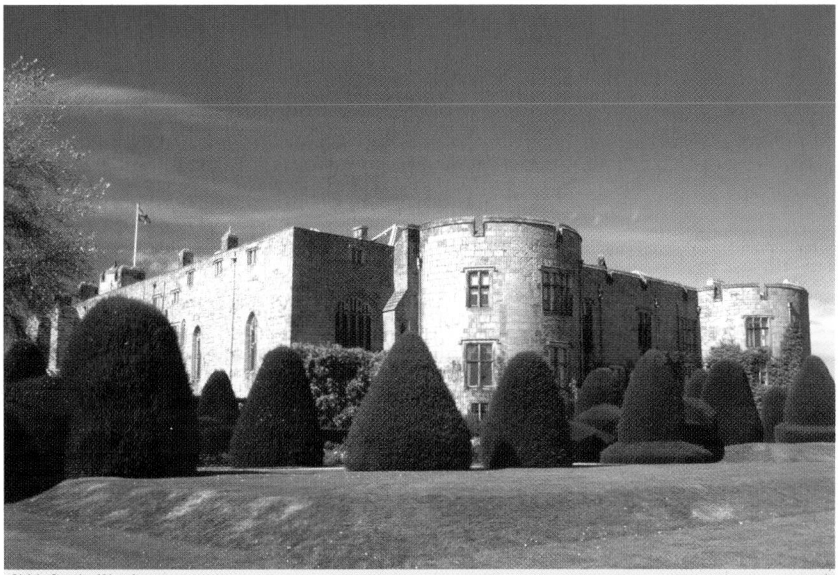

Chirk Castle, Wrexham

Buildings

Castles

Appleby Castle *Appleby-in-Westmorland, Cumbria* A Norman castle once owned by the kings of England and the stronghold of the Clifford lords, with a late-17th-century dwelling house, a Great Hall with paintings and furniture, and 25 acres of parkland with rare breeds and a weeping cedar. ☎01768 351402 **65 B8**

Beaumaris Castle *Castle Street, Beaumaris, Isle of Anglesey* An unfinished castle intended as one of Edward I's 'iron ring', with an ingenious symmetrical concentric design involving four successive lines of fortifications. ☎01248 810361 **28 D2**

Beeston Castle *Tarporley, Cheshire* A 13th-century ruined fortress built according to Middle-Eastern methods, with views of the Pennines to the east and the Welsh mountains to the west. ☎01829 260 464 **20 B4**

Bodelwyddan Castle *Bodelwyddan, Denbighshire* A 19th-century mock-medieval castle with turrets and battlements, designed by Joseph Hansom of Hansom cab fame and now an outstation of the National Portrait Gallery, with 260 acres of parkland, woodland trails, orienteering and WWI practice trenches. ☎01745 584060 **30 D2**

Bolton Castle *near Leyburn, North Yorkshire* A well-preserved medieval fortress on the border of the Yorkshire Dales National Park, built in 1399 by the 1st Lord Scrope of Bolton. The five floors have tableaux about castle life in the 15th century. ☎01969 623981 **61 B8**

Brough Castle *Brough, Cumbria* A ruined castle, parts of which date back to c.1100, with the semicircular Clifford's Tower added in the 13th century. English Heritage information panels retell its history. **66 D3**

Brougham Castle *Brougham, Cumbria* A 13th-century ruined riverside castle owned by English Heritage, built on the site of a Roman fort. The keep and gatehouse were restored by Lady Anne Clifford. ☎01768 862488 **71 F5**

Caernarfon Castle *Beaumaris, Isle of Anglesey* A commanding castle begun in 1283 as Edward I's seat of government and royal place, with unique polygonal towers and colour-banded masonry. ☎01248 810361 **28 D2**

Carlisle Castle *Carlisle, Cumbria* A medieval fortress with ancient chambers, stairways, dungeons and 'licking stones' where Jacobite prisoners tried to quench their thirst. Guided tours. ☎01228 591922 **75 E8**

Castell Dinas Bran *near Llangollen, Denbighshire* The medieval hilltop ruin of 'Crow Castle', 13th-century home of Madoc ap Gruffydd Maelor, founder of Valle Crucis Abbey, surrounded by the remnants of an Iron Age hill-fort and ditch and offering breathtaking views. **18 F5**

Chester Castle *Castle Square, Chester, Cheshire* A castle constructed by Hugh the Wolf shortly after 1066 but rebuilt for civic use between 1788 and 1822 by Thomas Harrison. Its Agricola Tower has some newly discovered early-medieval wall paintings. ☎01244 402008 **32 F2**

Chirk Castle *Chirk, Wrexham* A 1310 Marcher fortress, still home to the Myddelton family, with staterooms filled with Adam-style furniture, tapestries and portraits. The grounds include a thatched 'Hawk House', a classical pavilion, a 17th-century lime tree avenue and 18th-century parkland. ☎01691 777701 **10 A2**

Conwy Castle *Conwy* A ruin considered to have been of the greatest European fortresses, built by Edward I and accessed via an 1826 suspension bridge preserved by the National Trust. **28 D5**

Criccieth Castle *Castle Street, Criccieth, Gwynedd* A North Wales landmark on a headland between two beaches, originally a stronghold of the Welsh princes but annexed and extended by Edward I. ☎01766 522227 **6 A2**

Denbigh Castle *Denbigh, Denbighshire* A ruined hilltop castle with a triple-towered gatehouse, built as part of Edward I's 13th-century campaigns against the Welsh. ☎01745 813385 **18 A1**

Dolwyddelan Castle *Dolwyddelan, Conwy* A dramatically sited castle built by Welsh prince Llwelyn the Great in 1210-40, with a rectangular stone tower restored in Victorian times. ☎01690 750366 **16 D2**

Egremont Castle *Egremont, Cumbria* The ruins of a castle built by William de Meschines c.1130 on the site of a Norman mound, with well-preserved ditches and the remains of the gatehouse. ☎01946 820693 **62 D3**

Gwydir Castle *Llanrwst, Conwy* A Tudor courtyard house built c.1500, using material from the dissolved medieval Abbey of Maenan, and containing a 1640s panelled dining room reclaimed from the New York Metropolitan Museum. The 10-acre garden is Grade I listed. ☎01492 641687 **16 B4**

Gyrn Castle *Llanasa, Flintshire* An 18th- and 19th-century castle with a large picture gallery and panelled entrance hall. Visits by appointment. ☎01745 853500 **30 C4**

Halton Castle *Runcorn, Halton* One of two ruined Norman castles in Cheshire, probably laid out c.1071 by Nigel, 1st Baron of Halton. Not open to the public except for special events, but visitors can enjoy the Castle Hotel public house set into the castle wall. ☎01928 569895 **32 C5**

Harlech Castle *Castle Square, Harlech, Gwynedd* A spectacularly sited castle built by Edward I in the late 13th century as part of his 'iron ring' and later taken by Welsh leader Owain Glyn Dwr as the seat of his parliament, with a twin-towered gatehouse and stunning views from its battlements. ☎01766 780552 **6 B3**

Lancaster Castle★ *Lancaster, Lancashire* One of the UK's best-preserved castles, built on a site of Roman fortifications, owned by the Queen and still used as a court and prison. Visitors can see Gillow furniture, dungeons, the Shire Hall with its 600 heraldic shields, and the Crown Court from which convicts were transported to Australia. ☎01524 64998 **51 C8**

Lowther Castle *near Penrith, Cumbria* Sir Robert Smirke's first building (in 1806) and the Lonsdale family seat, dismantled after the death of the 5th earl, though the walls were retained as a memorial. The estate contains the 'Lowther Oak', said to be responsible for the good fortune of the Lonsdales. ☎01768 867466 **71 E5**

Middleham Castle *Middleham, North Yorkshire* A 12th-century fortress with one of the largest keeps in England, the childhood home of Richard III and subsequently his main castle in the north. The battlements have spectacular views. ☎01969 623899 **61 C8**

Mow Cop Castle *Congleton Edge, Congleton, Cheshire* A recently repaired hilltop folly, built in 1750 by the Wilbraham family of nearby Rode Hall, owned by the National Trust and offering wonderful views of the Cheshire Plain. Marks the beginning of the Staffordshire Way footpath. ☎0260 270795 **22 B3**

Muncaster Castle, Gardens and World Owl Trust★ *Ravenglass, Cumbria* An historic house with famous grounds, including the 77-acre Himalayan Gardens, the 'Meadowvolemaze' and the Terrace Walk, described by Ruskin as the 'Gateway to Paradise'. The Owl Trust runs 'Meet the Birds' flying displays and a 'Heron Happy Hour'. ☎01229 717614 **56 A2**

Pendragon Castle *near Kirkby Stephen, Cumbria* An isolated Norman ruin in Mallerstang Dale, razed by the Scots in 1541 and rebuilt in the 17th century by the powerful Clifford family. According to legend, Uther Pendragon, father of King Arthur, was poisoned here. **66 E3**

Artists' and poets' houses

Brantwood *Coniston, Cumbria* The home of John Ruskin from 1872 until he died in 1900, with the writer's furniture, books and other possessions, plus some of his drawings and watercolours. ☎015394 33002 **57 A7**

Dove Cottage and The Wordsworth Museum★ *Grasmere, Cumbria* The cottage where Wordsworth lived from 1799 to 1808, offering guided tours and with an adjoining award-winning museum about the poet's life and work. ☎015394 35544 **64 E1**

Hill Top★ *Near Sawrey, Cumbria* Beatrix Potter's holiday home, bought in 1905 and bequeathed to the National Trust on her death in 1943 on the proviso that it be kept as she left it. ☎015394 36269 **57 A8**

Lowry's House *117 Station Road, Swinton, Greater Manchester* The place where the painter lived from 1909 to 1948. By appointment only. ☎0161 794 5389 **40 D4**

Rydal Mount Close *Ambleside, Cumbria* Wordsworth's home from 1813 to 1850, containing some of his possessions, as well as portraits and poems. Visitors can see the dining room, part of the old Tudor cottage, and the drawing room and library added in 1750. ☎015394 33002 **64 F2**

Wordsworth House *Main Street, Cockermouth, Cumbria* The Georgian townhouse where the poet was born in 1770, now owned by the National Trust. As well as personal effects, there's a walled garden and terrace walk, and a tearoom in the old kitchen. ☎01900 824805 **69 E5**

Penrhyn Castle★ *Bangor, Gwynedd* An exuberant early-19th-century neo-Norman castle built by a local slate and sugar baron, with a one-ton slate bed made for Queen Victoria and paintings by the likes of Rembrandt, Gainsborough and Canaletto. The stable block has two railway museums, a doll museum and two galleries. ☎01248 353084 **27 E8**

Penrith Castle *Castle Park, Penrith, Cumbria* An imposing moated ruin begun in 1399 with the addition of a stone wall to an existing pele tower, mainly against Scottish raids, and later a fortress for Richard, Duke of Gloucester before he became King Richard III in 1483. ☎01768 867466 **71 E5**

Peveril Castle *near Castleton, Derbyshire* A ruined castle built in wood in 1080 and reconstructed in stone a century later, retaining its keep built by Henry I in 1176 and, in its curtain wall, some Roman tiles that may have been taken from the ruins of the fort at Navio (Brough). **36 C3**

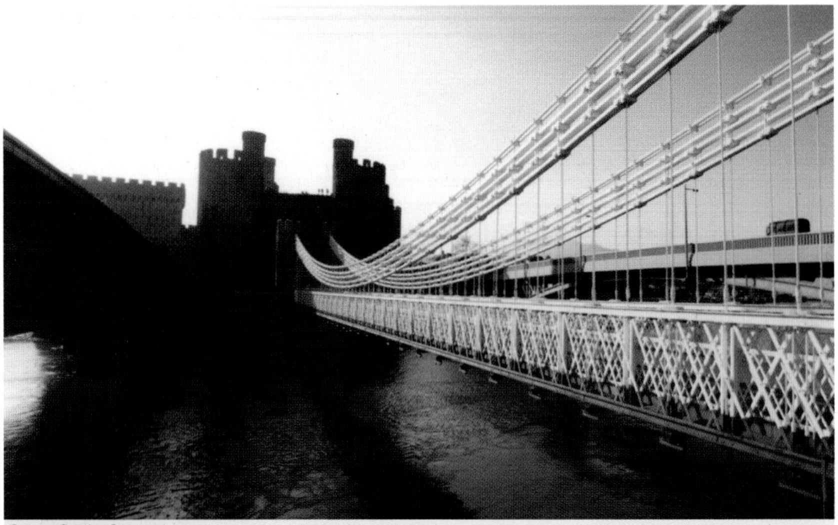

Conwy Castle, Conwy

Rhuddlan Castle *Rhuddlan, Denbighshire* A concentrically planned castle, the second of Edward I's 'iron ring', with a massive twin-towered gatehouse and diamond-shaped inner ward constructed in 1277. One side of its defences is formed by a protected dock dug out to allow ships access. ☎01745 590777 **30 D2**

Skipton Castle *Skipton, North Yorkshire* One of England's most complete medieval castles, famous for withstanding a three-year siege in the Civil War, with a banqueting hall, kitchen, bedchamber, privy, dungeon, watchtower and ancient well. ☎01756 792442 **54 E3**

Houses & gardens

Aberconwy House *Castle Street, Conwy* A medieval merchant's house with period rooms and an exhibition about life in the town from Roman times on. ☎01492 592246 **28 D5**

Arley Hall *Arley, Cheshire* An early-Victorian, Jacobean-style country house with an avenue of 'Quercus ilex' trees and a herb garden among 100 acres of gardens and parkland. Within the estate is Arley Green,with listed buildings and a village green. ☎01565 777353 **33 C8**

Astley Hall *Astley Park, Chorley, Lancashire* A 16th-century hall in 94 acres of parkland, containing boots Cromwell allegedly left behind, as well as furniture and ornate plaster ceilings and wall hangings. ☎01257 515555 **39 A8**

Bolton Abbey Estate *Skipton, North Yorkshire* The 30,000-acre working estate of the Duke and Duchess of Devonshire, with medieval buildings, moorland, woodland and riverside footpaths. ☎01756 718009 **54 E3**

Bramall Hall *Bramhall, Greater Manchester* A magpie half-timbered building boasting pre-Reformation passion paintings and an Elizabethan plaster ceiling, surrounded by a parkland with lakes and two playgrounds. ☎0161 485 3708 **34 B4**

Browsholme Hall *Bashall Eaves, Lancashire* A handsome mansion dating from the time of Henry VII, containing wood carvings, rare books, period furniture, textiles and arms and armour. ☎01254 86330 **46 B2**

Capesthorne Hall *Siddington, Cheshire* An 18th-century Jacobean-style red-brick hall containing silver, furniture, sculpture and paintings and surrounded by attractive gardens, parkland, woods and lakes. ☎01625 861221 **34 E3**

Chatsworth House★★ *Bakewell, Derbyshire* The Peak District's most popular tourist attraction, built in its current incarnation in 1686-1707 but retaining some Elizabethan interior walls and a 1580s hunting tower. The gardens were worked on by both 'Capability' Brown and Joseph Paxton. ☎01246 582204 **36 F4**

Croxteth Hall and Country Park *Muirhead Avenue East, Liverpool, Merseyside* The Earl of Sefton's Edwardian country estate, including his house, home farm and Victorian walled garden. ☎0151 228 5311 **32 A1**

Dalemain Historic House and Gardens *Dalemain, Cumbria* A medieval Tudor and early Georgian house with fine furniture, paintings and tapestries, and gardens with rare plants, trees, topiary and roses. ☎01768 486450 **70 F4**

Derwent Isle House *Keswick, Cumbria* A large National Trust house built on the biggest and most northerly of the four islands on Derwentwater in 1778, with a Gothic chapel-boathouse and Druid circle. Occasional trips are offered from the nearby landing stage. ☎017687 75936 **63 B8**

Dunham Massey Hall★ *Charcoal Lane, Altrincham, Greater Manchester* A 17th- and 18th- century red-brick stately home, with a collection of Huguenot silver and parklands with a parterre, moat, Elizabethan watermill, orangery, water garden and herd of fallow deer, plus a coach house with an exhibition about the park's natural history. ☎0161 941 1025 **34 B2**

Erddig House *near Wrexham* An 1680s house with 18th- and 19th-century furniture, impressive outbuildings (including a laundry, bakehouse and smithy) and an 18th-century walled garden with a Victorian parterre, yew walk and the National Collection of Ivies. ☎01978 355314 **19 D7**

Gawsworth Hall *Church Lane, Macclesfield, Cheshire* A half-timbered Norman manor house, site of a famous duel and host to open-air theatre productions in summer. Fitton Chapel, licensed in 1365, is still used by the family; Mary Fitton may have been the 'Dark Lady' of Shakespeare's sonnets. ☎01260 223456 **35 E5**

Haddon Hall *near Bakewell, Derbyshire* A medieval manor house restored by the 9th duke of Rutland in the 1920s, with a 17th-century kitchen and impressive gardens. ☎01629 812855 **36 F4**

Haigh Hall and Country Park *near Wigan, Greater Manchester* The former manor house of the Bradshaigh family, with a 250-acre wooded parkland complete with miles of trails and containing a model village, a childrens' playground, a narrow-gauge steam railway and golf ranges. ☎01942 832895 **39 C8**

Hall i'th'Wood *Green Way, off Crompton Way, Bolton, Greater Manchester* A timber-framed house extended in stone in 1591 and 1648, with fine 17th- and 18th-century furniture and a 'Lancashire Kitchen'. Once home to Samuel Crompton, inventor of the Spinning Mule. ☎01204 332370 **40 C3**

Hartsheath *Mold, Flintshire* An 18th- and 19th-century house in a small 19th-century parkland embracing formal gardens with flowering cherry and woodlands. By appointment only. ☎01352 770217 **18 B5**

Hoghton Tower *Hoghton, Lancashire* The 16th-century Renaissance hilltop home of the de Hoghton family, where James I knighted a loin of beef in 1617, creating the sirloin steak. Events include craft fairs and medieval weekends. ☎01254 852986 **45 E9**

Holker Hall and Gardens *Cark-in-Cartmel, Grange-over-Sands, Cumbria* A stately home in 25 acres of award-winning gardens boasting the world's biggest slate sundial. ☎015395 58328 **58 E2**

Hutton in the Forest *Penrith, Cumbria* The 14th-century house of Lord and Lady Inglewood, containing furniture, tapestries and portraits and surrounded by large gardens with topiary terraces and a woodland walk. ☎01768 484449 **71 E5**

Leighton Hall *Carnforth, Lancashire* The historic home of the Gillow family of furniture-makers, with Gothic towers and grounds with trained birds of prey. Events include craft fairs. ☎01524 734474 **52 A1**

Little Moreton Hall *Congleton, Cheshire* A well-preserved 15th-century timber-framed moated manor house with a wainscoated long gallery, owned by the National Trust. ☎01260 272018 **22 B3**

Lyme Hall and Park *Disley, Cheshire* A 1720 Palladian hall with Tudor origins, containing Grinling Gibbons carvings but most famous as 'Pemberley' in the BBC's 'Pride and Prejudice'. The vast parkland has red and fallow deer, an orangery and pools. ☎01663 762023 **35 C6**

Lytham Hall and Country Park *Ballam Road, Lytham, Lancashire* A hall built for Thomas Clifton by John Carr of York in the mid 18th century, currently closed to the public while being turned into a country park, though group tours are available by appointment. ☎01253 736652 **44 E4**

Meols Hall *Churchtown, Merseyside* An early-12th-century manor house in extensive private parkland, forming one of the oldest settlements in the area. There are open days and events such as Southport Spring Gardens Festival and Fireworks Night. ☎01704 28326 **38 A4**

Mirehouse Historic House and Gardens★ *Keswick, Cumbria* The 17th-century house of the Spedding family, set in award-winning landscaped gardens that include a 'poetry walk'. Inside are paintings and manuscripts by Tennyson, Southey and Wordsworth. ☎017687 72287 **63 B8**

Ordsall Hall *Ordsall Lane, Ordsall, Greater Manchester* A half-timbered manor house dating back more than 600 years, involved in the Gunpowder Plot and containing a furnished Tudor Great Hall and a Victorian kitchen. ☎0161 872 0251 **41 E5**

Peover Hall and Gardens *Knutsford, Cheshire* A 1585 Tudor manor house, with notable stables with plasterwork ceilings and gardens surrounded by a topiary-work hedge. ☎01565 722656 **34 D2**

Plas Mawr *Conwy, Conwy* One of the UK's best-preserved Elizabethan townhouses, with a gatehouse, stepped gables, a lookout tower and an original interior with elaborate plaster ceilings and wooden screens. ☎01492 580167 **28 D5**

Plas Newydd *Llanfairpwllgwyngyll, Isle of Anglesey* The 18th-century house of the 1st Marquess of Anglesey, built in a classical meets mock-Gothic style and boasting a 1930s interior, an exhibition about Whistler and a military museum. ☎01248 714795 **27 E7**

Plas Newydd★ *near Llangollen, Denbighshire* A black-and-white timbered house that belonged to the eccentric Irish 'Ladies of Llangollen', who dressed as men and entertained the likes of Sir Walter Scott and William Wordsworth here. The beautiful grounds are now a public park. ☎01978 861314 **18 F5**

Plas yn Rhiw *Rhiw, Gwynedd* A small 16th-century Welsh manor house in ornamental grounds, restored in 1938 by the Keating sisters and affording views across Cardigan Bay. ☎01758 780219 **4 C4**

Rufford Old Hall *Rufford, Lancashire* A 16th-century building with a great hall featuring elaborate timbering, a hammerbeam roof and a huge moveable screen, plus fine collections of furniture, tapestries, arms, armour and paintings, and magnificent gardens. ☎01704 821254 **39 A6**

Samlesbury Hall *Samlesbury, Lancashire* A 1325 black-and-white manor house formerly belonging to the Southworth family, with a Tudor parlour and fireplace. Hosts antique fairs. ☎01254 812010 **45 D8**

Smithills Hall and Country Park *Smithills Dean Road, Bolton, Greater Manchester* One of the area's oldest and best-preserved fortified manor houses, dating from the 14th century and containing Stuart furniture, a library with linenfold panelling, and a chapel. ☎01204 332377 **40 C3**

Speke Hall *The Walk, Speke, Merseyside* A half-timbered house dating from 1490, with grounds containing woodland trails and an 'Amazing Maze'. ☎0151 427 7231 **32 C3**

Sudley House *Mossley Hill, Merseyside* The home of Victorian shipping merchant and art collector George Holt, dating from the early 1800s and containing 18th- and 19th-century paintings, including Turners, Gainsboroughs and Reynolds, in their original setting. ☎0151 724 3245 **32 B2**

Tabley House *near Knutsford, Macclesfield, Cheshire* A Palladian mansion built in 1767 and visited by painters JMW Turner, Henry Thompson and James Ward, some of whose works can be seen here, along with Chippendale furniture. Next to it is the relocated St Peter's Chapel. ☎01565 750151 **35 E5**

Tatton Park★★ *Knutsford, Cheshire* A Georgian manor house (where 'Brideshead Revisited' was filmed) and Tudor Old Hall, with an art collection including works by Canaletto and Van Dyck. Its vast parkland has award-winning Japanese gardens and a working farm. ☎01565 654822 **34 D2**

The Ugly House *Ty Hill, Capel Curig, Conwy* A 'Ty Un Nos' or 'house built overnight' (under ancient law anyone who built a house between sunset and sunrise could claim the freehold), now the Snowdonia Society HQ with an exhibition about its work. ☎01690 720287 **16 C2**

Turton Tower *Chapeltown Road, Turton, Bolton, Greater Manchester* A country house dating from medieval times, with a defensive tower, period rooms, woodland gardens, temporary exhibitions and workshop demonstrations. ☎01204 85203 **40 C3**

Ty Mawr Wybrnant *Penmachno, Conwy* The restored 16th- and 17th-century house where Bishop William Morgan, the first translator of the whole Bible into Welsh, lived, now housing a display of Welsh Bibles. ☎01690 760213 **16 D3**

Ty n y Coed Uchaf *Penmachno, Conwy* A 19th-century farmhouse and outbuildings belonging to the National Trust, allowing an insight into life on a traditional smallholding. ☎01690 760229 **16 D3**

Walton Hall and Gardens *Walton Lea Road, Higher Walton, Cheshire* A hall built in the 1830s in the Elizabethan style, surrounded by a public park with picnic areas, a children's zoo and a heritage centre with a small Lewis Carroll exhibition. ☎01925 601617 **33 B6**

Wern Isaf *Penmaen Park, Llanfairfechan, Conwy* A 1900 Arts and Crafts house with original furniture and William Morris fabrics. ☎01248 680437 **28 D3**

Workington Hall *Curwen Park, Workington, Cumbria* The ruins of the manor house that provided shelter for Mary Queen of Scots on her last flight from Scotland, built around a 14th-century pele tower. ☎01900 606699 **68 F2**

Wythenshawe Hall *Wythenshawe Park, Northenden, Greater Manchester* A half-timbered Tudor house that played a dramatic role in the English Civil War, with oak-panelled interiors, glasshouses and a children's playground. ☎0161 998 2331 **34 A3**

Historic buildings

Adlington Hall *Macclesfield, Cheshire* A mainly 15th-century hall with magpie half-timbering, including a Great Hall with a 17th-century organ played on by Handel. In the grounds are a Temple of Diana, scented walkway, summerhouse, rose garden and maze. Group visits only. ☎01625 829206 **35 E5**

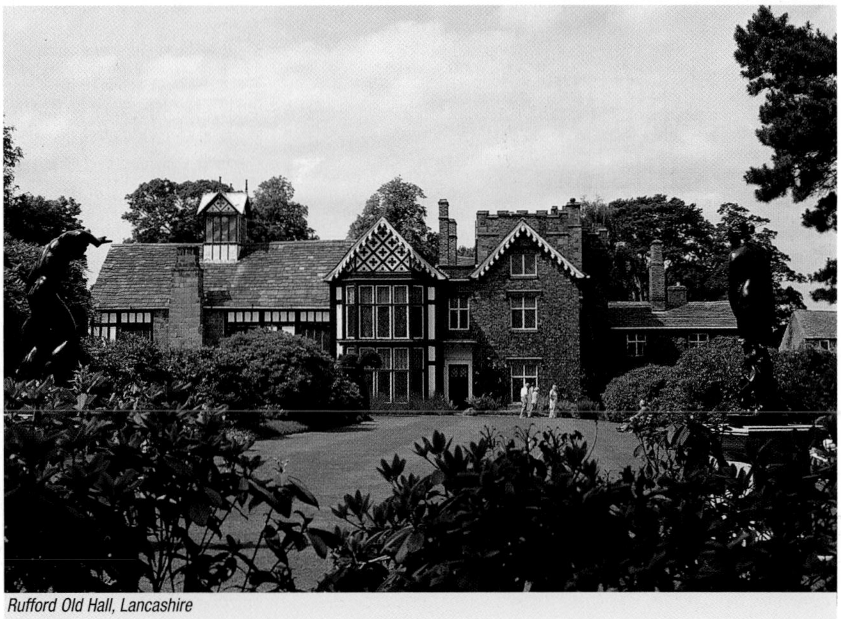

Rufford Old Hall, Lancashire

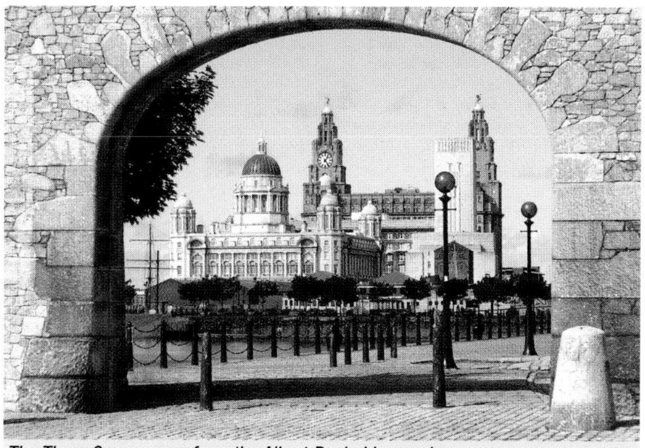

The Three Graces seen from the Albert Dock, Liverpool

Albert Dock★ *Liverpool, Merseyside* An 1846 dock that has undergone a £100-million transformation into a heritage attraction, boasting the largest group of Grade I listed buildings in the UK, plus attractions such as Tate Liverpool. ☎0151 708 8854 **32 A1**

Blackpool Tower *Blackpool* The famous 518ft tower, opened in 1894 and based on the Eiffel Tower, containing the brand-new Blackpool Tower Circus and the Ballroom. ☎01253 622242 **44 C3**

Cains Brewery *Stanhope Street, Liverpool, Merseyside* A Victorian brewhouse incorporating the Brewery Tap, a drinking landmark. Tours by arrangement. ☎0151 709 8734 **32 A1**

Citadel *English Street, Carlisle, Cumbria* Two huge oval towers at the southern entrance to the City of Carlisle, built in 1810-11 and until recently the civil and criminal courts; recently restored by English Heritage. ☎01228 606336 **75 E8**

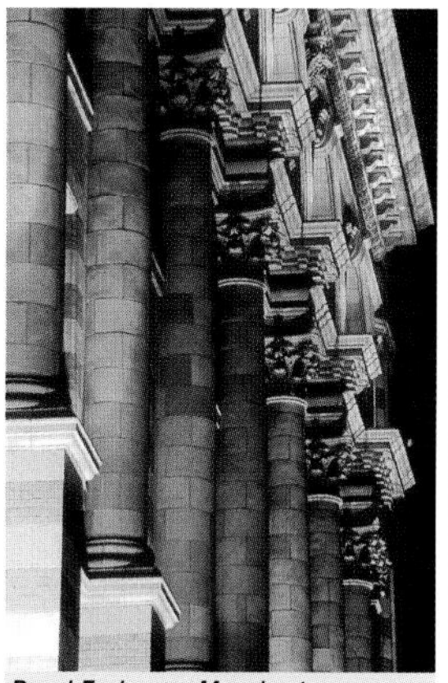

Royal Exchange, Manchester

Clifton Hall *near Penrith, Cumbria* An isolated three-storey pele tower thought to have been built in the 16th century, with information plaques showing how it probably looked when in use. ☎01768 867466 **71 E5**

Littleborough Coach House and Heritage Centre *Lodge Street, Littleborough, Greater Manchester* A Grade II listed, late-18th-century coach house within a conservation area, now a visitor centre covering the area. ☎01706 378481 **41 A7**

Liverpool Town Hall *High Street, Liverpool, Merseyside* A Grade I listed building with elegant staterooms, chandeliers and valuable paintings. By appointment only. ☎0151 707 2391 **32 A1**

Manchester Town Hall *Albert Square, Manchester, Greater Manchester* Manchester's Victorian-Gothic monument, with a giant clock tower and spire and a Great Hall described by Ruskin as 'the most truly magnificent Gothic apartment in Europe', with murals by Ford Madox Brown illustrating events in the city's history. ☎0161 234 5000 **41 E6**

Rochdale Town Hall *The Esplanade, Rochdale, Greater Manchester* A Victorian-Gothic town hall by William Crossland, with a stone tower by Alfred Waterhouse, architect of Manchester Town Hall. The Great Hall has a hammerbeam roof, a large mural of the Magna Carta and stained-glass windows picturing British monarchs. ☎01706 356592 **41 B6**

Royal Exchange *St Ann's Square, Manchester, Greater Manchester* A building constructed in 1729 and rebuilt after WWII and the IRA bomb of 1996, containing the former trading room of the global cotton industry, northern England's biggest room, with three glass domes and Corinthian columns, plus theatres and other amenities. ☎0161 833 9833 **41 E6**

Royal Liver Building *Pier Head, Liverpool, Merseyside* Liverpool's best-known landmark, built by the Royal Liver Friendly Society in the early 20th century and topped by two copper Liver Birds (the city's symbol). Tours by appointment. ☎0151 236 2748 **32 A1**

South Stack Lighthouse★ *Holyhead, Isle of Anglesey* A spectacular lighthouse on Holy Island, built in 1809 and accessed via 543 steps. The visitor centre, Ellin's Tower, has live footage of birds nesting on the cliffs. ☎01248 752444 **26 C2**

Stonyhurst College *Hurst Green, Lancashire* A boarding school with a museum collection boasting a 7th-century Gospel of St John. Cromwell stayed here in 1648; in 1811 it was the first gas-lit public building; Conan Doyle set 'The Hound of the Baskervilles here'; and Tolkien wrote in a guesthouse in the grounds. ☎01254 827073 **46 C2**

Swarthmoor Hall *Swarthmoor, Cumbria* The Grade II listed 16th-century building where George Fox, founder of the Society of Friends, dictated his journal, boasting an exhibition on Quaker history, 17th-century furniture and beautiful grounds. ☎01229 583204 **57 E6**

The Rows *Watergate Street, Northgate Street, Eastgate Street and Bridge Street, Chester, Cheshire* Unique half-timbered galleries forming a second row of shops above those at street level; the Three Old Arches in Bridge Street are the oldest shopfront in Britain. **32 F2**

Monuments & ancient sites

Barclodiad-y-Gawres *near Aberffraw, Isle of Anglesey* A chambered tomb spectacularly sited overlooking a bay, containing five carved stones. **26 F4**

Bryn-Celli-Ddum *Llanddaniel Fab, Isle of Anglesey* A late Neolithic tomb built on top of a previous circle henge, with a 27ft passage leading to the burial chamber. **27 E6**

Castlerigg Stone Circle *near Keswick, Cumbria* A ring of 38 stones up to 8ft tall enclosing a rectangular configuration of 10 stones, thought to have been a Druid place of worship 4000-5000 years ago. **63 B8**

Cenotaph *Market Place, Preston, Lancashire* A monument designed by Giles Gilbert Scott in the classical style, closely resembling the Cenotaph in Whitehall, London. **45 E7**

Countess Pillar *near Penrith, Cumbria* A pillar erected in 1656 by Lady Anne Clifford to her mother and restored by English Heritage. The nearby Dolestone is where Anne distributed alms once a year. ☎01768 867466 **71 E5**

Din Lligwy *near Ty-Mawr, Isle of Anglesey* A 4th-century settlement surrounded by a low stone wall, within which are the remains of nine huts, two of them circular. Nearby are the remains of Capel Lligwy, a 12th-century chapel. **27 B6**

Druids Temple *Birkrigg Common, Cumbria* An Iron and Bronze Age site with the remains of a double stone circle. **57 F6**

Hartshead Pike *Ashton-under-Lyne, Greater Manchester* The third tower built in the area (to commemorate the marriage of the Prince of Wales, later Edward VII, in 1863), known for its views of four counties. **41 E7**

Hendre Waelod *Llansanffraid Glan Conwy, Conwy* A neolithic burial chamber on the bank of the River Conwy, a rare portal dolmen with traditional high portal stones. **29 D6**

Lligwy Burial Chamber *near Ty-Mawr, Isle of Anglesey* A 28-ton capstone covering a burial chamber believed to have been used in the Neolithic period and the Bronze Age. **27 B6**

Long Meg and Her Daughters *Little Salkeld, Cumbria* The UK's second largest stone circle, c.350ft in diameter, probably a meeting place or site of religious ritual dating from c.1500 BC, described by Wordsworth as 'next to Stonehenge ... the most notable relick that this or probably any other country contains.' **71 D6**

Maen y Bardd (Stone of the Bard) *Rowen, Conwy* A neolithic burial chamber above the River Conwy, thought to date back to 3500BC, with sidestones and capstones that project to form a portal area. **28 E5**

Mayburgh Henge and King Arthur's Round Table *near Penrith, Cumbria* A circular bank containing a monolith probably dating from between 2000 and 1000 BC, possibly a prehistoric meeting place, next to an earthwork consisting of an irregular bank surrounding a circular ditch. **71 E5**

Ty Mawr Hut Circles *Holyhead, Isle of Anglesey* A small late Neolithic or early Bronze Age agricultural settlement comprised of about 19 structures spread over 15-20 acres of mountainside. **26 C2**

Ty Newydd *near Llanfaelog, Isle of Anglesey* A restored cromlech that is all that remains of a Neolithic tomb that remained in use into the Bronze Age. **26 E3**

Religious buildings

All Saints Church★ *Boltongate, Cumbria* A c.1400 Perpendicular church described by Pevsner as one of Cumbria's architectural sensations, with a steeply arched stone tunnel vault supported on 3ft-thick stone walls. **69 C7**

All Saints Church *Daresbury, Halton* An 1870 structure on the site of a 12th-century church, with a 16th-century tower, pulpit and screen with unusual grotesque carvings, and large stained-glass window depicting characters from 'Alice in Wonderland'. **33 C6**

All Saints Church *Whitefield, Greater Manchester* A landmark Gothic church by Sir Charles Barry (architect of the Houses of Parliament), built from the 'Waterloo' fund for the construction of churches after Napoleon's defeat. **41 C5**

Bakewell Church *Bakewell, Derbyshire* A late-Norman church, drastically renovated in the 1840s but retaining a 14th-century font, some ancient stone coffins, fragments of carved Saxon stonework, and two 9th-century Saxon crosses. **36 F4**

Birkenhead Priory and St Mary's Tower *Priory Street, Birkenhead, Merseyside* A Benedictine monastery established in 1150, possibly the oldest surviving building on Merseyside. The restored tower of St Mary's Church (1822) has views of the Liverpool waterfront. ☎0151 666 1249 **31 B8**

Blackburn Cathedral *Cathedral Close, Blackburn* Lancashire's only Anglican cathedral, on a site of Christian worship dating back to the 7th century and providing one of the earliest examples of the 19th-century Gothic revival, with noteworthy ceiling vaulting. ☎01254 51491 **46 E2**

Carlisle Cathedral *Castle Street, Carlisle, Cumbria* A restored red-sandstone cathedral, originally an 1122 priory, most notable for its great east window and carved oak misericords beneath the choir stalls. In the grounds is the Deanery, with the14th-century Prior's Tower containing a 16th-century heraldic ceiling. ☎01228 548151 **75 E8**

Cathedral Church of St John the Baptist *Chapel Street, Salford, Greater Manchester* A Victorian take on a medieval church, possibly the first built in the cruciform shape after the Reformation, with a stained-glass east window depicting the history of the Catholic Church in England. ☎0161 834 0333 **41 E5**

Chadkirk Chapel *Vale Road, Romiley, Greater Manchester* A simple medieval chapel on a site where St Chad is said to have arrived in the 7th century, with an audiovisual presentation on its history, and commissioned carvings and sculpture depicting scenes from the life of St Chad. ☎0161 430 5611 **35 A5**

Chester Cathedral★ *St Werburgh Street, Chester, Cheshire* A cathedral on the site of a Norman church begun in 1092, parts of which can still be seen, along with choirstalls with intricate misericords, well-preserved monastic cloisters, and a famous picture painted on cobwebs. Handel rehearsed his 'Messiah' here in 1742. ☎01244 324756 **32 F2**

Conishead Priory *Priory Road, Ulverston, Cumbria* A Victorian-Gothic mansion turned Buddhist centre and temple surrounded by woodlands. Guided tours. ☎01229 584029 **57 E6**

Eyam Church *Eyam, Derbyshire* A mainly 13th- and 14th-century church with two Norman columns, containing many relics of the Plague and a small exhibition about it. The churchyard has a 7th-century Saxon cross with pagan and Christian symbols and a fine sundial. **36 D4**

First Church of Christ Scientist★ *Edgar Wood Building, Daisy Bank Road, Manchester, Greater Manchester* A church of international importance, designed in the Arts and Crafts style by Edgar Wood in 1903 and lauded by Pevsner. Now a business centre; visits by pre-arrangement. ☎0161 248 3500 **41 E6**

Gosforth Church *Gosforth, Cumbria* A rural church boasting the tallest Viking cross in England (14ft, with Christian symbols on one side and Pagan and Norse symbols on the other) in its churchyard, as well as Europe's most northerly cork tree. **62 F4**

Great Altcar Church *Great Altcar, Lancashire* A parish church built in 1879 by the Earl of Sefton and one of the country's last authentic timber-framed buildings. The churchyard contains a pedestal font and stoup from earlier churches on the same site. **38 C3**

Great Budworth Church★ *Great Budworth, Cheshire* A mainly 15th-century masterpiece built under the supervision of the monks of Norton Priory, with an array of carvings. One of the friezes has a wild boar, emblem of Richard III. The churchyard contains the old grammar school building with the remains of a sundial. **33 D8**

Gujarat Hindu Society Temple *Preston, Lancashire* A new £3.6-million landmark built along traditional Indian lines. **45 E7**

Roman sites

Castlefield *Manchester, Greater Manchester* An 18th-century canal hub turned into the world's first Urban Heritage Park, looked after by 'urban rangers' on mountain bikes, with ruins dating from the first Roman settlement in the area in AD79, a recreated Roman fort, and bars, restaurants and hotels. ☎0161 834 4026 **41 E6**

City Walls *Chester, Cheshire* The most complete city walls in Britain, forming a two-mile circular promenade with information plaques and views of the surrounding countryside, built by the Romans in the first century AD. ☎01244 402008 **32 F2**

Deva Roman Experience *Pierpoint Lane, Bridge Street, Chester, Cheshire* Roman remains recently unearthed by archaeologists beneath the city, along with relics of Saxon and medieval life. The activity studio allows you to try on a replica suit of Roman armour, handle Roman pottery and animal bones and so on. ☎01244 343407 **32 F2**

Hadrian's Wall★★ *Cumbria* A World Heritage Site, some of the most accessible and interesting parts of which are in Cumbria, including the remains of Birdoswald Roman Fort, with its visitor centre; the well-preserved Poltross Burn Milecastle at Gilsland; the Banks East Turret and Pike Hill Signal Tower; and Bewcastle, the ramparts of an outpost fort with a small exhibition. ☎01434 322002 **74 D4 to 77 B9**

Hardknott Roman Fort *Hardknott Pass, near Ravenglass, Cumbria* A dramatic National Trust owned ruined fort above the valley of Eskdale, with views down to Ravenglass with its Roman ruins. ☎01900 81616 **56 A2**

Kanovium Roman Settlement *Caerhun, Gwynedd* A archaeological site with the remains of two prehistoric forts, a Roman fort, a Roman road, a chambered tomb, and Iron Age and medieval age farms and field systems. **27 F8**

Milefortlet 21★ *Crosscanonby, Cumbria* The first complete excavation of a milefortlet (part of a chain of evenly spaced defences that include Hadrian's Wall), allowing an insight into the lifestyle of Roman troops in Britain. **68 D4**

Minerva Shrine *Edgar's Field, Chester, Cheshire* A 2,000-year-old shrine carved into the rock in a Roman quarry; the only known Roman rock shrine in Britain. **32 F2**

Ribchester Roman Museum *Ribchester, Lancashire* A recently refurbished and expanded museum in the town that provided the only river crossing between Chester and Hadrian's Wall in Roman times, with artefacts excavated from the area. ☎01254 878261 **46 C1**

Roman Amphitheatre *Little Saint John Street, Chester, Cheshire* The partially excavated remains of Britain's largest Roman amphitheatre (it held about 7,000 spectators), one of only three legionary amphitheatres in the country. **32 F2**

Roman Garden *Souter's Lane, Chester, Cheshire* A 1949 garden containing Roman stone found during excavation work, a mosaic, and a reconstruction of a hypocaust Roman heating system. **32 F2**

Senhouse Roman Museum *Sea Brows, Maryport, Cumbria* An exploration of everyday life in Roman Britain next to the site of Maryport Roman fort, housing the largest collection of Roman altars from a British site. ☎01900 816168 **68 D3**

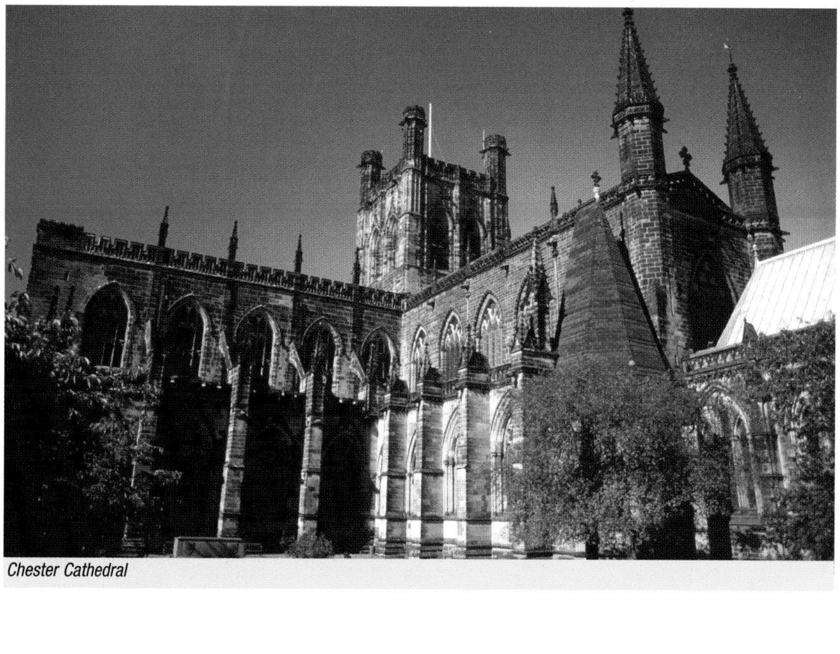

Chester Cathedral

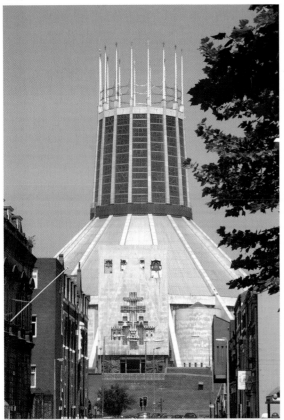

Metropolitan Cathedral, Liverpool

Gwydir Uchaf Chapel *Llanrwst, Conwy* A 17th-century family chapel in the woods above Llanrwst, famous for its painted ceiling. ☎029 2082 6185 **16 B4**

Holy Name of Jesus *Oxford Road, Manchester, Greater Manchester* A huge church by Joseph Aloyious Hansom of the Hansom cab fame, with an original reredos by the architect. The octagonal tower with its enormous windows was completed by Adrian Gilbert Scott. **41 E6**

Hope Church *Hope, Derbyshire* A mainly 14th-century church boasting a spire (unusual for the area), a Norman font, some fine gargoyles and the stump of a Saxon cross. **36 C3**

Ilam Church *Ilam, Staffordshire* A mainly Norman and Early English church, to which St Bertram's Chapel was added in 1618 to house the Saxon saint's tomb, still a place of pilgrimage. There's also a superb Saxon font and a walled-up Saxon doorway. **23 D8**

Irton Church *near Holmrook, Cumbria* A rural church with the early-9th-century 10ft Irton Cross in its churchyard and stained-glass windows by pre-Raphaelite artist Sir Edward Burne-Jones. **56 A2**

Lanercost Priory *Lanercost, Cumbria* A priory founded c.1166 by Henry II and dissolved by Henry VIII in 1536, with a nave restored for use as a parish church in 1740. The west front, dating from about 1200, is a fine example of early English architecture. Audio guided tours. ☎01697 73030 **76 D4**

Little Budworth Church *Little Budworth, Cheshire* A small sandstone church largely rebuilt in the early 19th century but retaining its 16th-century tower. Its font made of fossil marble contains fragments of sea lily stems; the churchyard has the grave of an 18th-century 'gypsy king'. **20 A4**

Liverpool Cathedral★★ *St James Mount, Liverpool, Merseyside* Britain's biggest Anglican cathedral, designed in 1901 by Giles Gilbert Scott and built over the course of the next half-century. Highlights include statues by Della Robbia and Dame Elisabeth Frink and the world's second largest organ. ☎0151 709 6271 **32 A1**

Llanaber and St Bodfan Church *Barmouth, Gwynedd* A 13th-century church housing the late-5th or early-6th-century Llanaber stones and boasting a south doorway held to be one of the country's best examples of Early English architecture. **6 E4**

Llanbadrig Church *Cemaes, Isle of Anglesey* The 'Church of Saint Patrick', built on a site of religious worship dating back to 440AD, with Islamic influences (stipulated by Muslim benefactor Lord Stanley of Alderly). **26 A4**

Llandrillo-yn-Rhos Church *Llandrillo-yn-Rhos, Conwy* A church with 13th-century pointed arches representing an early structure believed to have been the private chapel of Ednyfed Fychan Seneschal, and a 'Rector's Chair' built to hold flares in case enemy ships were sighted. **29 C6**

Llangar Church *Corwen, Denbighshire* A white-painted medieval church with early-Georgian furnishings and some restored 15th-century wall paintings. **18 F2**

Llangelynin Old Church *Llanaelhaearn, Gwynedd* A church with a 15th-century chancel and 16th-century north chapel, south porch and east window. The churchyard contains the Holy Well of St Celynin, said to cure sick children, and the footings of an ancient inn for mountain travellers. **14 F3**

Manchester Cathedral *Victoria Street, Manchester, Greater Manchester* A former parish church and collegiate church rebuilt by Joseph Crowther in the 19th century, with an ornate west front reconstructed by Basil Champneys for Victoria's Diamond Jubilee. There's a Regimental Chapel remembering Wilfred Owen and his comrades and a Fire Window in memory of the Blitz. ☎0161 833 2220 **41 E6**

Metropolitan Cathedral *Mount Pleasant, Liverpool, Merseyside* A Roman Catholic cathedral dubbed 'Paddy's wigwam', best known for its lantern tower made of multi-coloured glass. ☎0151 709 9222 **32 A1**

Middlewich Church *Middlewich, Cheshire* A Norman-built church with two columns and some carved stones from a 12th-century arch. A priest here was mentioned in the Domesday Book. **21 A7**

Princes Road Synagogue *Princes Road, Liverpool, Merseyside* Europe's finest piece of Moorish Revival synagogue architecture, viewable by pre-booked guided tour. ☎0151 709 3431 **32 A1**

Rug Chapel *Corwen, Denbighshire* A rare little-altered 17th-century private chapel, with an elaborately carved and painted ceiling, a chandelier decorated with cherubs, and a painted gallery. **18 F2**

Sacred Trinity *Chapel Street, Salford, Greater Manchester* The city's earliest church (1635), housing the colours of the local battalions of the Lancashire Fusiliers Regiment and a huge 18th-century wrought-iron organ screen. **41 E5**

St Ambrose Church *Grindleton, Lancashire* A former handweavers' parish church redesigned at the end of the 19th century but retaining its Georgian tower (1805). One of its 17th-century curates founded the 'Grindletonians' (forerunners of the Quakers). **46 A4**

St Andrew's Church *Aikton, Cumbria* A largely Norman church with an unusual kissing gate made from two large stone slabs, noteworthy roof timbers, exposed in 1869, and a 13th-century coffin lid. **75 F5**

St Andrew's Church *Dacre, Cumbria* A church on a site used for worship for more than 1000 years, boasting two ancient cross shafts, one of them pre-Viking, but most famous for the four carved stone bears, known as the Dacre Bears, in the corners of the churchyard. **64 A4**

St Andrew's Church *Greystoke, Cumbria* A church with features from an original medieval church, including a rood beam with emblems representing the Christ's wounds; ancient choir stalls with well-preserved misericords; and stained glass buried as Cromwell approached and restored in 1848. **70 E3**

St Andrew's Church★★ *Penrith, Cumbria* A 1720 church designed by Nicholas Hawksmoor, modelled on St Andrew's Holborn and incorporating the tower from the original 13th-century church. In the churchyard is the 'Giant's Thumb', a Norse cross erected by Owen Caesarius, King of Cumbria. **71 E5**

St Andrew's Church *Slaidburn, Lancashire* A mostly 15th-century church on an ancient worship site, with an 18th-century three-decker pulpit, a Jacobean chancel screen and unusual Georgian box-pews with the maker's adze marks. **53 E6**

St Asaph Cathedral *St Asaph, Denbighshire* Britain's smallest cathedral, founded on a site of worship dating back to 560AD and restored by Sir George Gilbert Scott in 1870. In the grounds are a monument to the first Welsh translations of the Book of Common Prayer and Bible by a local lawyer and bishop. ☎01978 852523 **30 E2**

St Chad's Church *Claughton, Lancashire* The 1100 church belonging to Lancashire's smallest parish, with some of the UK's oldest dated bells, dating back to at least 1296. **45 B7**

St Chad's Church *Over, Cheshire* A site where St Chad, first Bishop of Mercia in the 7th century, may have preached in an earlier church, with a circular churchyard indicating a pagan origin and a 1926 chapel added in memory of those who had died in WWI. **21 A5**

St Chad's Church *Sparrow Hill, Rochdale, Greater Manchester* A much-rebuilt medieval church with Saxon elements in its tower, stained glass by Burne-Jones and William Morris, and town stocks dated 1688 and the grave of local dialect poet Tim Bobbin in the churchyard. **41 B6**

St Cuthbert's Church *Bewcastle, Cumbria* A church built under Edward I, using stone from an outpost fort of Hadrian's Wall, and rebuilt in the 18th century. The best-known feature is the 14ft cross with runic inscription and sacred figures; inside is an exhibition about the carvings. **76 B4**

St Cuthbert's Church *Carlisle, Cumbria* A church rebuilt four times, most latterly in the Georgian style in 1778, but retaining a 14th-century stained-glass window and a rare moveable railed pulpit. Among the graves are some soldiers executed during Bonny Prince Charles' rising in 1745. **75 E8**

St Cuthbert's Church *Great Salkeld, Cumbria* An example of the fortified churches erected in the border area in the 14th century, with a typically narrow entrance. There was probably a church on the site from 880AD, when the body of St Cuthbert was rested here en route from Holy Island. **71 D5**

St Cwyfan Church *near Aberffraw, Isle of Anglesey* A seabound, largely Victorian church with 7th-century origins, cut off from the mainland by erosion but still holding services in summer. **26 F4**

St Deiniol's Church *Hawarden, Flintshire* A large church recorded in the Domesday Book, with a 14th-century nave, aisles and chancel arch, restored by Sir George Gilbert Scott after a fire in the 19th century. The Whitley Chapel has some fine 17th- and 18th-century monuments. **19 A7**

St Edmund's Church *Newbiggin, Cumbria* A church rebuilt in the 14th century but retaining a 12th-century pillar piscina with eight shafts in a square, crowned with a foliated capital and molded abacus. **50 B4**

St Giles' Church★ *Temple Row, Wrexham, Wrexham* A late-15th and early-16th-century church with a Perpendicular tower dubbed one of the 'seven wonders of Wales' and on which the tower of the Houses of Parliament is said to have been modelled. **19 D7**

St Helen's Church *Churchtown, Lancashire* A church known as 'the cathedral of the Fylde', dating back to the Norman Conquest and including architecture from almost every period since then. **45 B6**

St Helen's Church *Sefton, Merseyside* A Grade I listed church with Tudor woodwork, first built c.1170 as the private chapel of the Molyneux family and one of the oldest buildings in Merseyside. The tower dates from c.1320. **38 D4**

St James' Church *Great Ormside, Cumbria* One of Cumbria's oldest churches, with parts dating from c.1140. A Viking warrior was found buried here with his sword, as was the 'Ormside Bowl' (now in York Museum), about which there is a small exhibition in the Hilton Chapel. **66 C1**

St James' Church *Clapham, North Yorkshire* A church on the Craven Fault, originally built in the Perpendicular style and retaining its Perpendicular tower, plus the ends of the original Jacobean pews (now wall panellling). **53 B6**

St John the Baptist Church *Vicar's Lane, Chester, Cheshire* Chester's oldest church (and first cathedral) and one of the area's finest Norman churches, hidden behind a Victorian exterior. **32 F2**

St John the Baptist RC Church *Dowling Street, Rochdale, Greater Manchester* A 1925 church with a massive dome modelled on the Byzantine Santa Sofia in Istanbul, and a huge mosaic of Christ's Resurrection covering the apse, unique in an English church. **41 B6**

St John's Church *Newton Arlosh, Cumbria* A fortified 1303 church, restored and extended in 1843 thanks to Sarah Losh, who designed the stone ram's head by the altar, the eagle on the roof and the lecturn with its bog-oak base. **74 E3**

St John's Church *Over, Cheshire* The oldest known work by John Douglas, with a landmark spire, built as a memorial to Lady Delamere, whose initials are carved in stone and figure in stained glass. **21 A5**

St Kentigern's Church *Caldbeck, Cumbria* A much-altered structure on the site of a 6th-century church, with Norman arch stones with chevron and billet mouldings reset above the tower door. Behind is St Mungo's well, a 6th-century site of christian baptism. **70 D1**

St Kentigern's Church *Crosthwaite, Cumbria* A 1523 church with a unique full set of 16th-century consecration crosses marking spots where the bishop sprinkled holy water. There is also a mosaic floor, a 1602 sundial and an old Mass clock. Poet Laureate Robert Southey is buried here. **58 B2**

St Lawrence's Church *Crosby Ravensworth, Cumbria* A 'cathedral in miniature', the oldest part of which dates back to 1120. Early-19th-century restoration work was carried out by Sir Robert Smirke. The churchyard has a 7th-century cross shaft. **65 C7**

St Leonard's Church *opposite Jubilee Park, Middleton, Greater Manchester* A mainly 1524 parish church with a 1412 tower and porch and traces of a Norman structure, and one of the UK's three surviving wooden church towers. The stained-glass window dedicated to the Middleton Archers is the oldest known war memorial. **41 C6**

St Mark's Church *Worsley Brow, Worsley, Greater Manchester* A Victorian-Gothic church by George Gilbert Scott, with Matthew Nobel's marble effigy of the first Earl of Ellesmere, stained glass by Sir Edward Burne-Jones, and the Duke of Bridgewater's clock that strikes 13 instead of one. **40 D3**

St Martin's Church *Brampton, Cumbria* The only church designed by Pre-Raphaelite architect Philip Webb, in 1878, with an almost square main body and stained-glass windows designed by Sir Edward Burne-Jones and produced in the William Morris studio. **65 B8**

St Mary and St Bega Priory Church *St Bees, Cumbria* A 12th-century church that was a Benedictine priory until its dissolution by Henry VIII. The 'History Area' describes the discovery of 'St Bees Man', one of England's best-preserved medieval bodies, on the site of a ruined chapel in 1981 and includes his shroud. **62 D2**

St Mary the Virgin Priory Church *Lancaster, Lancashire* A parish church founded in 1094 on the site of an earlier Anglon Saxon church, with medieval carved choir stalls, impressive tapestries, a regimental chapel and views across Morecambe Bay. **51 C8**

St Mary's Church★ *Ambleside, Cumbria* A church designed in the neo-Gothic style by Sir George Gilbert Scott in 1850-4, with a chapel dedicated to Wordsworth. **64 F2**

St Mary's Church *Bodelwyddan, Denbighshire* A landmark church erected by Lady Willoughby de Broke in memory of her husband in 1856-60, known as the 'Marble Church' because of the 13 types of marble inside. It contains some of the finest Victorian wood carving in Britain. **30 D2**

St Mary's Church *Caerhun, Gwynedd* An ancient church built mostly of Roman stone blocks or 'ashlars' imported from Chester, built on the site of Kanovium Roman fort. Above the church door and the south chapel are three medieval carvings. **27 F8**

St Mary's Church *Church Street, Eccles, Greater Manchester* A church on the site of a 15th- and 16th-century parish church, with some early-16th-century Flemish glass, 17th-century English heraldic brass and an Anglo-Saxon cross shaft. **40 E4**

St Mary's Church *Cilcain, Flintshire* A mainly 15th-century church with a double nave; part of the north nave dates back to the 12th or 13th century, the south nave has a Perpendicular hammerbeam roof thought to have come from Basingwerk Abbey. **18 B4**

St Mary's Church *Hale, Halton* A simple village church on the site of an 1081 church, with a Venetian or Palladian window above the altar, an oak pulpit gifted by York Minster and a chestnut ceiling by a single carpenter. **32 C4**

St Mary's Church *Mellor, Lancashire* An 1829 church with a peal of Guildford Chimes and some early-19th-century Flemish stained-glass windows. Its chancel and organ screens are outstanding examples of woodcarving. **46 D2**

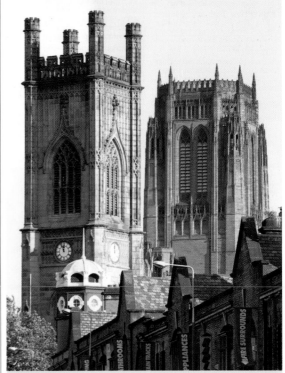

Spires, Liverpool

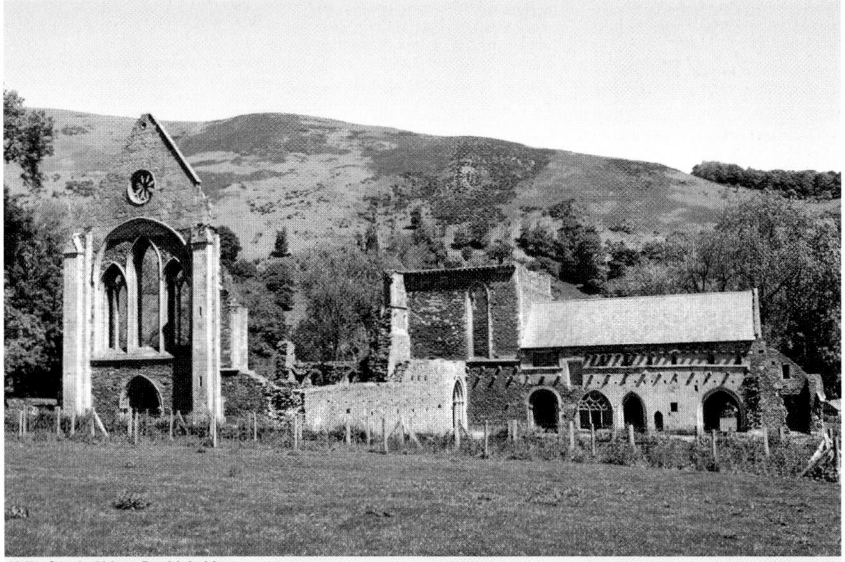

Valle Crucis Abbey, Denbighshire

St Mary's Church *Town Square, Nantwich, Cheshire* A mostly 14th-century church, the largest of its kind not forming part of a monastic settlement. It shares important features with Lichfield, Chester, Gloucester and Wells cathedrals, and its octagonal tower is a landmark. **21 D6**

St Mary's Church *Nercwys, Flintshire* A mainly 18th- and 19th-century church with a tower arch that may date back to Norman times, medieval masonry in its nave, fragments of medieval graveslabs, a late-medieval arched-braced roof and some some late-medieval stained glass. **18 B5**

St Mary's Church *Newchurch, Lancashire* A parish church known for its Eye of God tower, thought to protect parishioners from witchcraft (it is said to have been from St Mary's graveyard that the Pendle witches stole bones for use in spells). **47 F5**

St Mary's Church *Toad Lane, Rochdale, Greater Manchester* An early-20th-century church by Ninian Comper, foremost church architect of his time. The Rood Screen wood carving, also by Comper, is notable for its tracery and apostolic figures. By appointment. ☎01706 646272 **41 B6**

St Mary's Church *Ruabon, Wrexham* A Grade I listed church traceable back to 1253, when it was dedicated to St Collen, with a 14th-century tower and a restored early-15th-century wall-painting. **19 F7**

St Mary's Church *Wreay, Cumbria* An unusual church in the shape of a Roman basilica, designed by local Sarah Losh as a memorial to her family and incorporating French and Italian features. Outside are gargoyles, a sundial, a mausoleum and a replica of the Bewcastle Cross. **70 B3**

St Mary's RC Church *Mulberry Street, Manchester, Greater Manchester* An 1848 church christened the 'Hidden Gem' by a visiting bishop but dismissed by Pugin. The ornate interior includes Norman Adams' late-20th-century paintings of the Stations of the Cross. **41 E6**

St Michael and All Angels Church *Hubberholme, North Yorkshire* Originally a 12th-century forest chapel, a church best known for housing the remnants of a rood screen, one of only two to have survived in Yorkshire. **60 E4**

St Michael's Church *Burgh by Sands, Cumbria* A church built on the site of a Roman fort on Hadrian's Wall in the late 12th century, using stone from the fort or wall. Its west pele tower is probably one of three extant 14th-century fortified churches in the area. Edward I lay in state here after dying on the way to fight Robert the Bruce. **75 E6**

St Michael's Church★ *Torpenhow, Cumbria* One of only six of the 98 churches built in the 12th century that have remained unspoilt; some of the stone inside was brought from the great Roman camp of Old Carlisle, and during restoration work traces of a Saxon building were found. **69 D7**

St Michael's-on-Wyre *Lancashire* Founded between AD627 and 640, dedicated to St Michael the Archangel and one of only three churches in the Hundred of Amounderness mentioned in the Domesday book. **45 B6**

St Michaels and All Angels *Ashton-under-Lyne, Greater Manchester* A Grade I listed church mentioned in the Domesday Book, with outstanding 15th-century stained glass and a tower affording views of the area. **41 E7**

St Oswald's Church *Dean, Cumbria* A 12th-century church – one of only three in Cumbria with gargoyles – with a Norman font, 15th-century chancel and 17th-century sanctuary. Outside are ancient gravestones and a Preaching Cross with a base dating back to at least the 12th century. **62 A4**

St Oswald's Church *Kirkoswald, Cumbria* A partly 12th-century church with a 19th-century bell tower uniquely located on a hilltop 200ft above the village, probably used to signal the approach of Scots raiders, as well as summoning villagers. Outside are some ancient carved grave covers. **71 C6**

St Oswald's Church *Askrigg, North Yorkshire* The largest church in Wensleydale, built mainly in the late Perpendicular style in the 14th century, with a medieval font and an impressive 16th-century roof. **60 B4**

St Oswald's Church *Horton in Ribblesdale, North Yorkshire* A early-1100s church with a 14th-century tower, an entrance arch with chevron and dogtooth moulding, and a font with Norman herringbone carvings. **53 A8**

St Patrick's Chapel *near Heysham, Lancaster, Lancashire* A romantic ruined Anglo Saxon chapel on a headland, with rock-cut graves. **51 C8**

St Peter and St Paul Church *Ormskirk, Lancashire* One of only three churches in the country with both a spire (15th-century) and a tower (16th-century). There are also fragments of Saxon and Celtic masonry in the east wall and 12th-century Norman masonry in the north side of the chancel. **38 C5**

St Peter's Church *Kirkbampton, Cumbria* A Grade I listed Norman structure with a Saxon-style chancel arch and north doorway; above the latter is a rare sculptured tympanum. A Roman stone built into the south wall of the chancel was probably brought from Hadrian's Wall. **75 E6**

St Peter's Church (Bolton-le-Moors) *Bolton, Greater Manchester* An 1871 Victorian-Gothic building with a renovated 'Hill' organ case, a Saxon cross and coffin, and carved pews from the old church. The Museum Corner has fragments of stone and other artefacts from the previous Saxon and Norman buildings. **40 C3**

St Peter's RC Cathedral *East Road, Lancaster, Lancashire* A cathedral designed as a parish church in the early-14th-century Gothic style by Edward Paley in 1859, with newly restored stencilled walls and ceiling. ☎01524 61860 **51 C8**

St Stephen's Church *Market Place, Kirkby Stephen, Cumbria* A parish church known locally as the 'cathedral of the dales', built on the site of a Saxon church and containing various ancient relics, including the Viking 'Loki Stone'. **66 E3**

St Trillo's Chapel *Rhos on Sea, Conwy* A tiny 6th-century chapel built over a holy well, used as a place of special prayer. Visits by arrangement. ☎01938 553670 **29 C6**

St Tudno's Church *Great Orme, Llandudno, Conwy* A 12th-century church on the site where the 6th-century Celtic monk Tudno founded his cell in a small cave on the headland (still visible but difficult to get to), holding open-air services overlooking the sea. **28 C5**

St Wilfred's Church *Grappenhall, Cheshire* A parish church believed to be of Norman origin, with a buttress boasting one of only five scratch dials recorded in Cheshire. The graveyard contains village stocks, a sundial and a column dating from 1714. **33 B7**

St Winefride's Well *Greenfield Valley Heritage and Country Park, Holywell, Flintshire* The only shrine in Britain with an unbroken history of pilgrimage, at the spot where a local chieftain is said to have beheaded Winefride after she spurned his advances in 660AD. A chapel above the well has a camberbeam roof and carved corbels. ☎01352 713054 **31 D5**

Sawley Abbey *Sawley, Lancashire* A ruined Cistercian abbey in a picturesque village on the banks of the Ribble, founded in 1147. Remnants include part of the night stairs to the monks' dormitory, medieval mosaic tiling, and corbels and other decorative stonework. ☎01282 661702 **53 F7**

Shap Abbey *Shap, Cumbria* The last abbey founded in England (in 1199) and the last to be dissolved by Henry VIII (in 1540), now an isolated ruin in the care of English Heritage. A short path leads to the little 16th-century Keld Chapel, owned by the National Trust. ☎017683 51177 **65 C6**

The Oratory, Liverpool Cathedral *St James's Cemetery, Liverpool, Merseyside* The only surviving building by local architect John Foster Junior, containing monuments by 19th-century British sculptors. By appointment only. ☎0151 478 4102 **32 A1**

Tideswell Church★ *Tideswell, Derbyshire* Dubbed 'the cathedral of the Peak', one of the largest and finest churches in the area, largely unaltered since its construction c.1320-1400. Among features are a sedilla by the altar and traces of a previous Norman church in the chancel. **36 D3**

Valle Crucis Abbey *near Llangollen, Denbighshire* The Gothic stone ruins of a 13th-century Cistercian abbey founded by a Welsh prince, with an almost-intact chapterhouse. **18 F5**

Weaverham Church *Weaverham, Cheshire* A church with a tower bearing marks inscribed by the masons so they would get paid for each stone, a Victorian window with a picture of Edward I, who founded Vale Royal Abbey, and a communion table attributed to Chippendale. **33 E7**

Whalley Abbey *Whalley, Lancashire* A ruined Cistercian abbey, a protected Ancient Monument, moved here in 1296 from Stanlow in Cheshire and enlarged c.1320. **46 C3**

Whalley Church *Whalley, Lancashire* A parish church on the site of a wooden church believed to date back to 600AD, now known for its interior and pre-Conquest crosses. **46 C3**

Witton Church *Witton, Northwich, Cheshire* A largely 16th-century church with a magnificent ceiling, marks in its north wall said to be from musket balls during the Civil War, and carvings of 'barrows' (pointed salt baskets used to drain surplus brine). **33 E8**

Youlgreave Church *Youlgreave, Derbyshire* A 15th-century church with a Norman nave, north aisle and font, and a 14th-century south aisle and chance, the latter containing some medieval tombs. The east window was made by William Morris to a design by Edward Burne-Jones. **24 B2**

Museums & galleries

Art & crafts

Astley Cheetham Art Gallery *Trinity Street, Stalybridge, Greater Manchester* An impressive painting collection bequeathed to the town by John Frederick Cheetham in 1901, housed in a recently refurbished gallery. ☎0161 338 6767 **41 E8**

Atkinson Art Gallery *Lord Street, Southport, Merseyside* Victorian and 20th-century works by artists ranging from Lowry to Henry Moore. ☎01704 533133 **38 A3**

Beckstones Art Gallery *Greystoke Gill, Cumbria* Three hundred paintings and work in other media by more than 40 national artists. ☎01768 483601 **70 F3**

Bury Art Gallery and Museum *Moss Street, Bury, Greater Manchester* Oil paintings, watercolours, prints and ceramics collected by paper manufacturer Thomas Wrigley, including Turner's 'Calais Sands', plus the recreated 1950s 'Paradise Street'. ☎0161 253 5878 **40 B4**

Courtyard Gallery *Appleby-in-Westmorland, Cumbria* A gallery in a 300-year-old building, with paintings, etchings and ceramics by local and national artists. ☎01768 351638 **65 B8**

Gallery Oldham★ *Greaves Street, Oldham, Greater Manchester* A new gallery showing works by Constable, Turner and Lowry, and housing Oldham Museum with its displays on the town's industrial past. ☎0161 911 4653 **41 D7**

Harris Art Gallery and Museum *Market Square, Preston, Lancashire* A Grade I listed Greek Revival building housing a collection of fine, modern and decorative art, plus displays on social history. ☎01772 258248 **45 E7**

Haworth Art Gallery★ *Haworth Park, Manchester Road, Accrington, Lancashire* A refurbished gallery in an Arts and Crafts building, with a famous collection of 'Favrile' Art Nouveau Tiffany Glass, plus 19th- and early-20th-century oils and watercolours. ☎01254 233782 **46 E4**

Lady Lever Art Gallery *Lower Road, Port Sunlight, Merseyside* The first Lord Leverhulme's collection, including Napoleonic memorabilia, 18th- and 19th-century English paintings by the likes of Turner and Constable, furniture, Wedgwood pottery and Chinese porcelain. ☎0151 478 4136 **32 C1**

Manchester Art Gallery★ *Mosley Street, Manchester, Greater Manchester* The city's acclaimed art collection, with a new £35-million extension. ☎0161 235 8888 **41 E6**

Oriel Mostyn Gallery★ *12 Heol Vaughan, Llandudno, Conwy* An adventurous contemporary art gallery with exhibitions by major international artists. ☎01492 879201 **28 C5**

Plas Glyn y Weddw Art Gallery *Pwllheli, Gwynedd* One of Wales' oldest art galleries, set in a Victorian-Gothic mansion with landscaped gardens and displaying mainly Welsh work, plus Swansea and Nangarw porcelain. ☎01758 740763 **5 A7**

Platform Gallery *Station Road, Clitheroe, Lancashire* An award-winning gallery in a refurbished train station, with contemporary arts and crafts exhibitions. ☎01200 443071 **46 B3**

Royal Cambrian Academy★ *Crown Lane, Conwy* Wales' most prestigious art institution, showing work from Wales and the rest of Britain. ☎01492 593413 **28 D5**

Ruthin Craft Centre Gallery *Park Road, Ruthin, Denbighshire* An applied arts centre displaying contemporary pieces from around Britain. ☎01824 703992 **18 C3**

Tate Liverpool★★ *Albert Dock, Liverpool, Merseyside* A converted warehouse housing the National Collection of Modern Art in the north of England. Exhibitions are either art selected from the Tate Collection or special exhibitions of contemporary art. ☎0151 702 7400 **32 A1**

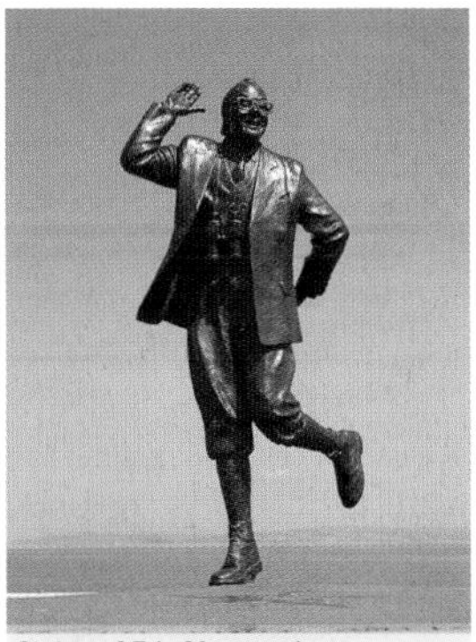

Statue of Eric Morecambe

Tern Public Art Project★ *Morecambe, Lancashire* An award-winning art project reflecting Morecambe Bay's role as a breeding ground for migratory birds, including the statue of Eric Morecambe (president elect of the RSPB), the poem-path 'A Flock of Words' and the Stone Jetty with its sculptures and games. ☎01524 582808 **51 C7**

The Lowry★★ *Pier 8, The Quays, Salford, Greater Manchester* Voted UK Building of the Year in 2001, this contains the world's biggest collection of works by LS Lowry, plus galleries for contemporary exhibitions, theatres, shops, cafes and bars. ☎0870 787 5780 **41 E5**

Towneley Hall Art Gallery and Museums *Towneley Park, Burnley, Lancashire* A 1,500-strong collection of oil paintings, sculptures, watercolours and illustrations, particularly strong on 19th-century British artists, plus local and natural history collections. ☎01282 424213 **47 D5**

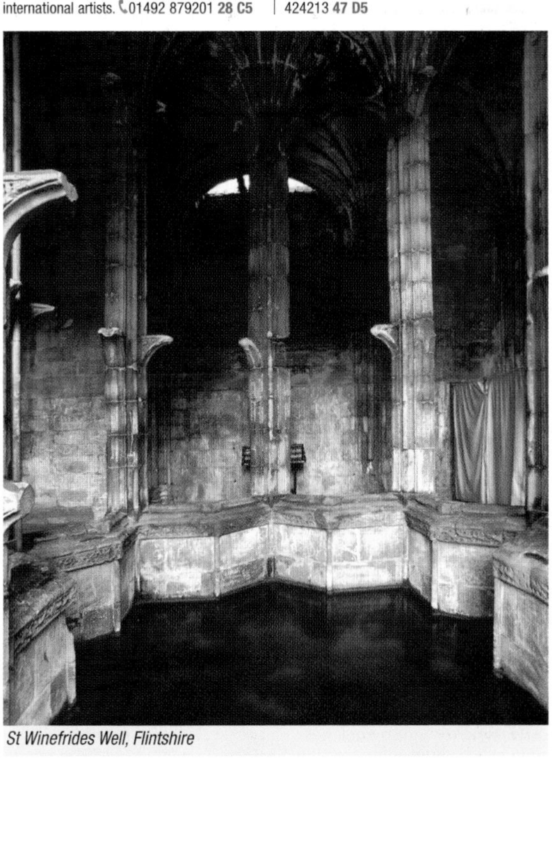

St Winefrides Well, Flintshire

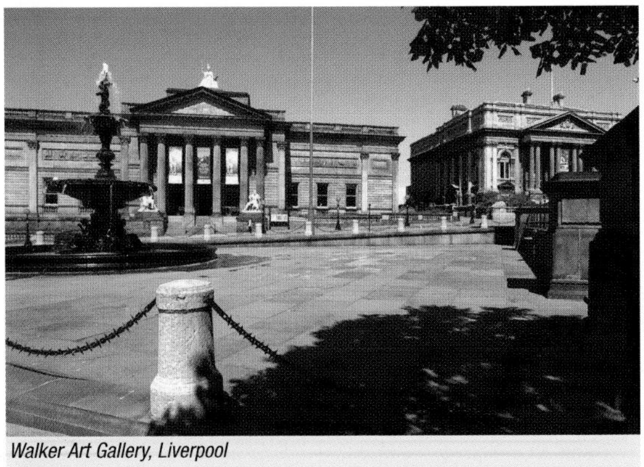

Walker Art Gallery, Liverpool

University of Liverpool Art Gallery *Abercromby Square, Liverpool, Merseyside* Contemporary and older art, including pieces by Audubon, Lucien Freud and Epstein. ☎0151 794 2348 **32 A1**

Voirrey Embroidery Centre *Brimstage Hall, Brimstage, Merseyside* The country's largest embroidery centre, with monthly exhibitions and courses. ☎0151 342 3514 **31 C8**

Walker Art Gallery★ *William Brown Street, Liverpool, Merseyside* One of Europe's foremost collections of fine and decorative art, massively refurbished to include a new Craft and Design gallery of decorative arts. ☎0151 478 4199 **32 A1**

Wetheriggs Pottery *Clifton Dykes, Cumbria* The UK's only steam pottery, with a ceramics museum, a 'create your own pot' studio, a children's play area and rare breeds of animal. ☎01768 892733 **71 F5**

Whitworth Art Gallery★ *Oxford Road, Manchester, Greater Manchester* An outstanding British watercolours collection, an array of historic textiles second only to that of the V&A, an important collection of wallpapers, and modern and contemporary pieces by the likes of Picasso and Lucien Freud. ☎0161 275 7450 **41 E6**

Williamson Art Gallery and Museum *Slatey Road, Birkenhead, Merseyside* Birkenhead's collection of Victorian oil paintings, English watercolours, Liverpool porcelain and Della Robbia Pottery, plus local history, ships models and temporary exhibitions. ☎0151 652 4177 **31 B8**

Science & technology

Catalyst *Mersey Road, Widnes, Halton* A chemistry-industry discovery centre with interactive exhibits, games and puzzles. ☎0151 420 1121 **32 C5**

Conservation Centre★ *Queen Square, Liverpool, Merseyside* The UK's first national conservation centre, voted European Museum of the Year in 1998, where precious items, from fine art and ancient archaeological artefacts to spacesuits, are preserved and restored. ☎0151 478 4999 **32 A1**

Electric Mountain Visitor Centre *Llanberis, Gwynedd* A complex on the edge of Snowdonia National Park, with interactive displays, models and exhibitions about the history of hydro-electricity. There's also a guided tour of Dinorwig Power Station, a 16th-century clinker and two art galleries. ☎01286 870636 **15 B7**

Ffestiniog Power Station Hydro Centre Tours and Stwlan Dam *Tanygrisiau, Gwynedd* Tours of Britain's first pump-storage hydro-electric power station, following by a trip up to Stwlan dam reservoir with its panoramic views. ☎01766 830465 **16 E1**

Godlee Observatory *Floor G, Main Building, UMIST, Sackville Street, Manchester, Greater Manchester* Built in 1902, this timber structure has a chamber with an original Grubb telescope and refractor. Panoramic city views from the balcony. ☎0161 200 4977 **41 E6**

Jodrell Bank Science Centre★★ *Lower Withington, Macclesfield, Cheshire* A planetarium and exhibitions on astronomy, satellites and the mysteries of the universe in the shadow of the Lovell Telescope. There's also a 35-acre. ☎01477 571339 **35 E5**

Museum of Science and Industry *Liverpool Road, Castlefield, Manchester, Greater Manchester* Exhibitions on Transport, Power, Past Present and Future, and Science. Events and activities range from science shows to puppet workshops. ☎0161 606 0174 **41 E6**

On the Air Broadcasting Museum *42 Bridge Street Row, Chester, Cheshire* The history of British broadcasting, from wireless to satellite TV; includes a re-created TV studio and a demonstration of how soundwaves work. ☎01244 348468 **32 F2**

Sellafield Visitor Centre *Seascale, Cumbria* Interactive displays and demonstrations about nuclear power at the famous power station. ☎019467 27027 **62 F3**

Southport Eco Visitor-Centre *Esplanade, Southport, Merseyside* Exhibitions on energy, transport and tourism, with the aim of inspiring people to consider the human impact on the environment. Scheduled to open in 2004. ☎0845 330 1342 **38 A3**

World of Glass *Chalon Way East, St Helens, Merseyside* Glass-blowing demonstrations and multimedia shows about one of the most common substances on earth Voted Best Small Visitor Attraction in the country in 2002. ☎08707 444777 **39 F8**

Transport

Anderton Boat Lift★ *Lift Lane, Anderton, Cheshire* The world's first and the UK's only working canal boat lift. A new operation centre was opened by the Prince of Wales in April 2003. ☎01606 786777 **33 D7**

Boat Museum *Ellesmere Port, Cheshire* An old dock housing the world's biggest collection of traditional canal boats, plus working engines and a resident blacksmith. Boat trips along the canal and lock demonstrations are offered. ☎0151 355 5017 **32 D3**

Bolton Abbey Station *Skipton, North Yorkshire* Steam train trips from the award-winning new Bolton Abbey Station to Embsay Station. ☎01756 710614 **54 E3**

British Commercial Vehicle Museum *Leyland, Lancashire* The history of British Commercial vehicles from horse-drawn contrivances to present-day models. ☎01772 451011 **45 F7**

Calatrava Bridge★ *Salford Quays, Greater Manchester* A flamboyant curving bridge designed by Spaniard Santiago Calatrava and opened in 1995, linking the five-star Lowry Hotel in Salford to Manchester city centre. **41 E5**

Cars of the Stars Motor Museum *Standish Street, Keswick, Cumbria* James Bond cars, a Batmobile and more, plus an autograph and memorabilia shop. ☎017687 73757 **63 B8**

Conwy Suspension Bridge *Conwy* An 1826 Thomas Telford designed bridge, now a National Trust property. **28 D5**

Cycle Museum *Old Police Station, Runcorn, Halton* Exhibits include a Sinclair C5 tricycle, a mini penny farthing, a unicycle and cycling artefacts from around the world. ☎01928 588532 **32 C5**

East Lancashire Railway *Bolton Street Station, Bury, Greater Manchester* Restored steam and diesel trains along the Irwell Valley, with stops at traditional station buildings and the scenic market town of Ramsbottom. In summer 2003 a Heywood-Rawtenstall line opened in Rochdale. ☎0161 764 7790 **40 B4**

Egerton Bridge *off Canning Street, Birkenhead, Merseyside* A working Birkenhead bascule bridge, plus models and information about the Birkenhead dock system of 1847. ☎0151 647 6780 **31 B8**

Ffestiniog Railway★ *Harbour Station, Porthmadog, Gwynedd* The world's oldest independent railway company, built to carry slate from Blaenau Ffestiniog, now crossing the spectacular scenery of the Snowdonia National Park. There's a sister railway, the Welsh Highland, between Caernarfon and Waunfawr. ☎01766 516024 **6 A3**

Great Orme Tramway *Llandudno, Conwy* The only surviving cable-hauled public road tramway still using the original Victorian carriages, providing access to Great Orme Country Park. The Halfway Station has a new tramway exhibition. ☎01492 575275 **28 C5**

Huddersfield Narrow Canal *Saddleworth, Oldham, Greater Manchester* Reopened in early 2001, a major local attraction allowing for towpath walks and boat rides through stunning countryside aboard the 'Pennine Moonraker'. **41 D7**

Lakeland Motor Museum *Holker Hall, Cark, Cumbria* Vintage vehicles and an exhibition about Sir Malcolm and Donald Campbell, who set more than 20 land and water speed records. ☎015395 58509 **57 E8**

Lakeside and Haverthwaite Railway *Haverthwaite Station, near Ulverston, Cumbria* Summer trips by restored steam locomotive from the Victorian station at Haverthwaite across the Leven Valley to Lakeside. ☎015395 31594 **57 E6**

Leeds-Liverpool Canal *Chorley, Lancashire* The one-time symbol of Chorley's strength during the industrial revolution and the longest canal in the country, now a route for narrow boats, walkers, cyclists and naturalists. ☎01257 481054 **39 A8**

Llanberis Lake Railway *Llanberis, Gwynedd* Forty-minute trips through the spectacular scenery of Padarn Country Park, with views of Snowdon and other mountains. ☎01286 870549 **15 B7**

Llangollen Motor Museum *Pentre Felin, Llangollen, Denbighshire* More than 60 vehicles, from cars to invalid carriages, a re-created 1950s village garage. and a smalll exhibition about the local canal network. ☎01978 860 324 **18 F5**

Llangollen Railway *Llangollen, Denbighshire* A restored line with mainly steam-hauled trains running through 7.5miles of stunning Dee Valley scenery, weekends in winter, daily June-Oct. ☎01978 860951 **18 F5**

Lowry Footbridge *Salford, Greater Manchester* A £5-million Millennium bridge by Spanish architect Carlos Fernandez Casado, engineered to lift vertically to allow boats to pass beneath, and linking The Lowry and the Imperial War Museum North across the revitalised docks. **41 E5**

Manchester Ship Canal *Eastham Locks, Merseyside* A canal created to link Manchester to the sea, opened in 1894 by Queen Victoria and running 35.5 miles to Salford Quays, where the Tourist Information Centre has a small exhibition about it. Cruises available with Mersey Ferries (0151 330 1444). ☎0161 848 8601 **32 C2**

Maritime Museum *St George's Quay, Lancaster, Lancashire* A museum set in the Richard Gillow Customs House, tracing the city's history as a busy Georgian seaport. ☎01524 64637 **51 C8**

Marple Canal Locks *Marple, Greater Manchester* The UK's second steepest flight of locks, taking the Peak Forest Canal down more than 200 feet through its 16 locks. Canal-related features of the village include an aqueduct, mills, lime kilns and old canal arms. **35 B6**

Maryport Maritime Museum *Senhouse Street, Maryport, Cumbria* Maryport's maritime heritage, including its links with the 'Titanic' and Fletcher Christian. ☎01900 326254 **68 D3**

Mersey Ferries★ *Pier Head, Liverpool, Woodside and Seacombe, Merseyside* Fifty-minute commentated river cruises on Europe's oldest ferry service, with views of the Liverpool waterfront, nominated for World Heritage Status. ☎0151 630 1030 **31 A8**

Merseyside Maritime Museum *Albert Dock, Liverpool, Merseyside* The story of Liverpool's seafaring heritage and the merchant navy told in a former bonded warehouse. ☎0151 478 4499 **32 A1**

Mouldsworth Motor Museum *Smithy Lane, Mouldsworth, Cheshire* A museum owned by motoring cartoonist James Peacop, with more than 60 cars, motorcycles and bicycles, plus other memorabilia. ☎01928 731781 **32 E5**

Museum of Transport in Manchester *Boyle Street, Cheetham Hill, Greater Manchester* A volunteer-run museum in a former bus depot, displaying vintage buses, fire engines and lorries. ☎0161 205 2122 **41 D5**

Pier Master's House and Offices *Albert Dock, Liverpool, Merseyside* An Edwardian house allowing a glimpse into the life of the pier master responsible for the day to day running of the dock. ☎0151 207 0001 **32 A1**

Pontcysyllte Aqueduct *Wrexham* A revolutionary 1795 Thomas Telford aqueduct, now on the list of possible future UNESCO World Heritage sites. Boat trips along the Llangollen Canal and across the aqueduct are available at Chirk Marina (01691 774558) and Trefor Basin (01978 821749). **19 D7**

Ravenglass and Eskdale Railway *Ravenglass, Cumbria* A narrow-gauge steam locomotive (which used to transport iron ore) through the scenic Eskdale Valley. ☎01229 717171 **56 A2**

Red House Stables Working Carriage Museum *Old Road, Darley Dale, Derbyshire* A unique collection of original horse-drawn vehicles and equipment, including one of the very few surviving Hansom cabs and a stage coach. ☎01629 733583 **24 B3**

Riversway *Preston, Lancashire* The largest single dock basin in Europe, with a marina, leisure facilities and shops. The Ribble Link, opened in 2002 to connect the Lancaster Canal to the Leeds-Liverpool Canal and join Preston to the national waterways network, was the UK's first new canal in 100 years. **45 E7**

Rochdale Canal *Rochdale, Greater Manchester* A newly restored 32-mile canal with 91 locks and more than 100 bridges. Boat trips (0161 627 5631) pass by eight reservoirs. **41 B6**

Romany's Vardo★ *Memorial Gardens, Wilmslow, Cheshire* The restored former caravan of author and environmentalist Reverend George Bramwell Even, which claims to be Britain's smallest tourist attraction. ☎01625 504507 **34 C3**

Snowdon Mountain Railway *Llanberis, Gwynedd* The UK's only public rack and pinion mountain railway, dating back to 1896 and offering spectacular views on its journey from Llanberis to the summit of Snowdon. ☎0870 458 0033 **15 B7**

Solway Aviation Museum *Aviation House, Carlisle Airport, Cumbria* Indoor and outdoor exhibits, including Vulcan, Canberra, Meteor and Vampire aircraft, plus displays about RAF stations in Cumbria. ☎01228 573823 **76 D2**

South Tynedale Railway *Railway Station, Alston, Cumbria* Trains hauled by preserved steam and diesel engines through the South Tyne Valley. ☎01434 381696 **72 B2**

Steam, Coal and Canal: the Bridgewater Canal Linear Industrial Heritage Park★ *Salford, Greater Manchester* A project to create Britain's first Linear Industrial Heritage Park, linking several important sites associated with the UK's first real canal and eventually extending from Castlefield to Wigan Pier. Major sights include Worsley Delphone with its underground canals, Barton Swing Aqueduct and a heritage and visitor centre. ☎0161 747 4414 **41 E5**

Talyllyn Railway *Wharf Station, Tywyn, Gwynedd* Two-and-a-half-hour trips by coal-fired narrow-gauge steam train through Snowdonia National Park, with stops for forest walks and a picnic beside a waterfall. ☎01654 710472 **2 C2**

The HUB Exhibition *Goods Shed Trust, Alston, Cumbria* Historic local vehicles and local photographs. ☎01434 382244 **72 B2**

Windermere Steamboat Museum *Rayrigg Road, Windermere, Cumbria* Steamboats, motorboats and Beatrix Potter's rowing boat, plus a 'Swallows and Amazons' exhibition and steamboat cruises on the lake. ☎015394 45565 **58 A2**

Wirral Museum *Hamilton Square, Birkenhead, Merseyside* The story of the the Cammell Laird shipyard, plus a collection of local Della Robbia pottery. The Grade II listed restored former town hall building also contains a gallery, theatre, cinema and concert hall. ☎0151 666 4010 **31 B8**

Military history

Border Regimental Museum *Queen Mary's Tower, The Castle, Carlisle, Cumbria* The history of Cumbria's county infantry regiment, the Border Regiment, the King's Own Royal Border Regiment and local militia told through uniforms, weapons and the like. The Castle also houses barracks and other 19th-century military buildings. ☎01228 532774 **75 E8**

Cheshire Military Museum *Chester Castle, Chester, Cheshire* The stories of the regiments of Cheshire told through exhibitions, events and activities. ☎01244 327617 **32 F2**

Fusiliers Museum *Wellington Barracks, Bolton Road, Bury, Greater Manchester* A museum about the regiment from its beginnings in 1688, including its role in the Napoleonic Wars and Gallipoli Landings. ☎0161 764 2208 **40 B4**

Historic Warships *East Float Dock, Birkenhead, Merseyside* A collection of 20th-century fighting ships, including the frigate HMS Plymouth and the German U-boat U534, raised after 50 years on the seabed; includes a new museum and visitor centre. ☎0151 650 1573 **31 B8**

HMS Bronington *Trafford Wharf Road, Trafford, Greater Manchester* A 425-tonne wooden minesweeper, once commanded by the Prince of Wales. ☎0161 877 7778 **41 E5**

Home Front Experience *New Street, Llandudno, Conwy* A museum re-creating civilian life during WWII. ☎01492 871032 **28 C5**

Hooton Park Aerodrome *The Hangers, West Road, Ellesmere Port, Cheshire* A WWI aerodrome later used for the assembling of more than 9,000 light aircraft in WWII. Viewable by guided tour (an exhibition centre is being created). ☎0151 350 2598 **32 D3**

Imperial War Museum North★★ *Trafford Wharf Road, Trafford, Greater Manchester* A museum exploring the impact of war, opened in 2002 in a metal-clad building designed by Daniel Libeskind. ☎0161 836 4000 **41 E5**

Museum of the Manchesters *Town Hall, Market Place, Ashton-under-Lyne, Greater Manchester* The story of the Manchester regiment (the most famous member of which was poet Wilfred Owen) from the Napoleonic Wars to their amalgamation in 1958. ☎0161 342 3078 **41 E7**

Museum of the Queen's Lancashire Regiment *Stanley Street, Preston, Lancashire* The North West's most extensive collection of military heritage. ☎01772 260362 **45 E7**

RAF Millom Museum *Bankside Estate, Haverigg, Cumbria* More than 3000 photographs tracing the history of the site, a restored Westland Whirlwind WM660 helicopter used in mountain rescues, and more. There's an Aircraft Restoration Workshop in Haverigg Prison. ☎01229 772636 **56 E4**

Regimental Museum of the Royal Welch Fusiliers *Caernarfon Castle, Beaumaris, Isle of Anglesey* An exhibition about Wales's oldest regiment. ☎01248 810361 **28 D2**

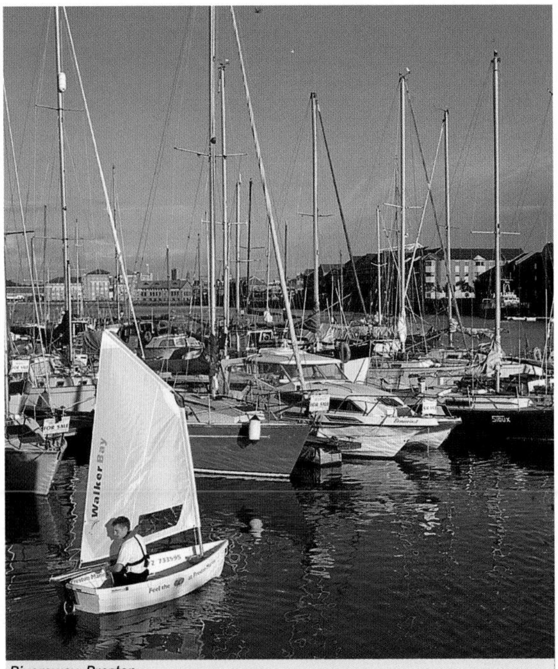

Riversway, Preston

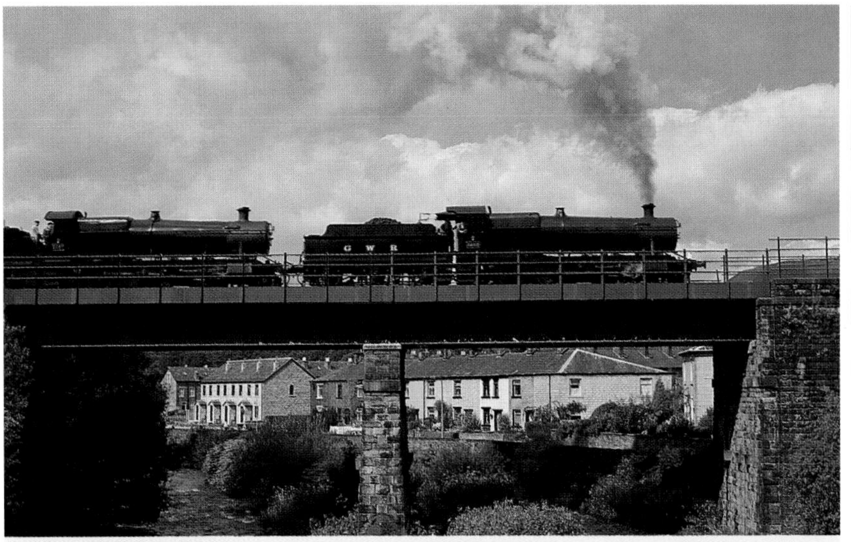

East Lancashire Railway, Bury

Stockport Air Raid Shelters *Chestergate, Stockport, Greater Manchester* Tunnels carved out of sandstone to protect locals during German air raids. Special explorer tours (hard hats and lamps provided) go deeper into the network. ☎0161 474 1940 **35 A5**

Western Approaches Museum *Rumford Street, Liverpool, Merseyside* A subterranean labyrinth of rooms that housed a top secret nerve centre in WWII. ☎0151 227 2008 **32 A1**

Local history

Astley Green Colliery Museum *Higher Green Lane, Astley Green, Greater Manchester* A listed building with a surviving headgear and engine house and containing 28 colliery locomotives and written and photographic records of the colliery, which closed in 1970. ☎01942 828121 **40 E3**

Blackpool Lifeboat Station and Visitor Centre *Central Promenade, Blackpool, Blackpool* An exhibition about the RNLI's work, locally and nationally. ☎01253 620424 **44 C3**

Buxton Museum and Art Gallery *Terrace Road, Buxton, Derbyshire* The history, archaeology and geology of the Peak District, plus an art gallery. ☎01298 24658 **35 E8**

Ceiriog Memorial Institute *Glyn Ceiriog, Wrexham* A memorial to local poet John 'Ceiriog' Hughes and other notable Welsh people, with a collection of memorabilia. ☎01691 718383 **9 A9**

Chester Heritage Centre *St Michael's Church, Bridge Street Row, Chester, Cheshire* Interactive displays, videos and scale models depicting the events and cultural influences, Roman, Viking and Norman, that have created Chester. ☎01244 402008 **32 F2**

Chester Visitor Centre *Vicars Lane, Chester, Cheshire* An information centre containing a mock-Victorian cobbled shopping street with real shops, a Hall of Names, a video on the history of Chester and crafts shops. ☎01244 402111 **32 F2**

City Museum *Market Square, Lancaster, Lancashire* The original town hall (1781), now housing exhibitions of paintings and artefacts relating to Lancaster's history and the King's Own Regiment museum of army life. ☎01524 64637 **51 C8**

Clitheroe Castle Museum *Castlegate, Clitheroe, Lancashire* Local history and geology, including a reconstructed lead mine, a clogger's shop and an Edwardian kitchen. ☎01200 424635 **46 B3**

Conwy Mussel Museum *Conwy* The history of pearl fishing in the area from Roman times, plus demonstrations of mussel harvesting today. ☎01492 592689 **28 D5**

Corgi Heritage Centre *53 York Street, Heywood, Greater Manchester* The history of locally manufactured Corgi diecast model vehicles. ☎01706 365812 **41 C6**

Cottage Museum *Castle Hill, Lancaster, Lancashire* A recreation of life in a artisan's family c.1825. ☎01524 64637 **51 C8**

Craven Museum *Town Hall, High Street, Skipton, North Yorkshire* A museum tracing the history of the Craven Dales, with a new 'family corner' with quizzes, puzzles and activities. ☎01756 706407 **54 E3**

Cumberland Pencil Museum *Southey Works, Keswick, Cumbria* A museum about graphite, its early uses and its discovery in Borrowdale, which led to Keswick becoming an important pencil-making town. ☎017687 73626 **63 B8**

Dock Museum *North Road, Barrow-in-Furness, Cumbria* A museum tracing the town's shipbuilding heritage, built over an original Victorian graving dock. ☎01229 894444 **50 A3**

Early Lead Mining Museum *Old Grammar School, School Lane, Lancashire* The history of the lead mining industry in the Yorkshire Dales and surrounds, told through 700 artefacts, including hand tools and mine wagons. Closed for refurbishment at the time of writing. ☎01282 841422 **45 E8**

Greater Manchester Fire Service Museum *Maclure Road, Rochdale, Greater Manchester* The history of firefighting, with horse-drawn and diesel fire engines and memorabilia, plus a Victorian street scene with a fire station and reconstruction of the Blitz. By appointment. ☎01706 341221 **41 B6**

Greater Manchester Police Museum *Newton Street, Manchester, Greater Manchester* A former police station with an exhibition tracing the story of policing in the city, through cells, uniforms, weapons and equipment. ☎0161 856 3287 **41 E6**

Grosvenor Museum★ *27 Grosvenor Street, Chester, Cheshire* An award-winning museum focussing on local history, with a new Timeline Gallery and displays on life in Roman times, and past and present wildlife. There's also the Chester silver collection, furniture, an art gallery and temporary exhibitions. ☎01244 402008 **32 F2**

Guildhall Museum *Fisher Street, Carlisle, Cumbria* A museum about the city's eight Trade Guilds (Butchers, Merchants, Shoemakers, Skinners, Smiths, Tailors, Tanners and Weavers), housed in Carlisle's only medieval house. ☎01228 534781 **75 E8**

Haig Colliery Mining Museum *Kells, Cumbria* Displays on the local coal and iron ore mining industries. ☎01946 599949 **62 C2**

Helena Thompson Museum *Park End Road, Workington, Cumbria* The history of the coal and iron ore mining industries, which brought prosperity to the area in the 18th and 19th centuries. ☎01900 326254 **68 F2**

Holyhead Maritime Museum *Newry Beach, Holyhead, Isle of Anglesey* A museum about the history of seafaring in the area, in reputedly the oldest lifeboat house in Wales (c.1858). ☎01407 769745 **26 C2**

Judges' Lodgings, Gillow Museum and Museum of Childhood *Upper Church Street, Lancaster, Lancashire* The residence of Thomas Covell, keeper of Lancaster, and the place where judges stayed from 1775 to 1975 when courts were in session in the castle. Exhibits include their robes, furniture, a 'below stairs' kitchen, a display on the local Gillow cabinet makers, and reproductions of traditional games in the Museum of Childhood. ☎01524 32808 **51 C8**

Keswick Museum and Art Gallery *Fitz Park, Station Road, Keswick, Cumbria* A late-Victorian museum charting Keswick's development from industrial mining centre to tourist town, with additional displays on natural history and famous locals, and paintings of the area. ☎01768 773263 **63 B8**

Llandudno Museum *Chardon House, 17-19 Gloddaeth Street, Llandudno, Conwy* A museum charting how the town developed as a resort. Other displays include a Roman tile with a footprint, a recreated Welsh kitchen and paintings and sculptures from around the world. ☎01492 876517 **28 C5**

Llanrwst Almshouses *Llanrwst, Conwy* A new museum about everyday life in a Welsh market town, created from almshouses established in 1610. ☎01492 642550 **16 B4**

Lloyd George Museum and Highgate Cottage *Llanystumdwy, Gwynedd* The childhood home of British PM David Lloyd George, now housing a museum dedicated to his life and times, a Victorian garden and a shoemaker's workshop. ☎01766 522071 **6 A1**

Macclesfield Silk Museums★ *Macclesfield, Cheshire* Four museums telling the story of the local silk industry: the Silk Museum (Park Lane), focussing on design; Paradise Mill, (Park Lane), with weaving demonstrations and restored jacquard handlooms; the Heritage Centre (Roe Street), with costumes and textiles; and West Park Museum (Prestbury Road), with fine and decorative art and local history artefacts. ☎01625 612045 **35 E5**

Manchester Jewish Museum *190 Cheetham Hill Road, Manchester, Greater Manchester* A museum housed in the former Spanish and Portuguese synagogue built in the Moorish style in 1874 by local Jewish architect Edward Salomans, telling the story of Jews in the city. Special events and exhibitions. ☎0161 834 9879 **41 E6**

Mgueddfa Syr Henry Jones Museum *Llangernyw, Conwy* A museum about rural life in Wales, including Henry Jones and his struggle for education, set in a restored cottage garden. ☎01492 575371 **29 F7**

Millom Folk Museum *Station Road, Millom, Cumbria* The history of the local coal and iron ore mining industries. ☎01229 774819 **56 D4**

Mining Museum *Matlock Bath, Derbyshire* A local-history museum in the pump room dating from Matlock Bath's days as a spa, with equipment and artefacts from the area's old lead mines. ☎01629 583834 **24 C3**

Museum of Lancashire *Stanley Street, Preston, Lancashire* The story of the county from the Middle Ages. ☎01772 260362 **45 E7**

Museum of Liverpool Life *Pier Head, Liverpool, Merseyside* A museum in a former boat hall, celebrating Liverpudlians' culture and contribution to national life; categories include faith, political activism and Liverpool bands. ☎0151 478 4080 **32 A1**

New York Cottages *Penmaenmawr, Conwy* Quarryworkers' dwellings from the 1840s; restored No.4 houses a small museum about the quarrying industry and the growth of Penmaenmawr in the 19th century. ☎01492 575371 **28 D4**

Nidderdale Museum *King Street, Pateley Bridge, North Yorkshire* An award-winning museum about life in the Yorkshire Dales, set in the former Victorian workhouse. ☎01423 711225 **55 B7**

Norton Priory Museum *Tudor Road, Manor Park, Runcorn, Halton* An award-winning museum re-creating life in medieval Cheshire, surrounded by woodland containing the ruins of a 12th-century priory and a 18th-century walled garden and orchard. ☎01928 569895 **32 C5**

NW Sound Archive★ *Clitheroe Castle, Clitheroe, Lancashire* A unique organisation holding about 100,000 sound-recorded items on all aspects of life in north west England, including coal-mining, canals and Jewish history. ☎01200 427897 **46 B3**

Old Gaol *Ruthin, Denbighshire* A new attraction based around Ruthin's Victorian prison, much of which has been preserved, including the baths, well, cell lighting and clock. ☎01824 708250 **18 C3**

Old House Museum *Bakewell, Derbyshire* A small local-history museum in Bakewell's oldest building, a 16th-century yeoman's house. ☎01629 813642 **36 F4**

Old Lifeboat House *East Beach, Lytham, Lancashire* A museum of Lytham's seafaring past, operated by the local Lifeboat Society. ☎01253 725610 **44 E4**

Oriel Ynys Mon *Rhosmeirch, Isle of Anglesey* A purposebuilt museum with a Heritage Gallery relating the cultural history of Anglesey and an art gallery exhibiting work in all media. ☎01248 724444 **27 D6**

Pacific Road Arts and Exhibition Centre *Birkenhead, Merseyside* A 19th-century warehouse housing a performing arts and exhibition centre (part of the Birkenhead Heritage Trail) and a recreated Victorian street with historic vehicles. ☎0151 666 2756 **31 B8**

Pankhurst Centre★ *60-62 Nelson Street, Manchester, Greater Manchester* The Georgian home of Emmeline Pankhurst, where the Women's Social and Political Union ('suffragettes') was formed. Displays trace the group's history, and there's a reconstruction of Pankhurst's living room. ☎0161 273 5673 **41 E6**

Pendle Heritage Museum *Park Hill, Barrowford, Lancashire* An historic building containing a museum on the history of the area, including the story of the Pendle witches, and an 18th-century walled garden and cruck barn with livestock. ☎01282 661702 **47 C6**

Penrith Museum *Middlegate, Penrith, Cumbria* A newly refurbished museum in an Elizabethan building, with displays on the history, geology and archaeology of the area, including Roman pottery, and temporary exhibitions on local interest. ☎01768 867466 **71 E5**

Portland Basin Museum *Portland Place, Ashton-under-Lyne, Greater Manchester* An award-winning reconstruction of the 1834 Ashton canal warehouse, portraying local life and industry, including a typical Tameside street of 1928. There are also canal displays and boat trips. ☎0161 343 2878 **41 E7**

Prescot Museum of Clock and Watchmaking *Church Street, Prescot, Merseyside* The history of the area, including its clock- and watch-making industry, once central to the town's development. ☎0151 430 7787 **32 A4**

Queen Street Mill Museum *Harle Syke, Lancashire* A museum about the area's weaving industry, based in Lancashire's last 19th-century steam-powered weaving mill. ☎01282 412555 **47 C6**

Rhyl Museum and Arts Centre *Church Street, Rhyl, Denbighshire* The history of the town as a seaside resort, plus displays on other topics, including the submarine 'Resurgam' and photography. ☎01745 353814 **30 C2**

Rochdale Pioneers Museum *31 Toad Lane, Rochdale, Greater Manchester* A museum in the building where the UK's first viable working-class co-operative shop started in 1844, set in a conservation area, with a restored shop and other displays. ☎01706 524920 **41 B6**

Saddleworth Museum *High Street, Uppermill, Greater Manchester* Changing exhibitions about the Pennine community of Saddleworth, plus the history of the Roman fort in Castleshaw Valley and an art gallery. ☎01457 87493 **42 C1**

Salford Museum and Art Gallery *Peel Park, The Crescent, Salford, Greater Manchester* Local-history displays including Lark Hill Place, a re-created Victorian northern street with original shopfronts, a new LifeTimes gallery tracing 200 years of the city's social and industrial heritage, and a Victorian Gallery with art, crafts and fine furniture. ☎0161 736 2649 **41 E5**

Salt Museum *162 London Road, Northwich, Cheshire* The history of the Cheshire salt industry told through artefacts, models, photographs and interactive exhibits, in a museum housed in the old Northwich workhouse. ☎01606 41331 **33 E8**

Stockport Hatworks *Wellington Road North, Stockport, Greater Manchester* A new museum in a former mill, tracing the history of the hatmaking, a local industry, through permanent and temporary exhibitions. ☎0161 355 7770 **35 A5**

Swaledale Folk Museum *Reeth Green, Reeth, North Yorkshire* An exhibition about life in Swaledale and Arkengarthdale in the past, with farming implements, lead mining tools and artefacts relating to pastimes and Wesleyan Methodism. ☎01748 884373 **61 A6**

The Beacon *West Strand, Whitehaven, Cumbria* An award-winning centre exploring the social, industrial and maritime heritage of Whitehaven, once a larger port than Liverpool, and containing the Met Office Weather Gallery. ☎01946 592302 **62 C2**

The Rum Story *Lowther Street, Whitehaven, Cumbria* The history of the 'dark spirit' in Whitehaven, including a virtual rainforest and a slave ship. ☎01946 592933 **62 C2**

Threlkeld Quarry and Mining Museum *Threlkeld, Cumbria* Miners' tools, photos, maps and plans, plus a Geology Room with a mineral collection and a tabletop relief map of the Lake District. ☎017687 79747 **64 A1**

The Beatles

Casbah Club *8 Haymans Green, West Derby, Liverpool, Merseyside* Liverpool's first beat club, where the Mersey Beat Music Scene took seed and The Beatles came into being. ☎0151 291 9764 **32 A1**

Cavern Quarter *around Mathew Street, Liverpool, Merseyside* The area around the legendary Cavern Club, including a statue of Lennon and the Cavern Wall of Fame with names of the musicians and bands who played at the club. ☎0151 236 5000 **32 A1**

Magical Mystery Tour *from Queen's Square and Albert Dock, Liverpool, Merseyside* Two-hour bus tours of various sites associated with The Beatles, including their birthplaces, Strawberry Fields and Penny Lane. ☎0871 222 1967 **32 A1**

Mathew Street Gallery *Mathew Street, Liverpool, Merseyside* A gallery specialising in artwork by John Lennon, with than 50 limited-edition prints on display and for sale. ☎0151 236 0009 **32 A1**

Mendips and 20 Forthlin Road★ *251 Menlove Avenue, Liverpool, Merseyside* John Lennon's childhood home, donated to the National Trust by Yoko Ono and opened to the public (guided tours only) in March 2003, plus Paul McCartney's family home in Allerton, where the pair wrote and rehearsed early songs. ☎0870 900 0256 **32 B3**

The Beatles Story★ *Britannia Vaults, Albert Dock, Liverpool, Merseyside* An exhibition charting the rise of The Beatles, including rare film footage and the piano on which Lennon composed 'Imagine'. ☎0151 709 1963 **32 A1**

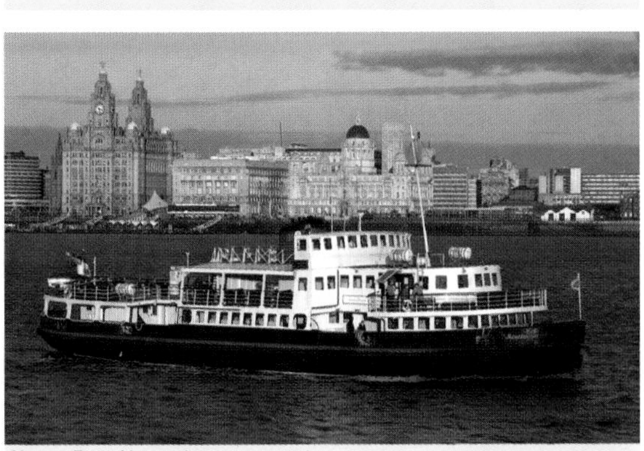

Mersey Ferry, Liverpool

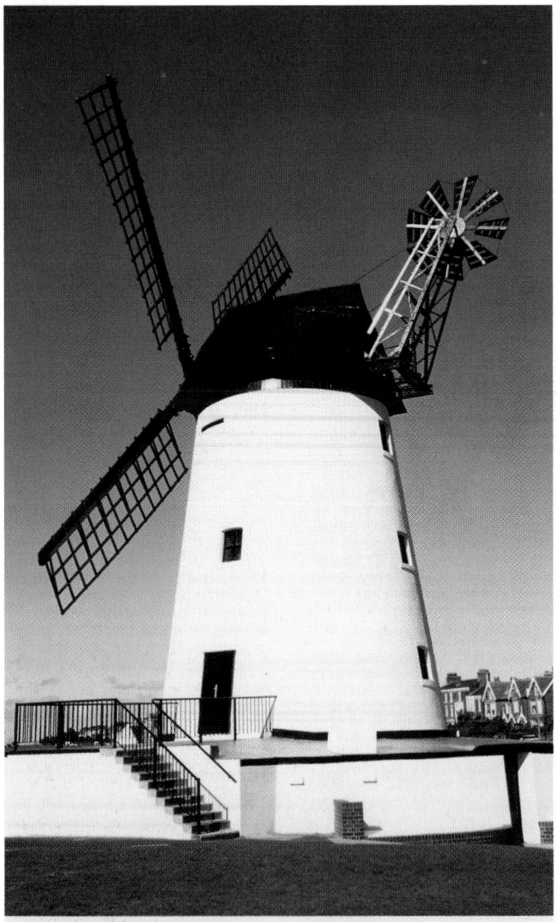

Lytham Windmill, Lancashire

Townhead Barn *Buckden, North Yorkshire* A National Trust exhibition about how the area of Upper Wharfedale around Buckden has been shaped since the last Ice Age, plus displays on the local lead industry and Langstrothdale Chase. ☎01729 830416 **60 E4**

Tullie House Museum and Art Gallery *Castle Street, Carlisle, Cumbria* An award-winning museum on the history of Carlisle and surrounds, including Hadrian's Wall and the Border Reivers, plus a contemporary art gallery and a herb garden. ☎01228 534781 **75 E8**

Upper Wharfedale Folk Museum *The Square, Grassington, North Yorkshire* A museum about lead mining, farming and crafts in the area, as well as its geology, set in two converted leadminers' cottages. There are also displays on period costume, folklore, the railway and WWI. ☎01756 753059 **54 C4**

Welsh Slate Museum *Padarn Country Park, Llanberis, Gwynedd* The history of slate quarrying in North Wales, with machinery and railway equipment, a waterwheel, slate-splitting and iron-forging demonstrations, a cinema and photographs. ☎01286 870630 **15 B7**

Wigan Pier Experience★ *Trencherfield Mill, Wigan, Greater Manchester* An 8.5-acre site beside the redeveloped Leeds and Liverpool Canal, with The Way We Were museum depicting Wigan life in 1900, Opie's Museum of Memories tracing 20th-century British domestic life, a waterbus, the world's largest working mill steam engine, and the Machinery Hall recreating the harsh working conditions at the mill. ☎01942 323666 **39 C8**

Factories, mills & mines

Acorn Bank Mill *Temple Sowerby, Cumbria* An early-19th-century mill on an older mill site, undergoing long-term restoration by the National Trust but offering working demonstrations. ☎017683 61893 **71 F7**

Arkwright's Mill *Cromford, Derbyshire* Sir Richard Arkwright's first and most important cotton mill (1771), where he pioneered the water frame spinning machine, one of the cornerstones of the Industrial Revolution. ☎01629 823256 **24 C3**

Bancroft Mill Engine Trust *Gillians Lane, Barnoldswick, Lancashire* A 1920 textile mill with a working steam engine, offering textile displays and weaving demonstrations on Lancashire and Northrop Looms. ☎01282 865626 **54 F1**

Caudwell's Mill *Rowsley, Derbyshire* A working 19th-century mill with water turbines, roller and bagging equipment, plus a craft centre and flour shop. ☎01629 734374 **24 A3**

Eskdale Mill *Boot, Cumbria* A 1578 mill with free tours, including working demonstrations of a rare two-wheel water cornmill, plus a picnic area and woodlands. ☎019467 23335 **63 F6**

Great Orme Bronze Age Copper Mines *Great Orme Country Park, Llandudno, Conwy* An old metal mine with 3500-year-old passages leading to a prehistoric cavern and a Visitor Centre with displays about Bronze Age life and archaeological artefacts. ☎01492 870447 **28 C5**

Helmshore Textile Museum *Holcombe Road, Helmshore, Lancashire* The story of Lancashire's textile industry, with a new interactive Revolution Gallery featuring an original Spinning Jenny, the unique Arkwright's Water Frame and a Lancashire Loom. ☎01706 226459 **46 F4**

Heron Corn Mill and Museum of Paper Making *Beetham, Cumbria* One of the area's few working mills, dating back to at least 1096, plus a museum dedicated to the local papermaking industry. ☎015395 65027 **58 E3**

Heysham Heritage Centre *Heysham, Lancashire* A museum about the history of this ancient settlement, in a Grade II listed 17th-century barn. ☎01282 661702 **51 C7**

Inigo Jones Slateworks *Groeslon, Gwynedd* The last fully operational slateworks in North Wales. ☎01286 830242 **15 B6**

Linton Mill Visitor Centre *Shaddon Mills, Carlisle, Cumbria* A 1912 weaving mill producing wool for Chanel and other prestigious fashion houses. Visitors can watch designs being woven on 100-year-old handlooms. ☎01228 527569 **75 E8**

Llechwedd Slate Caverns *Blaenau Ffestiniog, Gwynedd* Guided tours of an old slate quarry by former miners, including the Deep Mine, accessed via the steepest funicular railway in Britain, plus a re-created Victorian village. ☎01766 830306 **16 E2**

Lytham Windmill *East Beach, Lytham, Lancashire* An 1805 windmill with milling and local-history exhibitions and a tourist information point. ☎01253 794879 **44 E4**

Marsh-Mill-in-Wyre *Thornton, Lancashire* A restored 1794 windmill with guided tours, temporary exhibitions, demonstrations and workshops. ☎01253 860765 **44 B3**

Minera Lead Mines and Country Park *Wern Road, Minera, Wrexham* The remnants of a 19th-century lead mine, a reconstructed engine house and a visitor centre with displays on the geology and social and industrial history of lead mining in the area, including during Roman times. ☎01978 261529 **19 D6**

Muncaster Water Mill *Ravenglass, Cumbria* 01229 717232 ☎A water-powered corn mill producing flour since 1455 (organic produce is sold in its shop); tours include viewings of the 19th-century machinery in action. **56 A2**

Nenthead Mines Heritage Centre *Nenthead, Cumbria* A lead mine with interactive displays and mineral panning demonstrations. ☎01434 382037 **72 C3**

Priests Mill *Caldbeck, Cumbria* A restored riverbank watermill built by a rector of Caldbeck, used as a stone-grinding cornmill, sawmill and joiner's workshop, with a display of old farm implements, goldsmith's workshop and secondhand bookshop. ☎016974 78369 **70 D1**

Quarry Bank Mill *Quarry Bank Road, Styal, Cheshire* A Georgian cotton mill with a giant working waterwheel and an award-winning museum featuring the child millworkers' Apprentice House and the picturesque village built for the millworkers. ☎01625 527468 **34 C3**

Saltpans *Crosscanonby, Cumbria* An Elizabethan salt workings where the tradition of saltmaking from seawater along the Cumbrian coast was carried out for nearly 700 years. ☎01900 326333 **68 D4**

Shore Road Pumping Station *Woodside, Birkenhead, Merseyside* Part of the Birkenhead Heritage Trail, with a restored and functioning 'Giant Grasshopper' steam pump used to clear water from the Mersey tunnel (Europe's first underwater rail tunnel) plus a reconstruction of a 1901 Birkenhead street scene. ☎0151 650 1182 **31 B8**

Sygun Copper Mine *Beddgelert, Gwynedd* A re-creation of the life of Victorian miners in Snowdonia National Park, with tours of the old workings, tunnels and chambers. ☎01766 510100 **15 E7**

Temple Mine *Matlock Bath, Derbyshire* A former fluorspar mine with displays, the small ore-carrying railway, a chute and hopper system for taking the ore down to the lower level, and a view of the mineral vein. ☎01629 583834 **24 C3**

General museums

Bolton Museum and Art Gallery *Le Mans Crescent, Bolton, Greater Manchester* One of the largest galleries in the North West, embracing archaeology, art, botany, social history, geology and zoology, and hosting national touring exhibitions. ☎01204 332211 **40 C3**

British in India Museum *Newtown Street, Colne, Lancashire* A museum about the Raj, with uniforms, paintings, postcards, dioramas, stamps and model soldiers. ☎01282 613129 **47 B6**

British Lawnmower Museum *106-114 Shakespeare Street, Southport, Merseyside* The history of garden machinery, including Victorian and Edwardian mowers and 'lawnmowers of the rich and famous'. ☎01704 501336 **38 A3**

Cuckooland *Tabley, Macclesfield, Cheshire* A collection of antique Black Forest cuckoo clocks, plus tools and machines used by clockmakers and five Black Forest fairground organs. ☎01565 633039 **35 E5**

Dales Countryside Museum★ *Station Yard, Hawes, North Yorkshire* An award-winning museum in a converted railway station about the landscape and inhabitants of the Yorkshire Dales, with interactive exhibits and demonstrations, including a recreated lead mine. ☎01969 667450 **60 C3**

Gallery of Costume *Platt Hall, Rusholme, Greater Manchester* One of the UK's most extensive collections of costume and accessories. By appointment only. ☎0161 224 5217 **41 E6**

HM Customs and Excise National Museum *Albert Dock, Liverpool, Merseyside* The national collection of the Department of Customs and Excise, tracing the story of smuggling and contraband from the 1700s. ☎0151478 4499 **32 A1**

Laurel and Hardy Museum *4C Upper Brook Street, Ulverston, Cumbria* A museum in Ulverston, where Stan Laurel was born in 1890, with a large collection of Laurel and Hardy memorabilia. ☎01229 582292 **57 E6**

Liverpool Museum *William Brown Street, Liverpool, Merseyside* A large museum embracing archaeology, ethnology and the natural and physical sciences. Current expansion may mean some galleries are temporarily closed; call for details. ☎0151 478 4399 **32 A1**

Manchester Museum *Manchester University, Oxford Road, Manchester, Greater Manchester* The university museum, embracing archaeology, archery, botany, Egyptology, ethnology, geology, numismatics, Oriental Studies and zoology, and boasting the new Science for Life gallery, an interactive exploration of the human body and medicine. ☎0161 275 2634 **41 E6**

Printing House Museum *102 Main Street, Cockermouth, Cumbria* An exhibition charting the development of printing from the 15th century. ☎01900 824984 **69 E5**

Pumphouse People's History Museum *Bridge Street, Left Bank, Manchester, Greater Manchester* A museum in a former pumphouse, depicting the lives and political struggles of working-class Brits, including the Trade Union Movement and pastimes such as football. ☎0161 228 7212 **41 E6**

Stockport Museum *Vernon Park, Turncroft Lane, Offerton, Greater Manchester* A general museum, with the 'One Round Hill' exhibit tracing the history of Stockport through artefacts dating back as far as the Stone Age. ☎0161 474 4460 **35 B5**

Teapot World *Castle Street, Conwy* Novelty and humorous teapots ranging in date from the mid 18th century to the present. ☎01492 596533 **28 D5**

The Teapottery *Keswick, Cumbria* A small museum charting the history of tea through displays and videos, with a cafe serving the real thing. ☎017687 73983 **63 B8**

Urbis - Museum of the Modern City★ *Cathedral Gardens, Manchester, Greater Manchester* A stunning new glass building in Manchester's medieval heart, exploring the experiences of people in cities around the world through an archive, videos and pictures. ☎0161 907 9099 **41 E6**

Warrington Museum and Art Gallery *Bold Street, Warrington, Cheshire* A museum with a new Earth's History gallery, plus local and social history displays. Art is displayed throughout the building, and there are temporary exhibitions. ☎01925 442392 **33 B7**

Williamson's Tunnels *Smithdown Lane, Liverpool, Merseyside* An underground labyrinth created by local eccentric Joseph Williamson in the early 19th century, the purpose of which remains obscure. ☎0151 709 6868 **32 A1**

Family Attractions

See also *Outdoors:* ANIMAL ATTRACTIONS and *Outdoors:* BEACHES & RESORTS

Alice in Wonderland Centre *The Rabbit Hole, 3-4 Trinity Square, Llandudno, Conwy* An animated walk-through life-size displays of some of the best-known scenes from the Alice books. ☎01492 860082 **28 C5**

Anglesey Model Village *between Dwyran and Newborough, Isle of Anglesey* A scale model village featuring many of Anglesey's landmarks, in an acre of landscaped gardens with water features. ☎01248 440477 **27 F5**

Beech End Model Village *Commercial Square, Leyburn, North Yorkshire* An indoor model village with hands-on exhibits. ☎01969 625400 **61 B8**

Blackpool Model Village *East Park Drive, Blackpool, Blackpool* A model village in 2.5 acres of peaceful landscaped gardens. ☎01253 763827 **44 C3**

Blackpool Pleasure Beach★ *Ocean Boulevard, Blackpool* A huge adventure park with more than 145 rides and attractions, including the Pepsi Max Big One, the tallest and fastest rollercoaster in Europe. ☎0870 444 5566 **44 C3**

Camelot Theme Park *Charnock Richard, Lancashire* An award-winning theme park with rides, magic shows and jousting. ☎01257 453044 **39 A8**

Central Pier *Promenade, Blackpool* One of three piers in Blackpool; a family-oriented attraction with a funfair. ☎01253 623422 **44 C3**

Cumberland Toy and Model Museum *Market Place, Cockermouth, Cumbria* Mainly visitor-operated exhibits, including toy trains, Scalextric, Lego and dolls' houses. ☎01900 827606 **69 E5**

Derwent Bay Bears *Derwent Bay Sawmill, Portinscale, Cumbria* A sawmill displaying chainsaw sculptures of timber bears and other animals, with a children's playground. ☎017687 78788 **63 B7**

Dinosaur World *Eirias Park, Colwyn Bay, Conwy* The UK's biggest collection of life-size model dinosaurs, in a mock-up prehistoric environment. There's also an audio-visual room and a children's play area. ☎01492 518111 **29 D7**

Forbidden Corner *Tupgill Park Estate, Coverham, North Yorkshire* A four-acre walled garden with an underground grotto. Advance booking necessary. ☎01969 640638 **61 C8**

Gulliver's World *Old Hall, Warrington, Cheshire* A theme park set in fine grounds, with more than 50 rides and attractions. ☎01925 230088 **33 A6**

Harlequin Puppet Theatre *Rhos on Sea, Conwy* Britain's oldest permanent puppet theatre, set up in 1958. ☎01492 548166 **29 C6**

Knights Cavern★ *Rhyl, Denbighshire* A hi-tech entertainment centre with rides themed around Ancient Wales. ☎01745 338562 **30 C2**

Lakeland Miniature Village *Flookburgh, Cumbria* A model village with more than 140 buildings crafted in local Coniston slate, including Beatrix Potter's Hill Top. ☎015395 58500 **57 E8**

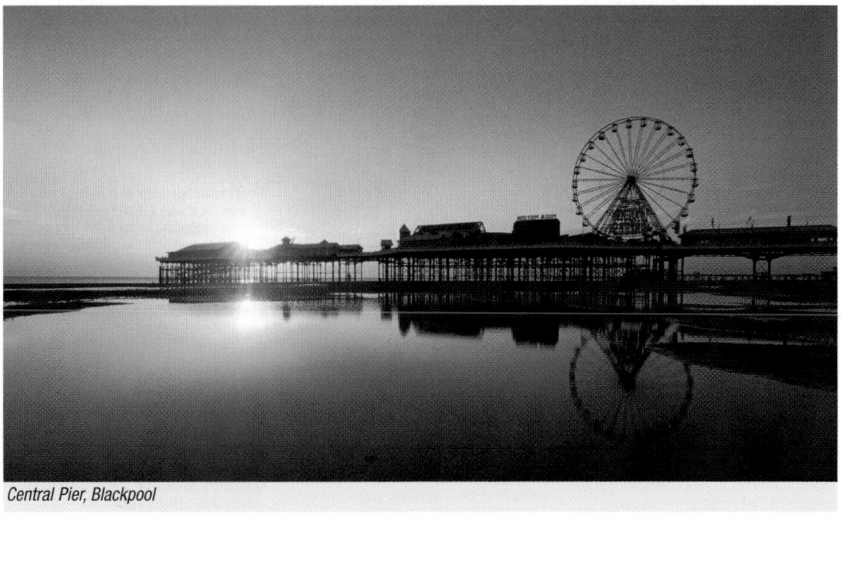

Central Pier, Blackpool

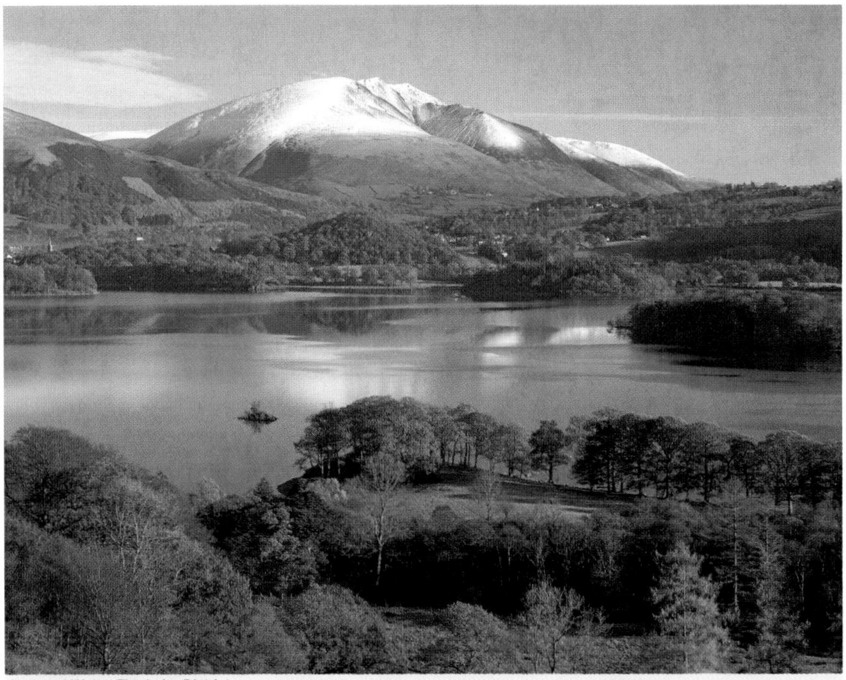

Derwent Water, The Lake District

Llandudno Pier★ *Llandudno, Conwy* A recreational pier in an Indian-Gothic style with iron lacework, built in 1878 and the longest in Wales. **28 C5**

Llangollen Exhibition Centre *Lower Dee, Llangollen, Denbighshire* An attraction combining the BBC Doctor Who Experience, Dapol Model Railway World and Toy Factory, and new Llangollen Museum of local history with its digital picture archives and history tours. ☎01978 860584 **18 F5**

Louis Tussaud's Waxworks *Promenade, Blackpool* A five-storey museum with more than 150 waxworks. ☎01253 625953 **44 C3**

Museum of Childhood Memories *1 Castle Street, Beaumaris, Isle of Anglesey* A museum exploring family entertainment over the past 150 years, including clockwork tin-plate toys, teddy bears and early cycles. ☎01248 712498 **28 D2**

North Pier *Blackpool* An old-fashioned, Grade II listed pier with a range of traditional family entertainment. ☎01253 621452 **44 C3**

Ocean Beach Fun Fair *Rhyl, Denbighshire* A pleasure park combining sponsored attractions such as the Skoda Big Wheel and Pepsi Loop Roller Coaster with more traditional rides. ☎01745 343246 **30 C2**

Pleasureland Southport *Marine Drive, Southport, Merseyside* More than 100 rides and attractions, including the Casablanca family entertainment centre and the 'Traumatizer', Britain's fastest and tallest suspended looping coaster. ☎01704 532717 **38 A3**

Southport Pier *Southport, Merseyside* Britain's second longest pier (and its first iron pier, built in 1860), which re-opened in 2002 after a £7-million restoration. **38 A3**

The Sandcastle *Promenade, Blackpool, Blackpool* One of the biggest waterworlds in the country, with giant waterslides, white-knuckle waterchutes and the like. ☎01253 343602 **44 C3**

The World of Beatrix Potter *The Old Laundry, Bowness-on-Windermere, Cumbria* A indoor re-creation of the Lakeland countryside depicted in Beatrix Potter's tales. ☎015394 88444 **58 A2**

Toy and Doll Museum *13a Lower Bridge Street Row, Chester, Cheshire* Dolls, teddies and other classic toys, including Matchbox cars, Meccano, Hornby trains and an original Punch and Judy, plus a shop for collectors. ☎01244 346297 **32 F2**

Toy and Teddy Bear Museum of Childhood *Clifton Drive North, St. Anne's, Lancashire* Classic toys and childhood memorabilia, plus a collection of children's photographs. ☎01253 713705 **44 E3**

Victoria Pier *Colwyn Bay, Conwy* A Victorian pier with a variety of amusements. **29 D7**

Victorian School of the 3 R's and Heritage Centre *Parade Street, Llangollen, Denbighshire* A re-creation of the harsh life of Victorian schoolchildren; visitors dress in Victorian costume and use authentic writing implements, inkwells, books and slates. There's also a collection of Victorian toys and games. ☎01978 860794 **18 F5**

Sport

Activity centres

See also individual activities below

Eden Valley Centre *Ainstable, Cumbria* Activities in the northern Lake District, including caving, climbing, abseiling, walking, canoeing/kayaking and scrambling. ☎01768 896202 **71 B5**

Kepplewray Centre *Broughton in Furness, Cumbria* An activity centre in the southern Lake District, offering climbing, abseiling, canoeing/kayaking, scrambling, walking and the like. ☎01229 716936 **57 C5**

Outward Bound Trust★ *Eskdale Green, Cumbria* A range of activities in the western Lake District, including walking, climbing, abseiling, canoeing/kayaking, scrambling and cycling/mountain biking. ☎019467 23281 **63 F5**

ProAdventure *23 Castle Street, Llangollen, Denbighshire* Adventure holidays, including canoeing, whitewater rafting, rock climbing, abseiling and gorge walking. ☎01978 861912 **18 F5**

Total Adventure *Holehird Farm, Patterdale Road, Windermere, Cumbria* A multi-activity centre in the Lake District, offering walking, climbing, abseiling, canoeing/kayaking, scrambling, cycling/mountain biking and more. ☎015394 47302 **58 A2**

Climbing & caving

See also ACTIVITY CENTRES; ***Outdoors:*** CAVES, CAVERNS & POTHOLES

British Mountaineering Council *177-9 Burton Road, Manchester, Greater Manchester* Details of mountaineering clubs around the country. ☎0161 445 4747 **41 E6**

Derwent Hill Centre *Portinscale, Cumbria* A Lake District activity centre offering climbing and caving, as well as walking, abseiling, canoeing/kayaking, scrambling and cycling/mountain biking. ☎017687 72005 **63 B7**

High Trek Snowdonia *Tal y Waen, Deiniolen, Gwynedd* Rock-climbing courses in Snowdonia for beginners and more advanced climbers, with accommodation in an old farmhouse. ☎01286 871232 **15 B7**

Plas-y-Brenin National Mountain Centre *Capel Curig, Conwy* Mountaineering, rock climbing, canoeing and orienteering courses at the national centre for mountain activities. ☎01229 716936 **16 C2**

Cricket

Lancashire County Cricket Club Museum *Old Trafford Cricket Ground, Old Trafford, Greater Manchester* Memorabilia recalling the history of the Lancashire team, at the ground where test matches have been held for more than 100 years. ☎0161 282 4000 **41 E5**

Cycling

See also ACTIVITY CENTRES

Berwyn Mountain Biking *Glyn Ceiriog, Wrexham* Bike hire, equipment and maps for mountain biking in the scenic Ceiriog Valley. ☎01691 718845 **9 A9**

Dales Mountain Biking *Reeth, North Yorkshire* A group mountain biking specialist in the Yorkshire Dales, offering hire and weekend packages. ☎01748 884356 **61 A6**

Lakeland Mountain Bike Experience *9 Acorn Street, Keswick, Cumbria* Cycling and mountain biking breaks in the Lake District. ☎017687 73216 **63 B8**

Rhiw Goch Ski and Mountain Bike Centre *Bronaber, Gwynedd* An award-winnng skiing and mountain biking centre in Snowdonia National Park. ☎01766 540578 **7 B6**

Football

Everton Football Club *Goodison Park, Liverpool, Merseyside* Stadium tours of the Everton homeground. ☎0151 330 2400 **32 A1**

Liverpool Football Club★ *Anfield Road, Liverpool, Merseyside* The Liverpool FC museum, including a film about a day in the life of the club and a recreation of Bill Shankly's 1965 dressing room, plus tours of the stadium. ☎0151 263 9199 **32 A1**

Manchester United Museum and Tour Centre★ *Sir Matt Busby Way, Old Trafford, Greater Manchester* Backstage tours of Old Trafford, including the manager's dugout and the players' tunnel, plus a museum with memorabilia and interactive exhibits and archives. ☎0870 442 1994 **41 E5**

National Football Museum★★ *Deepdale Stadium, Sir Tom Finney Way, Preston, Lancashire* A major museum housing world-class collections and interactive exhibits relating to the 'beautiful game', including the official FIFA collection, plus social history displays. ☎01772 908442 **45 E7**

Reebok Stadium *Middlebrook Leisure and Retail Park, Burnden Way, Bolton, Greater Manchester* The home of Bolton Wanderers, with an interactive Museum and Tour Centre. ☎01204 673670 **40 C3**

Golf

Royal Birkdale Golf Course *Waterloo, Merseyside* A course set among spectacular sand dunes; a regular venue for the Open. ☎01704 567920 **38 E4**

Royal Liverpool Golf Club *Hoylake, Merseyside* A famous golf club hosting the 2006 Open. ☎0151 632 3101 **31 B6**

Royal Lytham and St Annes Golf Club *Links Gate, St. Anne's, Lancashire* A championship course that hosted the 2001 British Open Championships. ☎01253 724206 **44 E3**

Hanggliding & paragliding

Derbyshire Soaring Club *Derbyshire and Lancashire Gliding Club Clubhouse, Camphill, near Bradwell, Derbyshire* One of the UK's largest hang gliding and paragliding clubs. ☎0709 201 7770 **36 C3**

Lakes Paragliding Centre *Graeber, Maulds Meaburn, Cumbria* A centre for paragliding and hanggliding over the Lake District. ☎01931 715050 **65 C7**

Peak Hang Glide *York House, Ladderedge, Leek, Staffordshire* The oldest BHPA registered school in the country. ☎07000 426445 **23 C5**

Horseracing

Aintree★ *Ormskirk Road, Liverpool, Merseyside* The famous racecourse, with a stables tour and interactive displays such as a Grand National simulator. ☎0151 522 2929 **32 A1**

Chester Racecourse *The Roodee, Chester, Cheshire* Britain's oldest horseracing course, on the site of the massive Roman harbour (part of the wall of which can still be seen). One of the few UK courses where horses race anticlockwise. Races are held May-Sept (the Chester Cup is in May). ☎01244 323 70 **32 F2**

Haydock Park★ *Newton-le-Willows, Merseyside* The UK's most-visited racecourse, hosting the group 1 Stanley Leisure Sprint and the De Vere Gold Cup in September and February respectively. ☎01942 725963 **39 E8**

Riding

John Pughe Pony Trekking *Glyn Ceiriog, Llangollen, Denbighshire* A trekking centre in the spectacular Ceiriog Valley, also offering quad off-road riding for all levels. ☎01691 718333 **18 F5**

Kilnsey Trekking and Riding Centre *Conistone with Kilnsey, Skipton, North Yorkshire* Pony trekking and riding for all ages and abilities in the Yorkshire Dales. ☎01756 752861 **54 E3**

Parkfoot Trekking Centre *Pooley Bridge, Cumbria* An off-road Lake District pony trekking centre catering for all ages and abilities. ☎01768 486696 **64 B4**

Snowdonia Riding Stables *Waunfawr, Gwynedd* Riding, hacking and trekking for all abilities on bridleways between Snowdon and the sea. ☎01286 650342 **15 C6**

Sockbridge Pony Trekking Centre *The Cottage, Sockbridge, Cumbria* Pony trekking along pretty country lanes and fells overlooking Ullswater, for all age groups and levels of ability. ☎01768 863468 **70 F4**

Yorkshire Dales Trekking Centre *Malham, North Yorkshire* Riding lessons and treks in the Yorkshire Dales National Park. ☎01729 830352 **54 C2**

Motorsport

See also ACTIVITY CENTRES; ***Outdoors:*** BEACHES & RESORTS

Oulton Park *Little Budworth, Cheshire* Cheshire's famous motor racing circuit, celebrating its 50th anniversary in 2003. ☎01829 760301 **20 A4**

Watersports

Canolfan Tryweryn National Whitewater Centre *Frongoch, Gwynedd* Whitewater rafting amidst spectacular Snowdonia scenery. ☎01678 521083 **8 A3**

Derwentwater Marina *Portinscale, Cumbria* A variety of watersports activities and courses for different levels of expertise. ☎017687 72912 **63 B7**

Glenridding Sailing School and Boat Hire *The Spit, Glenridding, Cumbria* Lake District boat and yacht hire, and courses in sailing, canoeing, kayaking and archery. ☎017684 82541 **64 C2**

Hafan Pwllheli Marina★ *Pwllheli, Gwynedd* A European Centre of Excellence in sailing, and the venue for various national and international sailing and watersports events. ☎01758 701219 **5 A7**

JJ Canoeing and Rafting *Mile End Mill, Berwyn Road, Llangollen, Denbighshire* A canoeing and rafting centre with its own section of the River Dee, also offering whitewater rafting, climbing, abseiling, gorge walking, laser clay shooting, archery, quad biking, horse riding, and guided country walks. ☎01978 860763 **18 F5**

Llyn Brenig *Cerrigydrudion, Conwy* A deep artificial lake in a superb setting, with a watersports centre, a sailing club and flyfishing facilities. There's also a visitor centre, adventure playground and lakeside cafe plus a fleet of mountain bikes for hire. ☎01490 420463 **17 E7**

Royal Chester Rowing Club *The Groves, Chester, Cheshire* Britain's first open rowing club, now organising the Chester Regatta dating back to at least 1733. ☎01244 322468 **32 F2**

Sailing School *Marine Lake, New Brighton, Merseyside* Sailing, angling, powerboating, jetskiing, waterskiing, windsurfing and raft-building; equipment provided. ☎0151 691 0941 **38 F3**

Wirral Sailing Centre *Marine Lake, South Parade, West Kirby, Merseyside* Sailing, canoeing and wind-surfing facilities on a massive saltwater lake with constant wind conditions. ☎0151 625 2510 **31 B6**

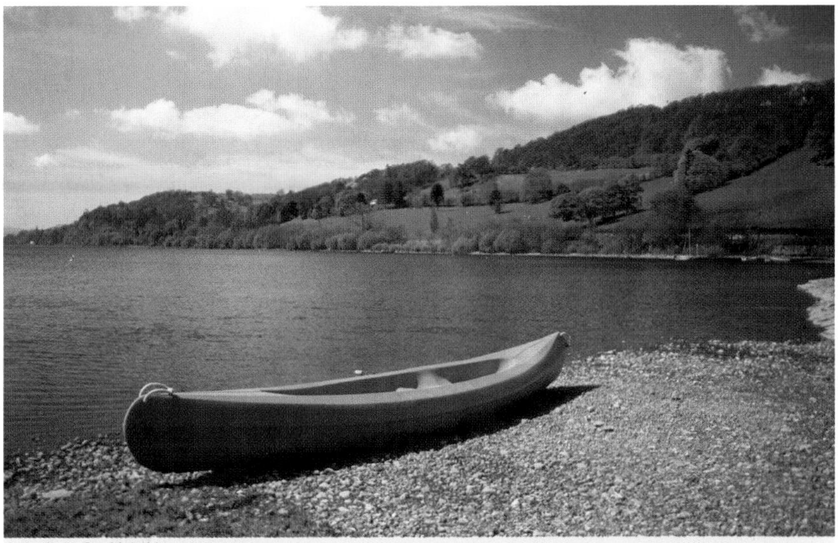

Lake Bala, Denbighshire

Isle of Man

NATURE RESERVE

Ayres Nature Reserve and Visitor Centre *Point of Ayre, Isle of Man* The sandy northernmost part of the island, with rich plant- and birdlife, the 100ft Point of Ayre lighthouse, designed by Robert Stevenson in 1818, a dunes trail and a visitor centre. ☎ 01624 801985 **80 A4**

Calf of Man *The Sound, Isle of Man* A nature reserve and bird sanctuary on an islet off the southern tip of the Isle of Man, visitable by summer boat trips. ☎ 01624 832339 **80 E1**

Scarlett Point *Castletown, Isle of Man* A Manx Wildlife Trust site with a coastal nature trail and a visitor centre with displays about local flora and fauna and industrial heritage. ☎ 01624 801985 **80 E2**

Silverdale Glen *Ballasalla, Isle of Man* An attractive glen with a lake and Edwardian-era boating and sailing centre, radio-controlled boats, a play park and a new craft centre. ☎ 01624 823474 **80 B3**

PARKS & GARDENS

Ballalheannagh Gardens *Glen Roy, Lonan, Laxey, Isle of Man* About 30 acres of formal gardens, glen trails, streams and waterfalls, with an arboretum. ☎ 01624 861875 **80 C4**

Curraghs Wildlife Park *Ballaugh, Isle of Man* A wetland habitat created from the boggy Ballaugh Curraghs, a relic of the Ice Ages. with more than 100 animal species (including Manx Loghtan sheep, brought to island by the Vikings), a walk-through aviary, a children's farm and nature trails. ☎ 01624 897323 **80 B3**

ANIMAL ATTRACTIONS

Home of Rest for Old Horses *near Douglas, Isle of Man* A 92-acre country site housing 50 retired horses and donkeys, with a small museum and cafe. ☎ 01624 674594 **80 D3**

Mann Cat Sanctuary *Ash Villa, Main Road, Santon, Isle of Man* A home for rescued cats and kittens, including Manxes, plus other pets and farm animals. ☎ 01624 824195 **80 D3**

BEACHES & RESORTS

Port Erin *Isle of Man* A family holiday resort with an almost circular bay and sandy beach and the key-shaped landmark of Milner's Tower. **80 E1**

Port St Mary *Port St Mary, Isle of Man* A quaint family and yachting resort, with a fine sheltered beach in Chapel Bay and a marine walk over rocks to the harbour. **80 E2**

TOWNS & VILLAGES

Castletown *Isle of Man* One of Britain's oldest towns, dating back to 1090, with narrow streets and fishing cottages. **80 E2**

Buildings Castle Rushen • Old House of Keys
Family Attractions Old Grammar School
Military history Nautical Museum
Outdoors Scarlett Point and Visitor Centre

Peel★ *Isle of Man* A small harbour city with a sandy beach, a promenade and narrow streets, the scene of smuggling in the 18th century and now the centre of the island's fishing industry, with curing houses producing the famous Manx kippers. **80 C2**
Buildings Cathedral Church of St German • Peel Castle
Local history & industry House of Manannan • Leece Museum • Moore's Traditional Museum

St John's *Isle of Man* A sleepy little village, home to Tynwald Hill, said to be made of soil brought from the 17 parishes of the island and the focal point for Manx National Day celebrations. Its arboretum has trees donated by the parishes in 1979 to mark the Millennium of Tynwald, plus a lake and picnic spots. **80 C2**

CASTLES

Castle Rushen *Castletown Square, Castletown, Isle of Man* The restored medieval limestone fortress of the kings and lords of Mann, with a limestone keep with a one-fingered clock said to have been donated by Elizabeth I, a drawbridge, dungeons and historical displays. ☎ 01624 648000 **80 E2**

Peel Castle *Peel Harbour, Peel, Isle of Man* A ruined ancient sandstone castle and cathedral on St Patrick's Isle, with foundations and surviving walls built by the early English kings of Man at the end of the 14th century. There's also a round tower built by monks as sanctuary against the Vikings. Recent archaeological findings have included the grave of the Viking 'Lady of Peel'. ☎ 01624 648000 **80 C2**

HISTORIC BUILDINGS

Corrin's Tower *Contrary Head, near Peel, Isle of Man* A four-storey hilltop tower built around 1806 for landowner Thomas Corrin, known as Corrin's Folly, with stone memorial tablets and inscriptions on the inner walls. **80 C2**

Molly Carrooin's Cottage *Church Road, Onchan, Isle of Man* A restored thatched cottage once inhabited by the local washerwoman, possibly the oldest house in the village and occasionally open to the public. **80 D3**

Old House of Keys *Castletown, Isle of Man* The restored 19th-century Manx Parliament building, where visitors can relive the debates and votes that shaped the island's history. ☎ 01624 648000 **80 E2**

RELIGIOUS BUILDINGS

Cathedral Church of St German *Peel, Isle of Man* A tiny building largely built between 1879 and 1884, a cathedral since 1980 (the remains of the original cathedral can be seen on St Patrick's Isle). **80 C2**

Kirk Maughold Church★ *Kirk Maughold, Isle of Man* A parish church with a cross

Old House of Keys

shelter containing 44 Manx crosses, many of them Celtic and some bearing the names of priests and bishops of the former monastery. **80 B4**

Kirk Michael Church★ *Kirk Michael, Isle of Man* A parish church with the outstanding 10th-century Gaut's cross, with a ring-chain pattern and the runic inscription 'Gaut made this and all in Mann'. Other crosses bear figures from both Norse and Christian mythology. **80 B3**

Rushen Abbey★ *Ballasalla, Isle of Man* A ruined abbey founded in 1134 by monks from Furness Abbey in Cumbria, currently being excavated by Manx National Heritage. There's a viewing room for live digs, exhibition rooms with a model of the abbey, a children's section and a herb garden. ☎ 01624 648000 **80 B3**

St Thomas's Church *Douglas, Isle of Man* An early-Victorian-Gothic church by local architect Ewan Christian, with nave and chancel walls painted by Manx artist John Miller Nicholson between 1896 and 1910. **80 D3**

TRANSPORT

Douglas Horse Trams *Douglas, Isle of Man* Two-mile trips by Victorian horse-drawn

passenger trams, open and closed, along Douglas Promenade. ☎ 01624 675222 **80 D3**

Groudle Glen Railway *Onchan, Isle of Man* An 1896 narrow-gauge steam railway running summer trips through the biggest and most spectacular of the islands' glens, developed in the 1890s as a pleasure glen and extending to the coast. ☎ 01624 622138 **80 D3**

Isle of Man Steam Railway *Douglas, Isle of Man* Britain's longest narrow-gauge steam railway, running 16 miles between Douglas and Port Erin (where there's a steam rail museum) via Castletown and Port St Mary. ☎ 01624 663366 **80 D3**

Manx Electric Railway *Douglas, Isle of Man* An 1893 electric tramway running 18 miles between Douglas and Ramsey via Laxey, using the world's oldest working tramcars and offering rural and coastal views. ☎ 01624 663366 **80 D3**

Murray's Motorcycle Museum *Isle of Man* An exhibition of more than 120 motorcycles and motoring memorabilia dating from 1902 to 1961 and including Mike Hailwoods' 1961 TT winning Honda. ☎ 01624 861719 **80 C3**

Snaefell Mountain Railway *Laxey, Isle of Man* Five-mile trips on Britain's only electric mountain railway, from Laxey to the summit of Snaefell, with views of England, Ireland, Scotland and Wales. ☎ 01624 675222 **80 C4**

MILITARY HISTORY

Manx Military and Aviation Museum *between Ballasalla and Castletown, Isle of Man* A volunteer-run museum open on weekends and holidays, with displays about military, wartime and civil aviation, including guns, photos and recovered aircraft parts. **80 E2**

Nautical Museum *Castletown Harbour, Castletown, Isle of Man* An exhibition about the Isle of Man's naval connections, focussing on the late-18th-century armed yacht 'Peggy' in her original boathouse. ☎ 01624 648000 **80 E2**

Regimental Museum of the Manx Regiment *MacClellan Hall, Tromode Road, Douglas, Isle of Man* A small museum commemorating the Regiment's role in World War II. ☎ 01624 803146 **80 D3**

LOCAL HISTORY

Cregneash Folk Museum *Port St Mary, Isle of Man* A 'living village' recreating life in a Manx upland crofting and fishing community at the end of the 19th century, with a working farm. ☎ 01624 648000 **80 E2**

Grove Museum of Rural Life *Andreas Road, Ramsey, Isle of Man* A 19th-century country house with period furnishings and outbuildings with displays of old agricultural equipment. ☎ 01624 648000 **80 B4**

House of Manannan *Peel, Isle of Man* A heritage centre with interactive exhibits about the history of the Isle of Man. ☎ 01624 648000 **80 C2**

Laxey Heritage Trust *Mines Road, Laxey, Isle of Man* A centre providing information about Laxey, Laxey Wheel and Mines and local crafts, with displays of farm implements. ☎ 01624 862007 **80 C4**

Laxey Wheel and Mines *Laxey, Isle of Man* The still-functional 'Lady Isabella', claimed to be the world's largest water wheel, built in 1854 to pump water from the flooding zinc ore mines, of which there are tours. ☎ 01624 675522 **80 C4**

Leece Museum *The Old Courthouse, East Quay, Peel, Isle of Man* The municipal museum of Peel, with historic photographs of the town. ☎ 01624 845366 **80 C2**

Manx Museum★ *Douglas, Isle of Man* The 'Story of Mann', told through a short video and displays on natural history, social development, local art, and archaeology, including some of the 204 Manx crosses found on the island, serving as grave markers and memorial stones since the 5th century AD. ☎ 01624 648000 **80 D3**

Moore's Traditional Museum★ *Mill Road, Peel, Isle of Man* A curers offering working demonstrations of how Manx kippers have been cured over oak chips since c.1770. ☎ 01624 843622 **80 C2**

FACTORIES, MILLS & MINES

Laxey Wheel and Mines *Laxey, Isle of Man* The still-functional 'Lady Isabella', claimed to be the world's largest water wheel, built in 1854 to pump water from the flooding zinc ore mines, of which there are tours. ☎ 01624 675522 **80 C4**

St George's Woollen Mills *Glen Road, Laxey, Isle of Man* A traditional Manx woollen mill where visitors can watch Manx tweed and tartan being woven. ☎ 01624 861395 **80 C4**

FAMILY ATTRACTIONS

Old Grammar School *Castletown, Isle of Man* The one-time Manx capital's first church, built in 1200AD, subsequently a school (1570-1930) and now housing a recreated Victorian schoolroom. ☎ 01624 648000 **80 E2**

Onchan Pleasure Park *Onchan, Isle of Man* A family-oriented park with boats, crazy golf, kiddie cars, tennis, stock car racing and more. ☎ 01624 675564 **80 D3**

WATERSPORTS

Isle of Man Yacht Club *Club House, Lime Street, Port St. Mary, Isle of Man* A training club catering for all levels of yachting experience. ☎ 01624 832088 **80 E2**

Laxey Wheel

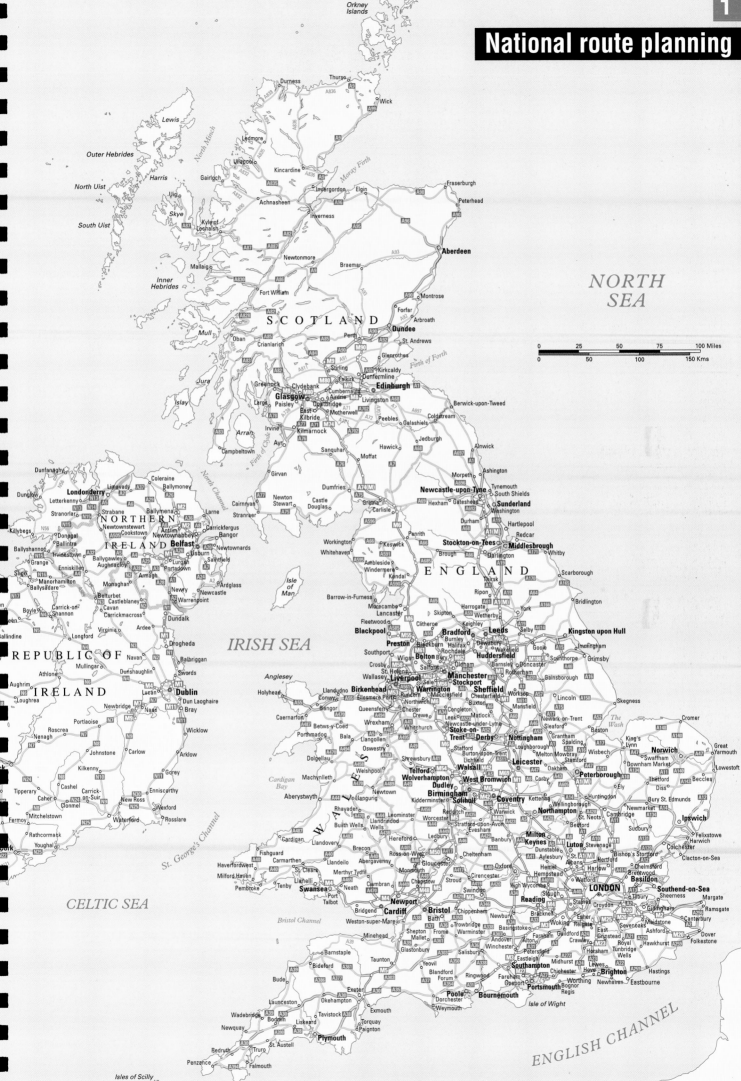

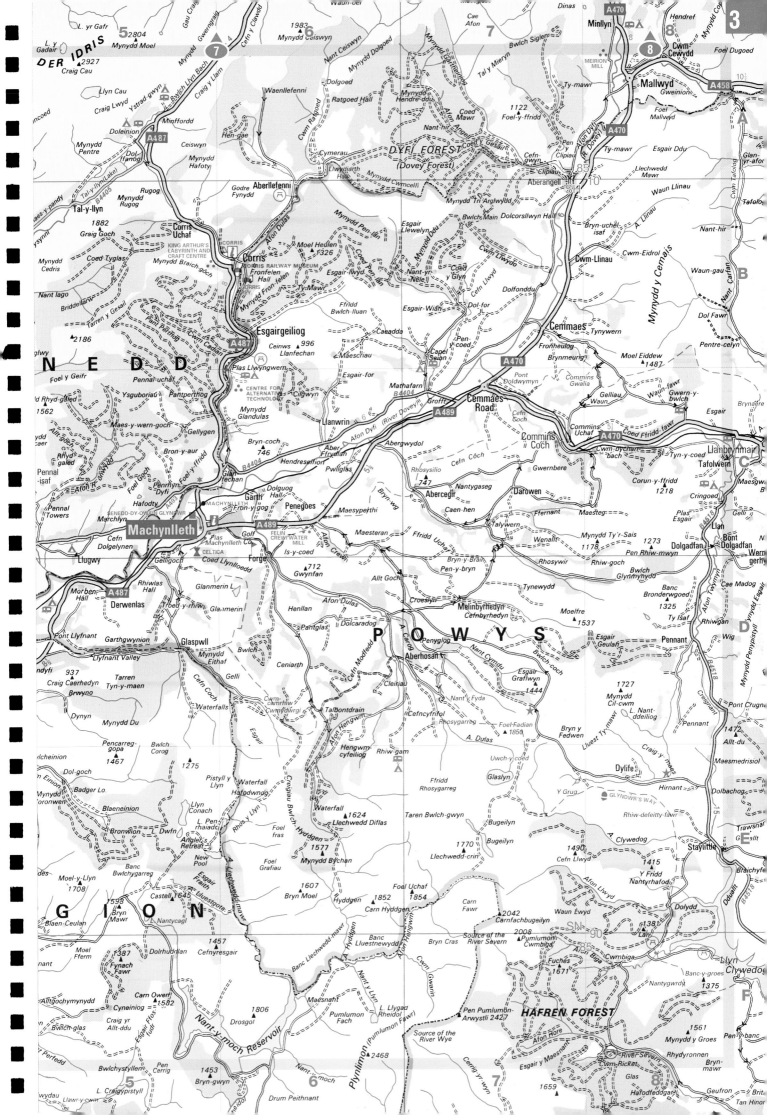

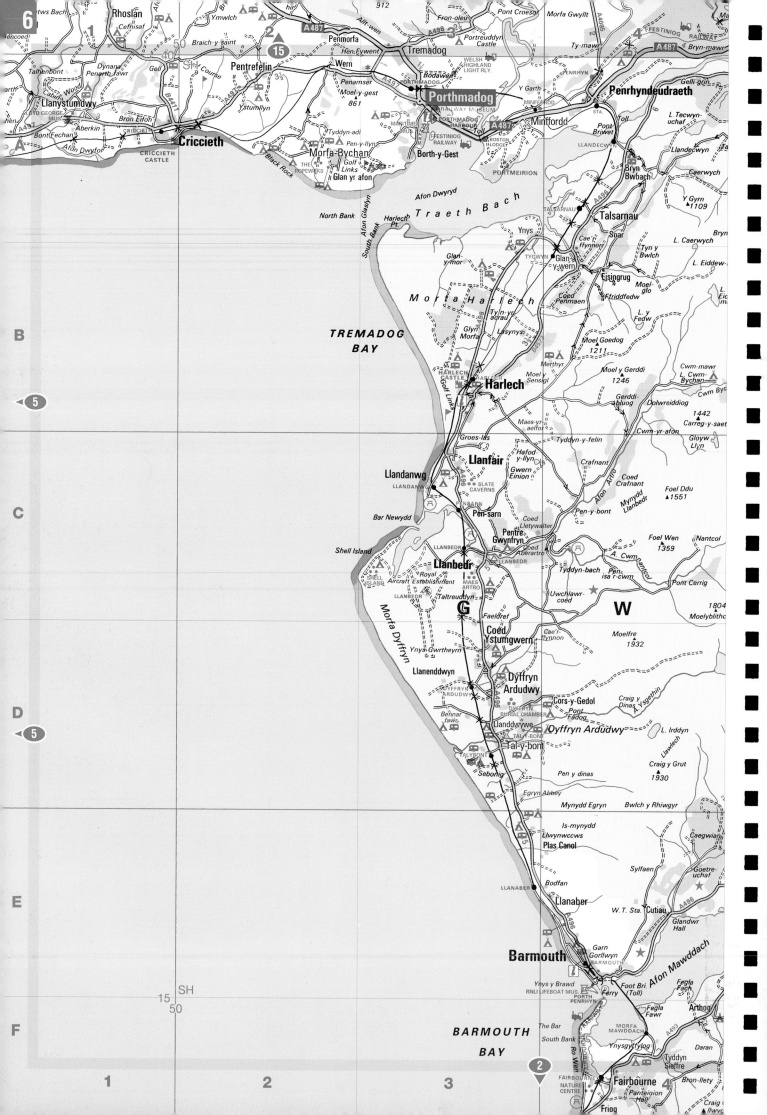

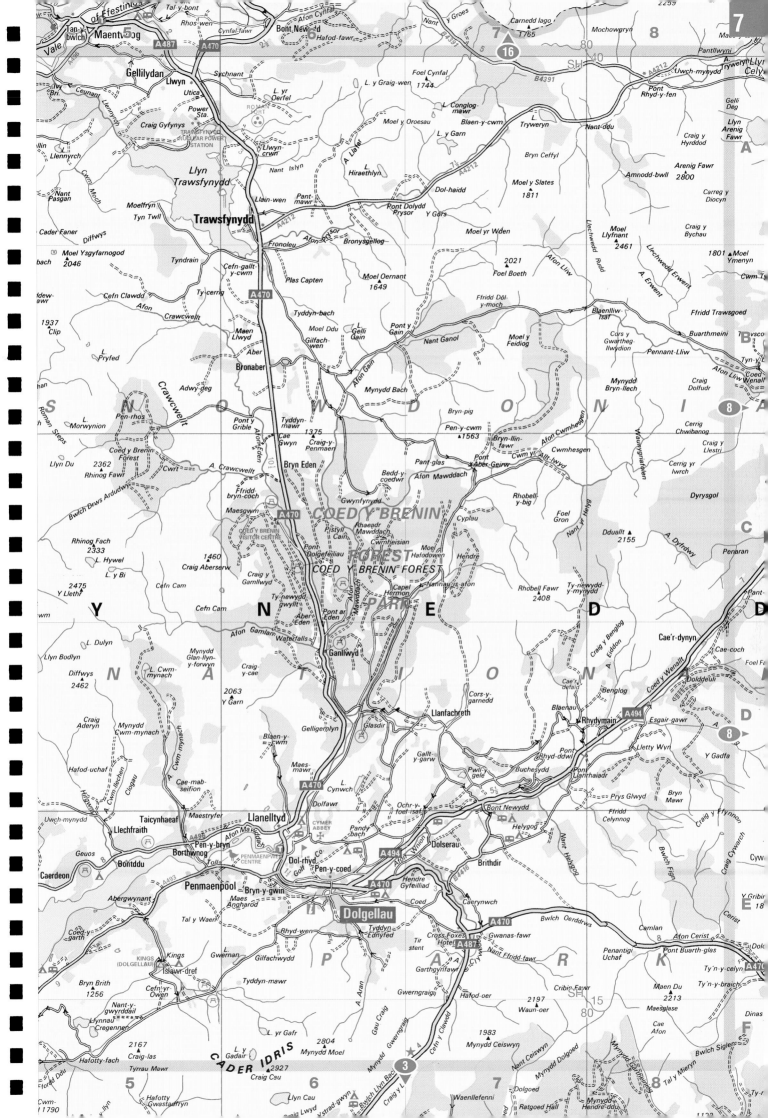

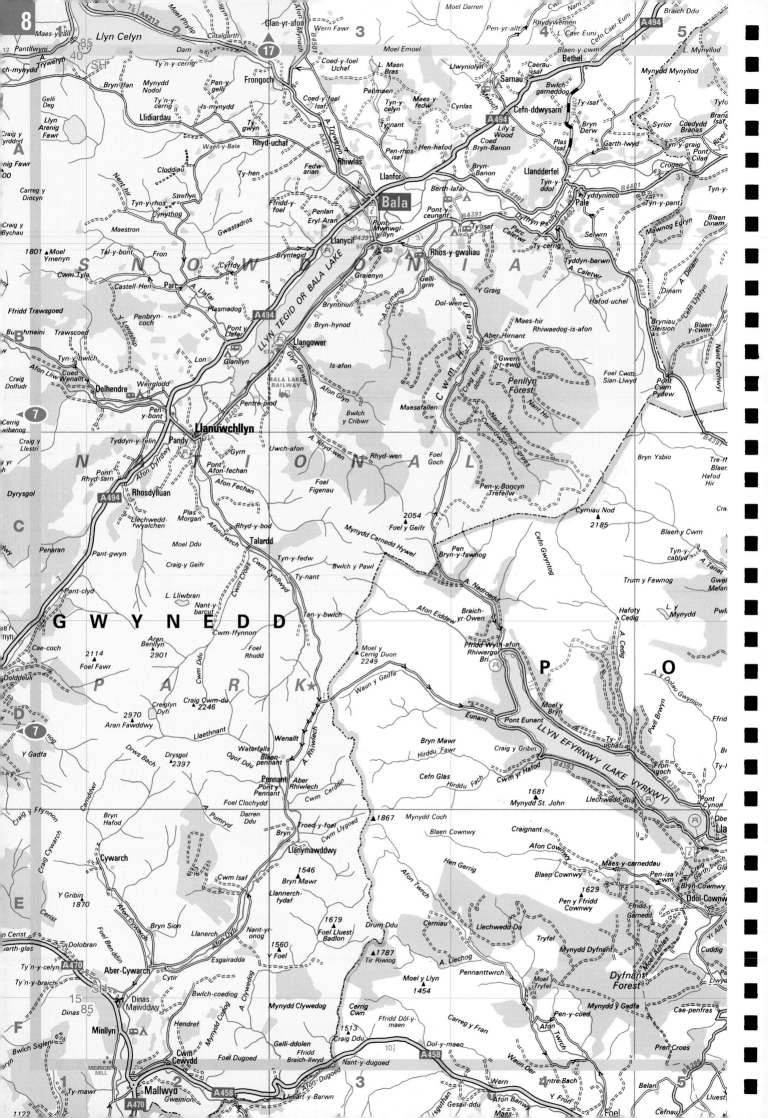

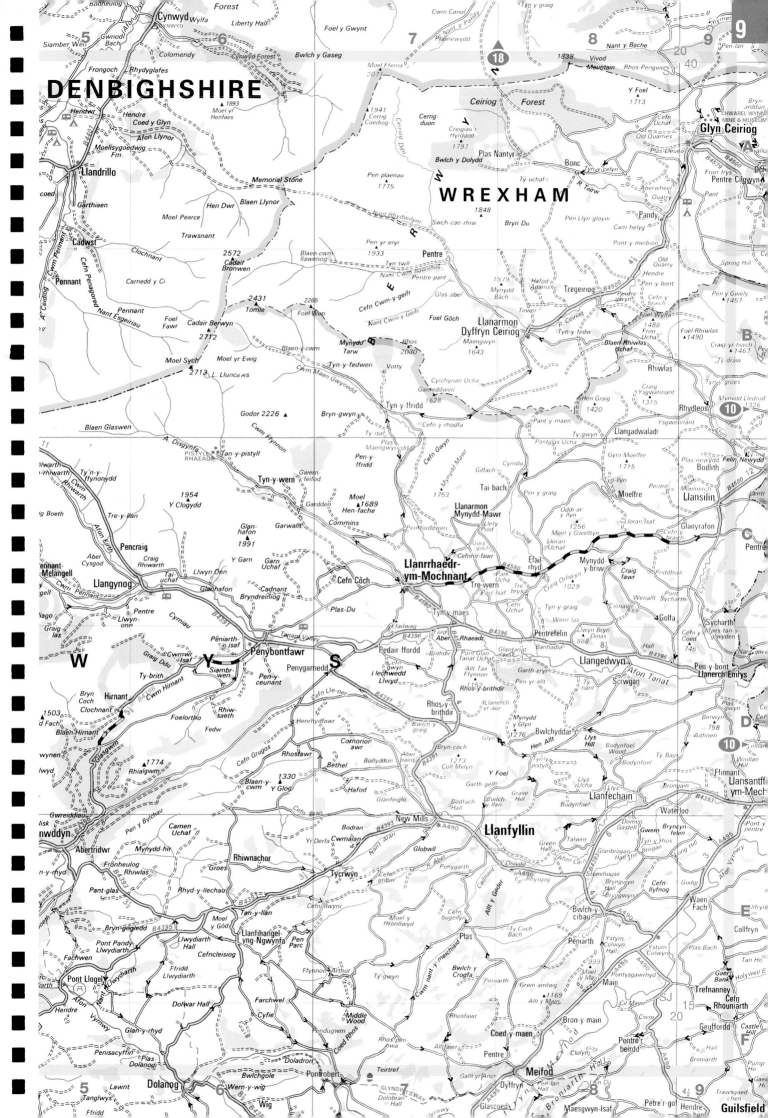

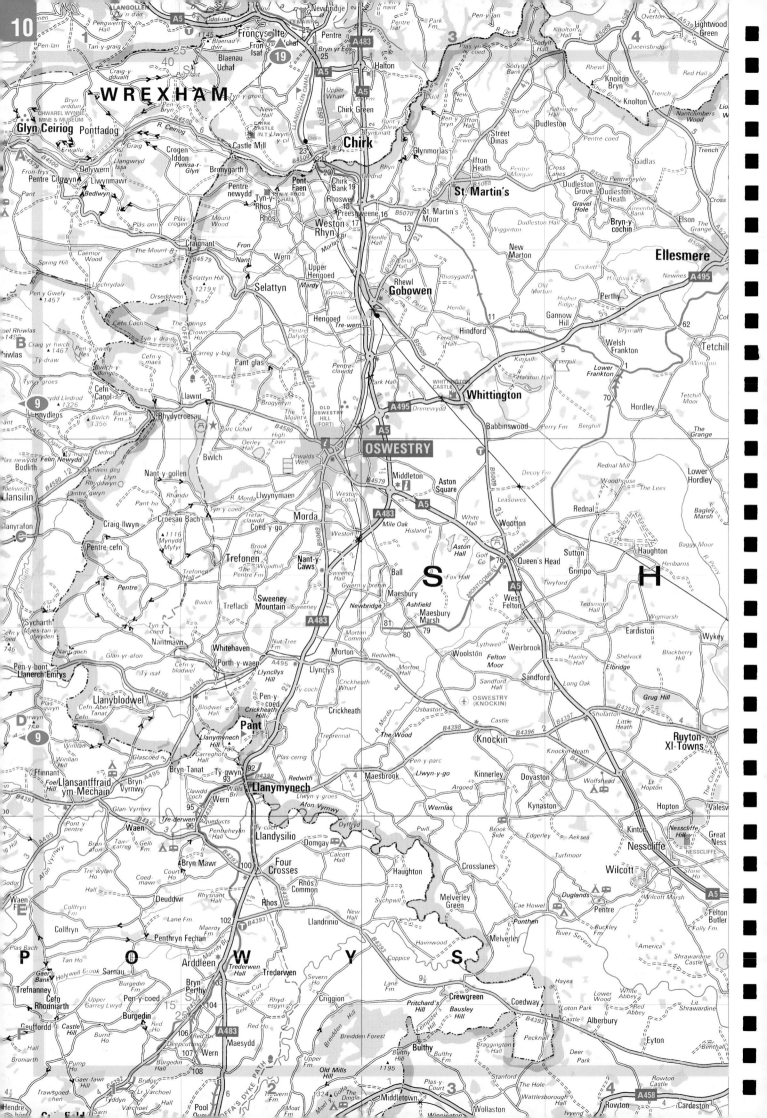

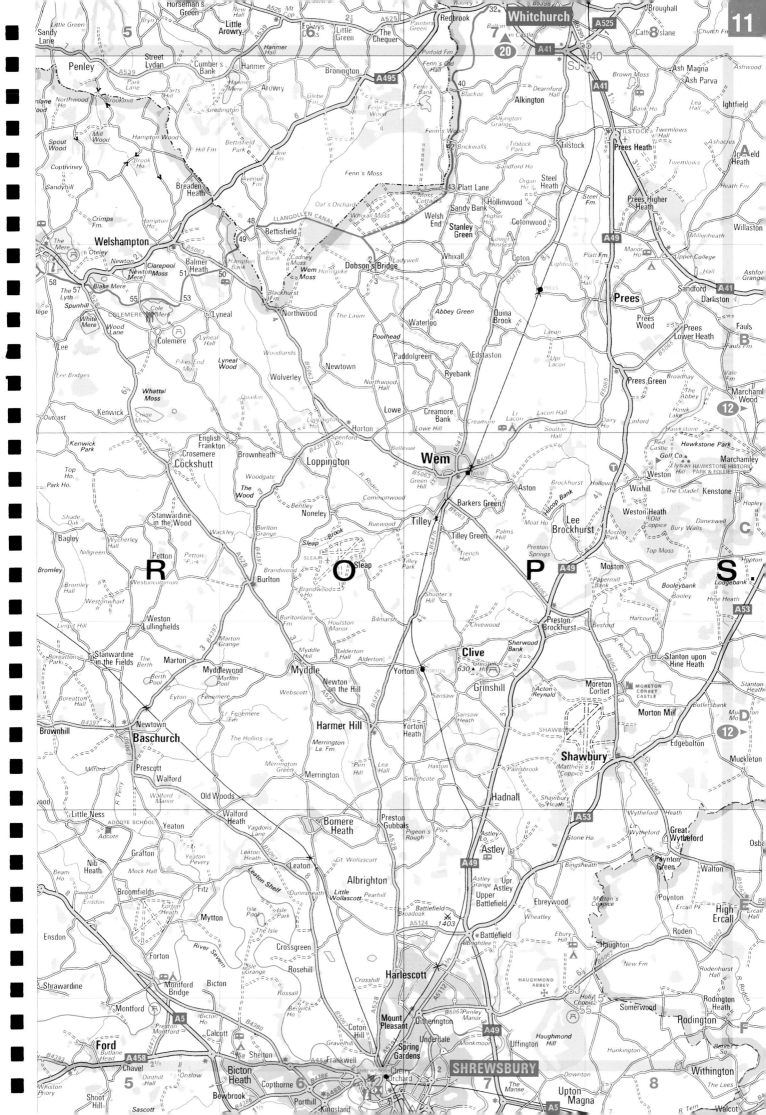

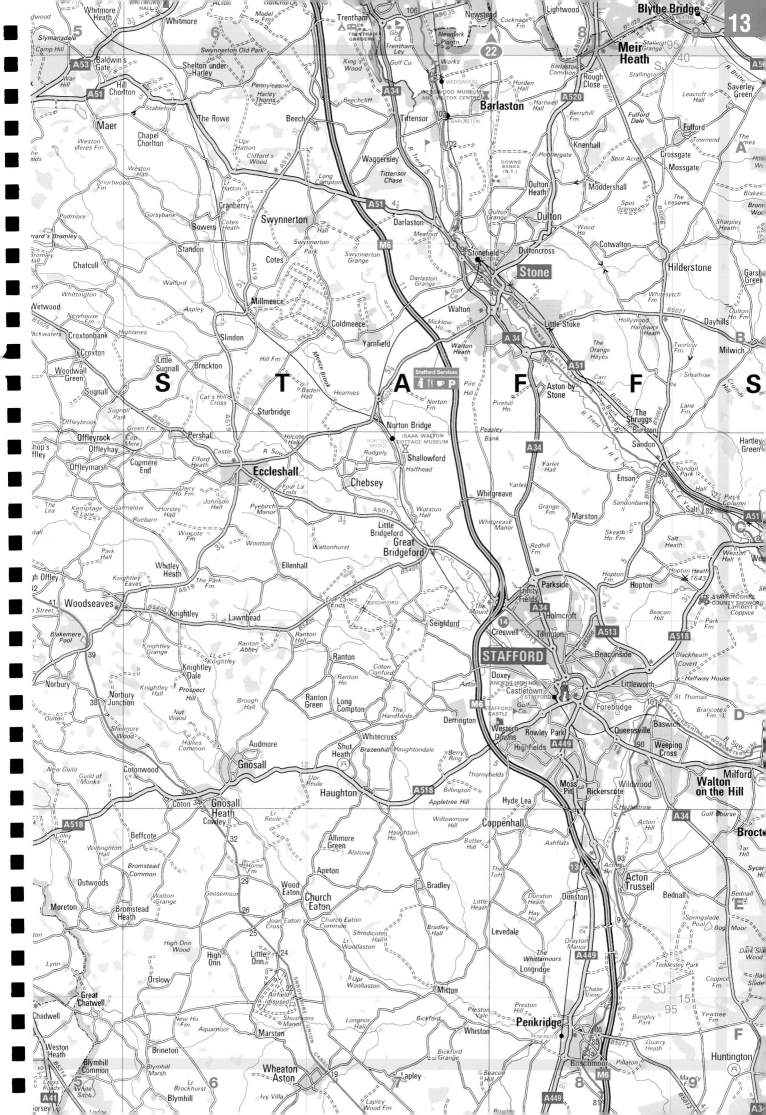

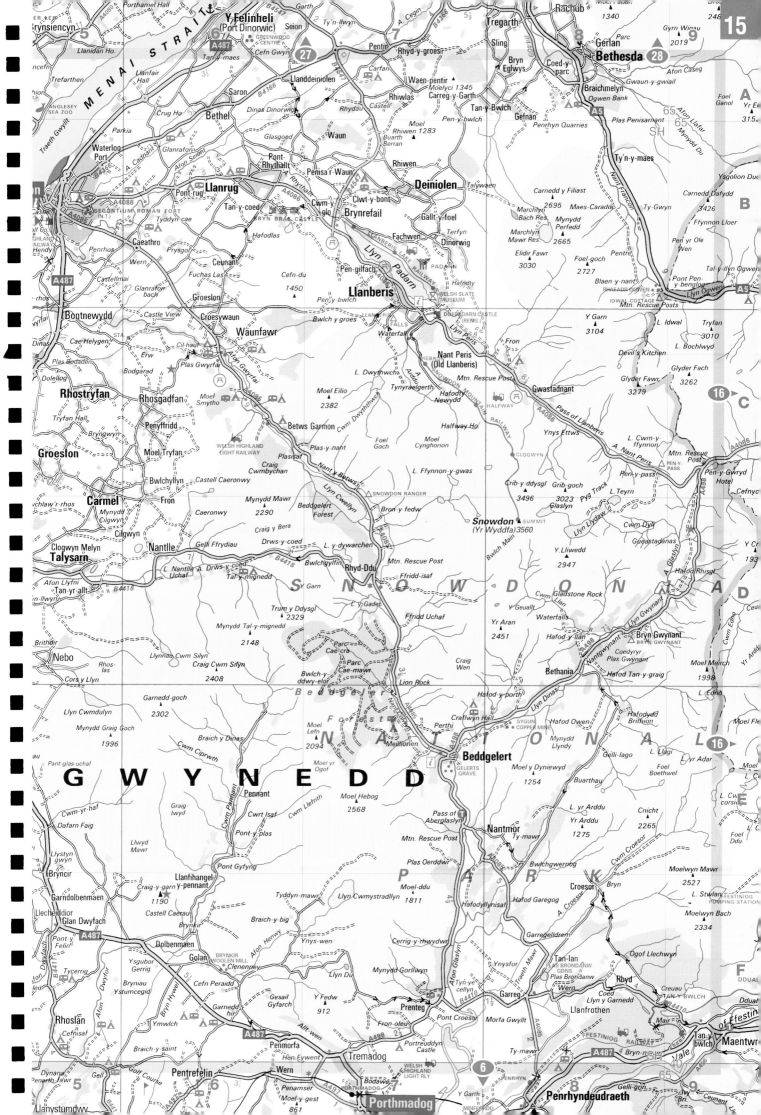

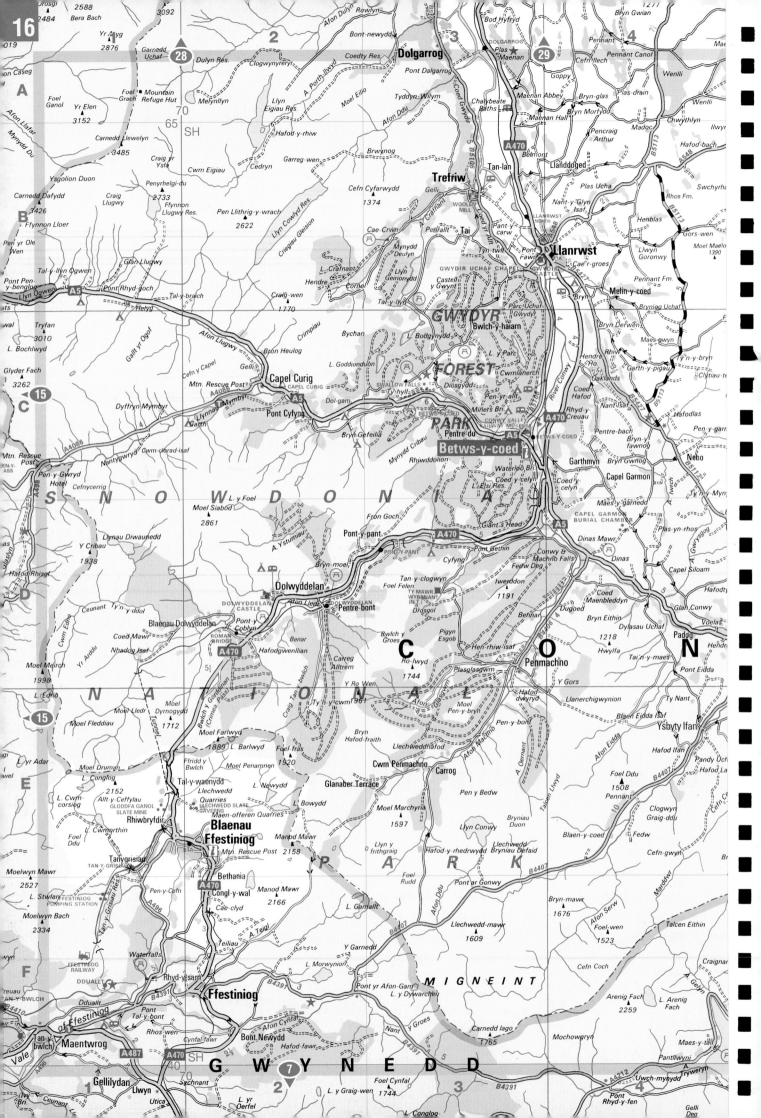

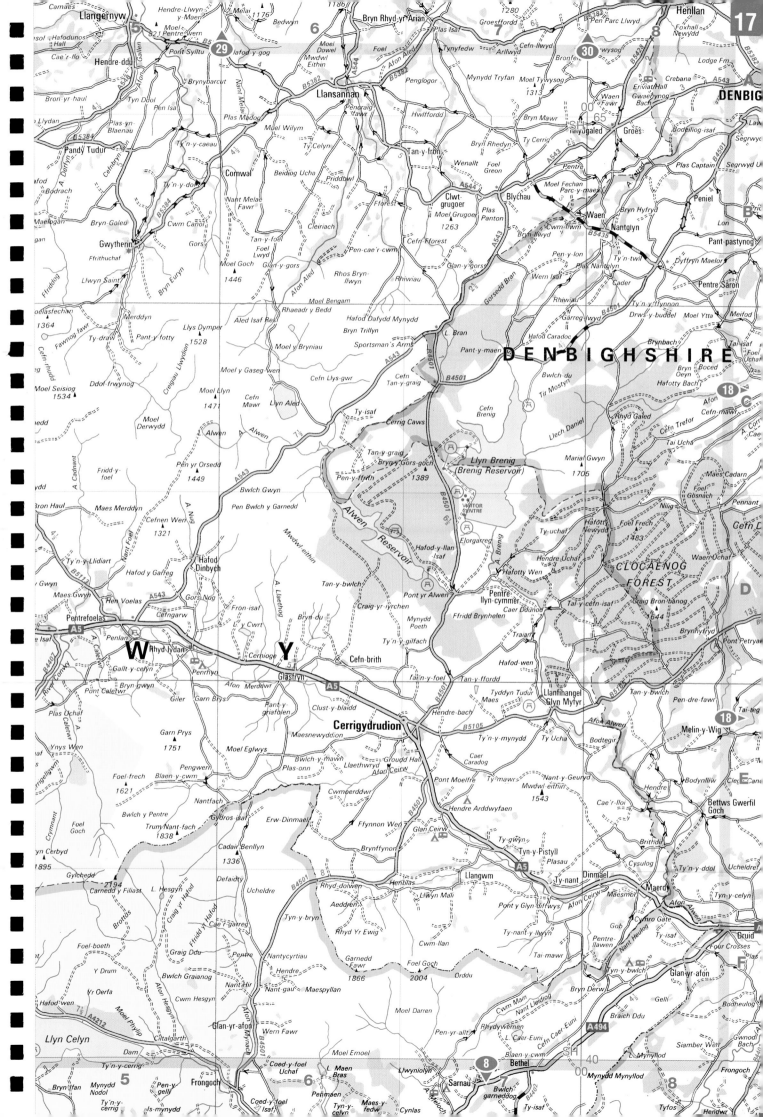

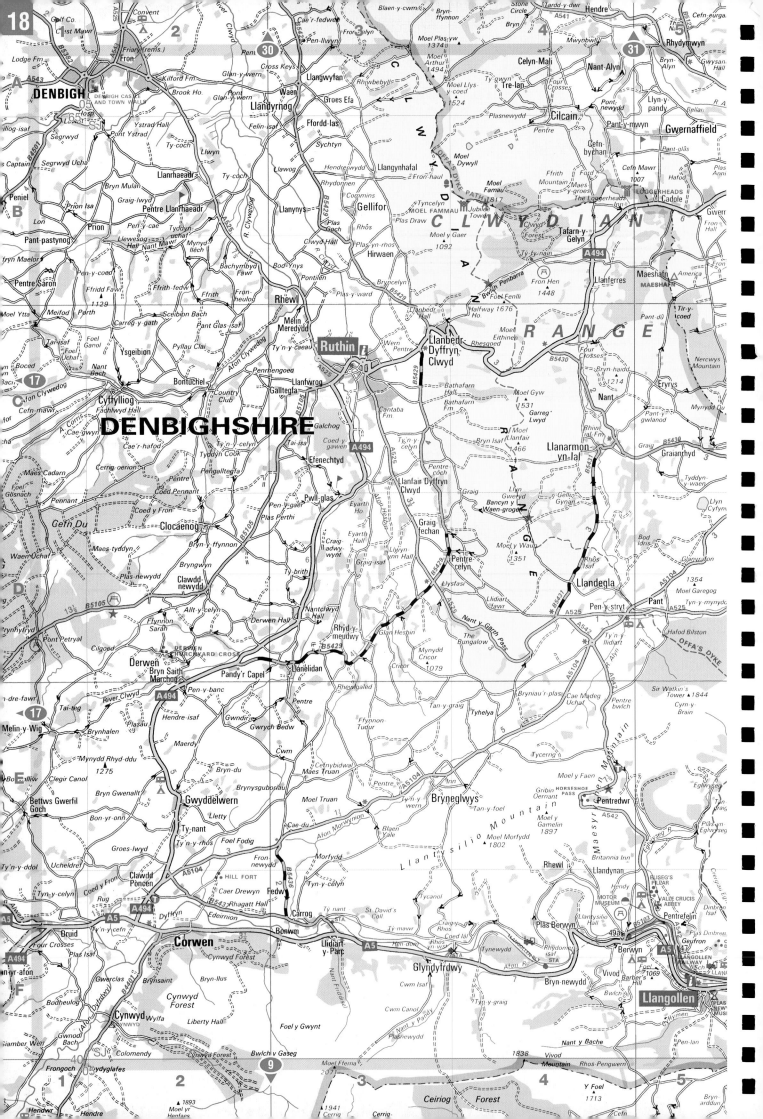

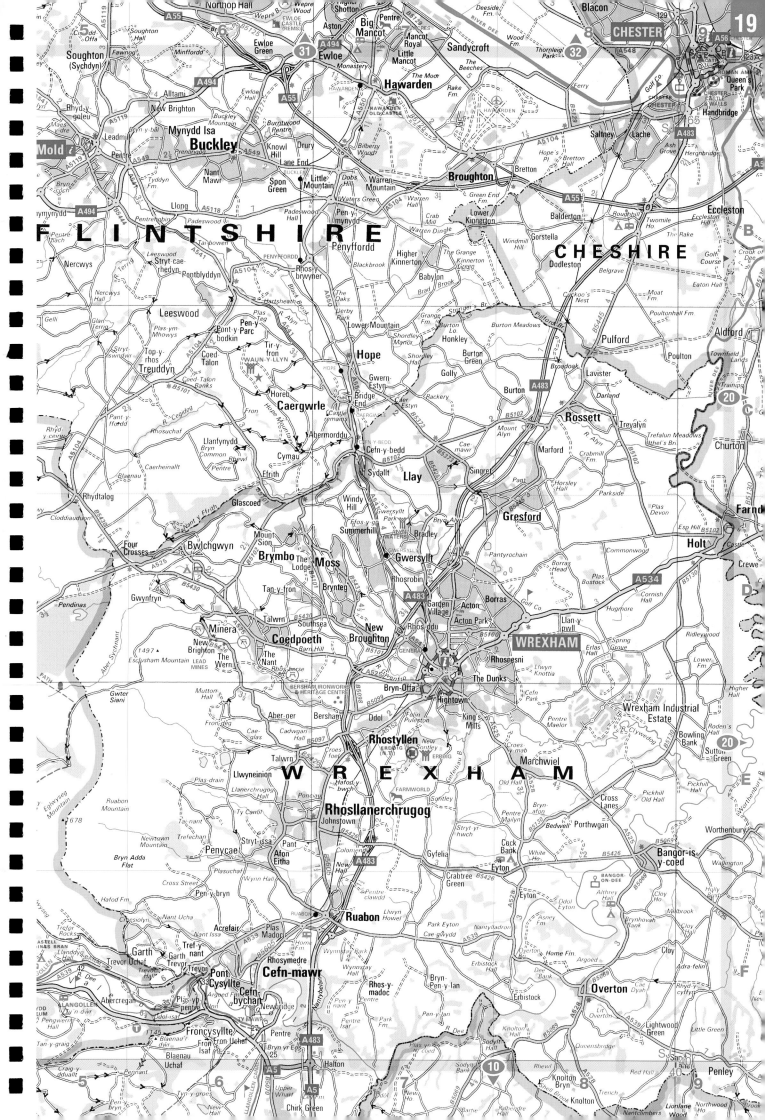

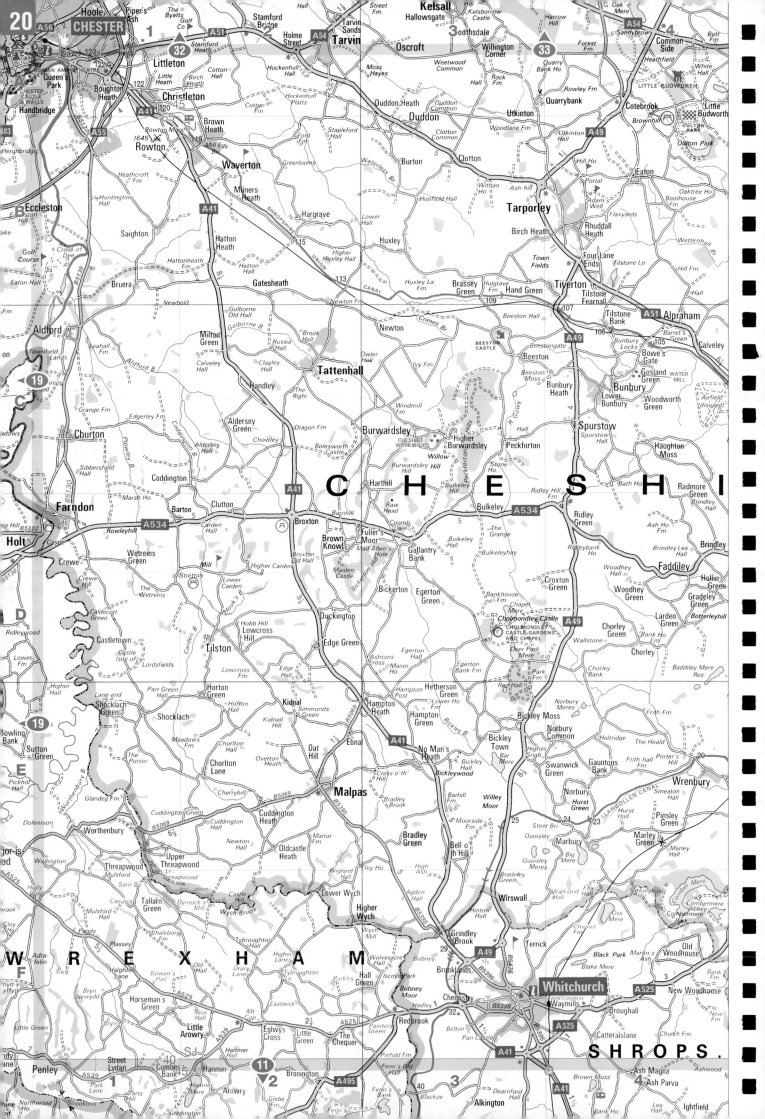

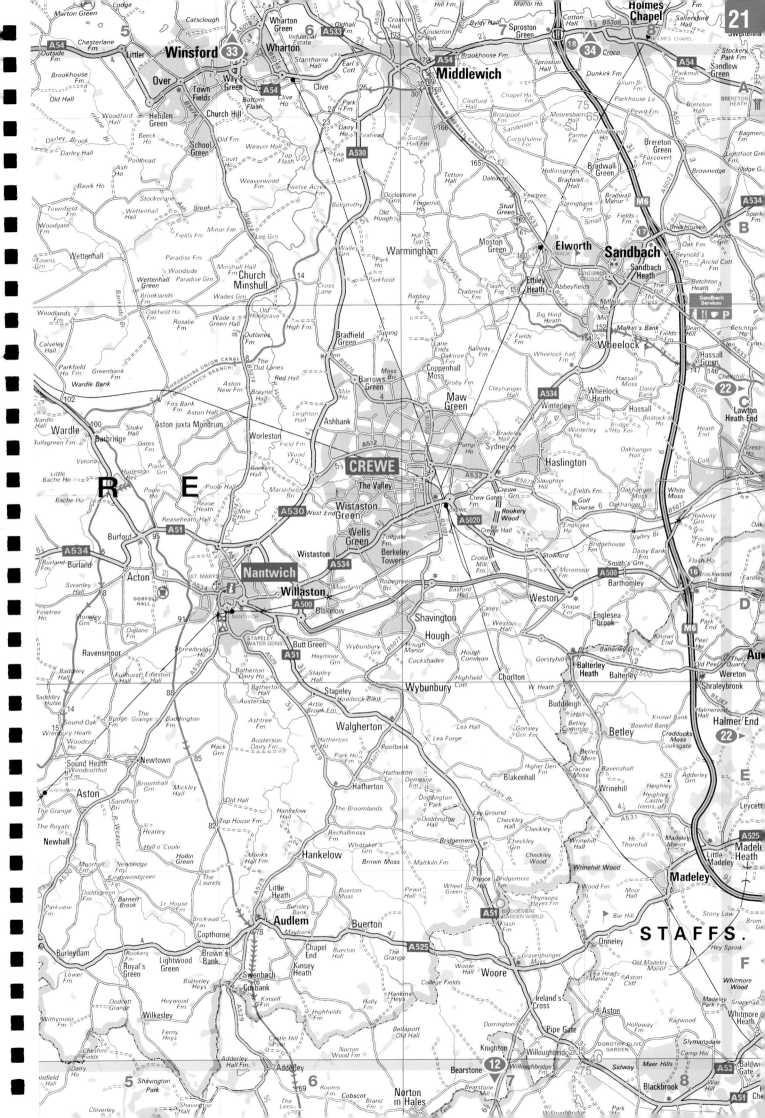

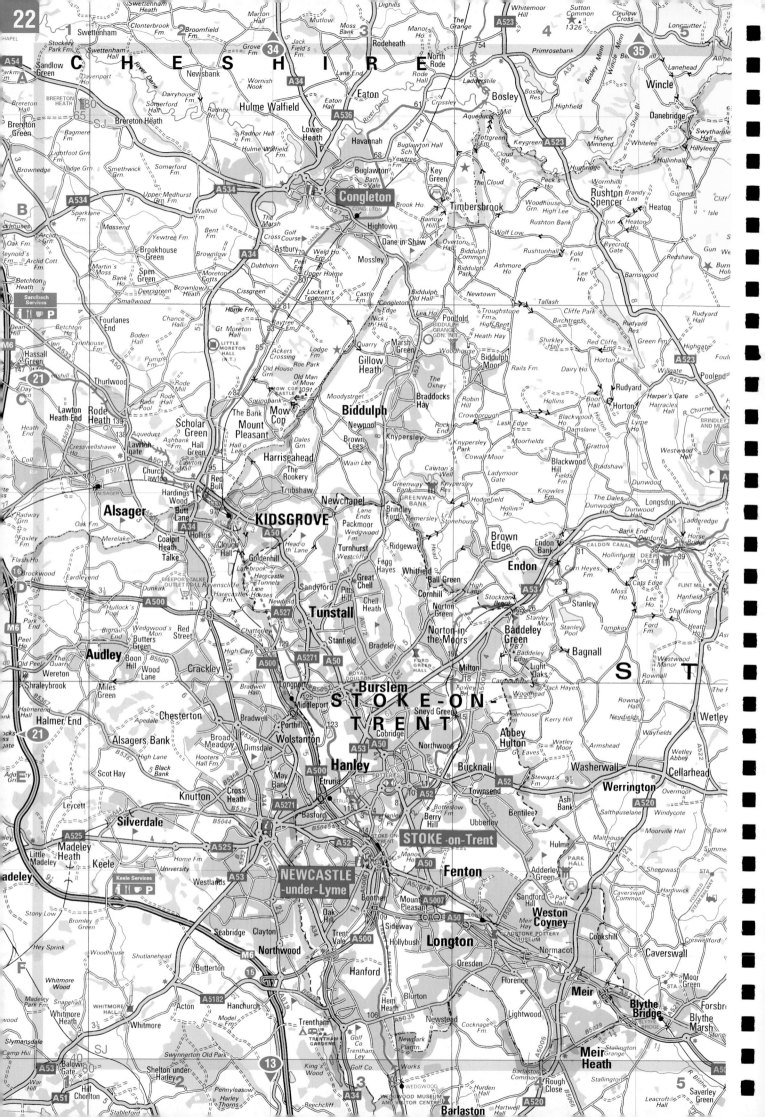

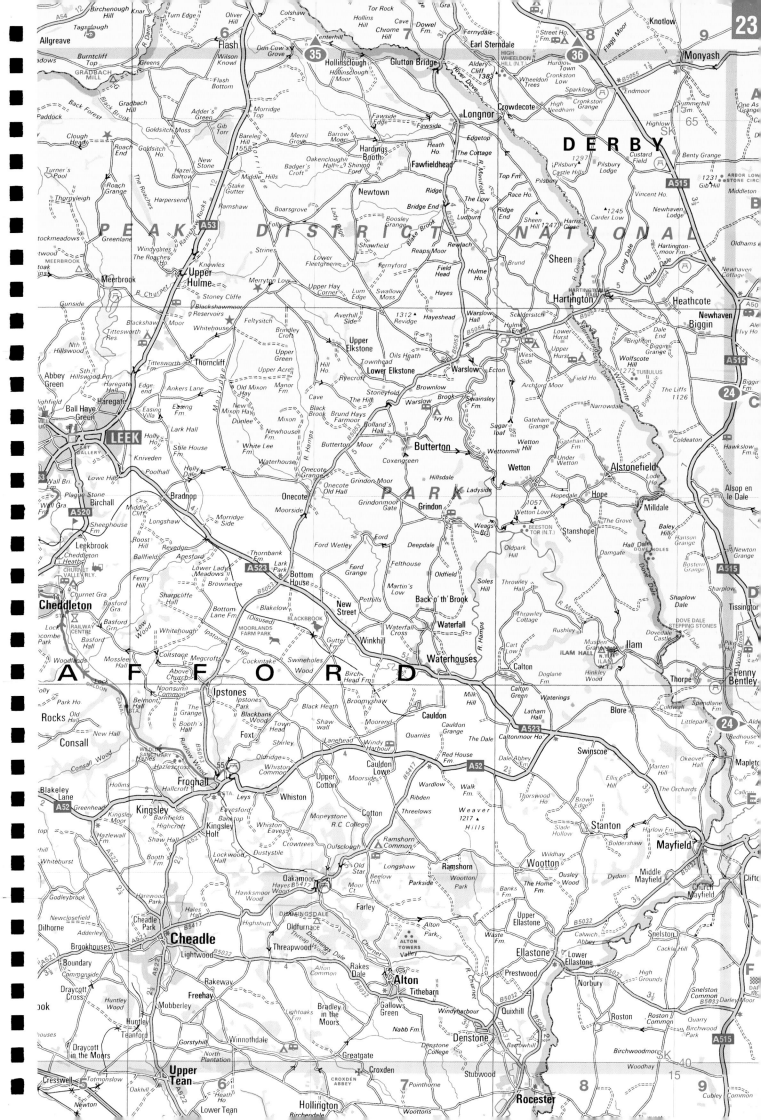

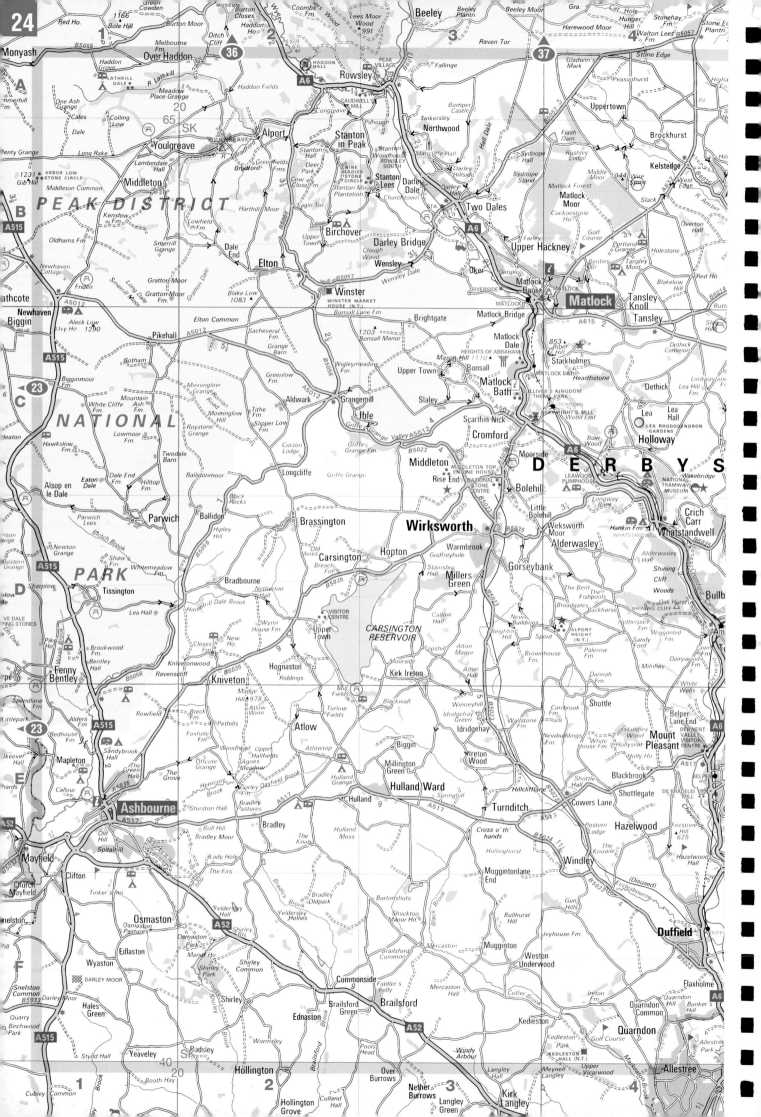

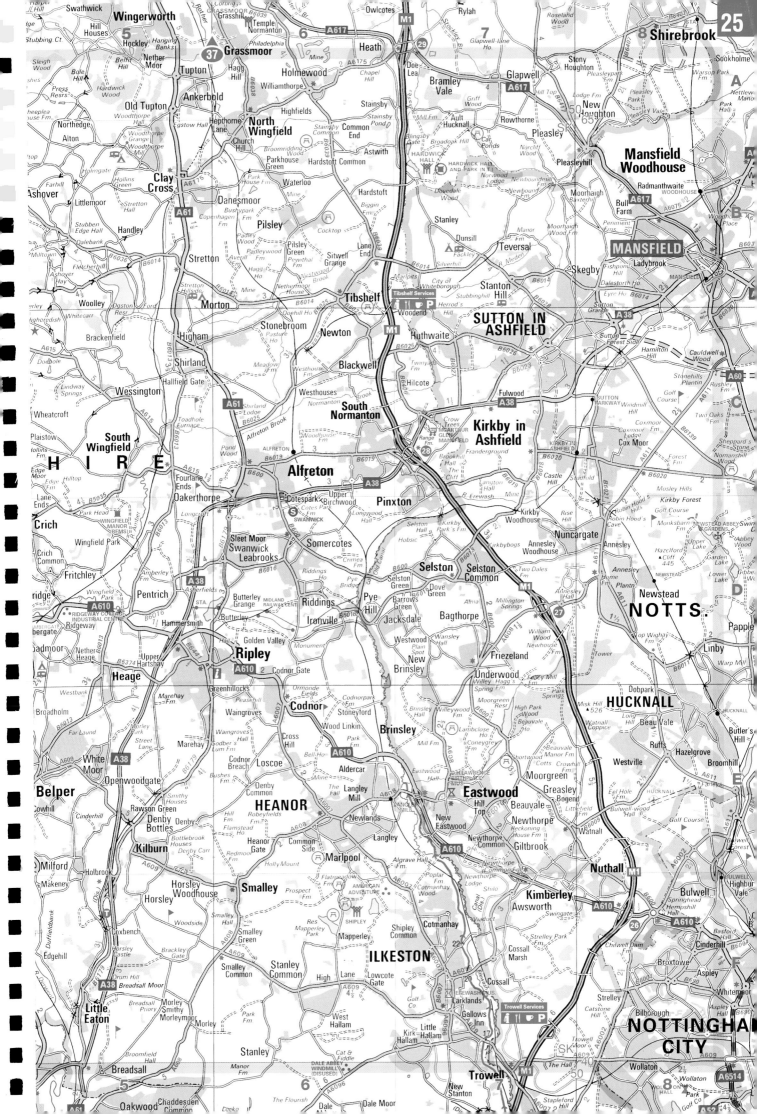

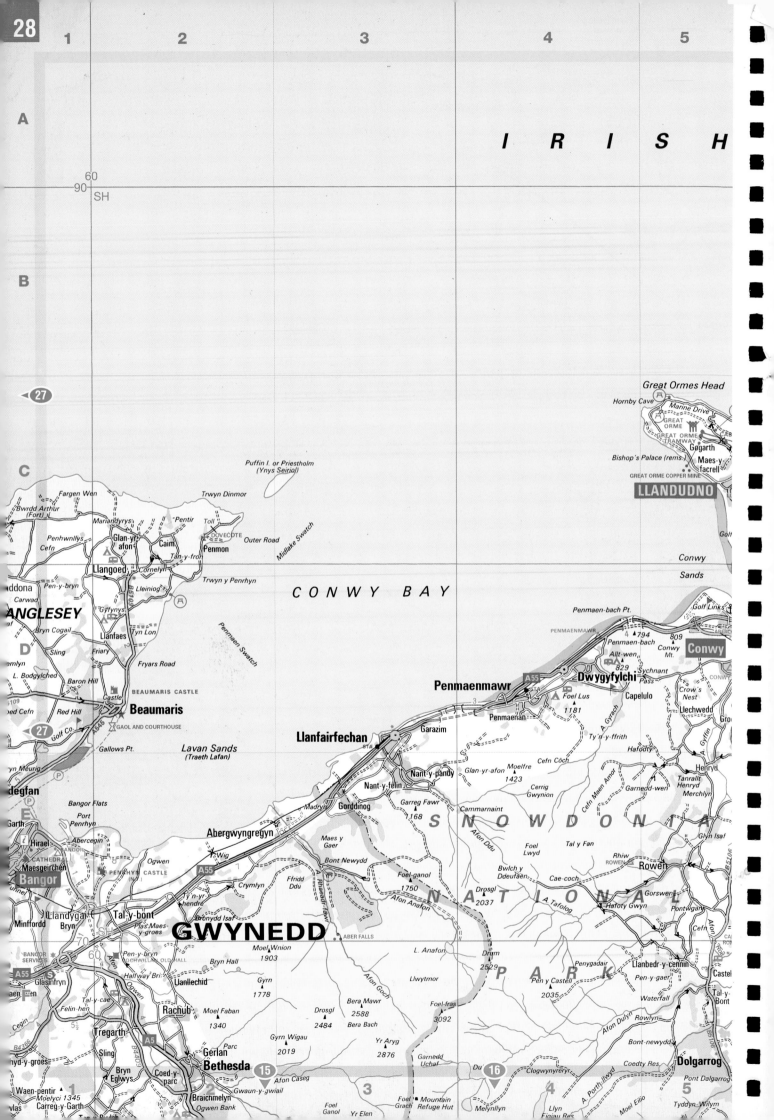

1 2 3 4 5

A

I R I S H

60
90 SH

B

◁ 27

Great Ormes Head

Hornby Cave
Marine Drive
GREAT
ORME
GREAT ORME
TRAMWAY
Gogarth

Puffin I. or Priestholm
(Ynys Seiriol)

Bishop's Palace (rems.)
Maes-y-facrell

GREAT ORME COPPER MINE

C

Fargen Wen
Bwrdd Arthur
(Fort) ⌐
Trwyn Dinmor

LLANDUDNO

Penhwnllys
Cefn
Mariandyrys
Pentir
Toll
Glan-yr-afon
Caim
DOVECOTE
Penmon
Outer Road
Midlake Swatch

Conwy

Llangoed
Tan-y-fron
Cornelyn

Sands

addona
Pen-y-bryn
Lleiniog
Trwyn y Penrhyn

Carwad
R

ANGLESEY
Gyfynys

C O N W Y   B A Y

Penmaen-bach Pt.

Golf Links

af
Bryn Cogail
Tyn Lon
Penmaen Swatch
PENMAENMAWR
4 ▲794
Penmaen-bach
809

Conwy

D

Llanfaes
Friary
▲ 1423
Allt-wen
Conwy
Mt.
CONW

L. Bodgylched
Sling
Fryars Road
A55
829
Sychnant

emlyn
Baron Hill
Penmaenan
Dwygyfylchi
Pass

ed Cefn
Castle
BEAUMARIS CASTLE
Penmaenmawr
Foel Lus
1181
Capelulo
Crow's
Nest

9 Cefn
Red Hill
Llechwedd

27
Golf Co.
A545
Beaumaris
Penmaenan
Gro

yn Meurig
P
GAOL AND COURTHOUSE
Llanfairfechan
Garazim
Ty'n-y-ffrith
Hafodty

Gallows Pt.
Lavan Sands
(Traeth Lafan)
Garreg Fawr
A. Gyrach
A. Gyffin

degfan
P
Nant-y-pandy
Glan-yr-afon
Moelfre
Henryd

Bangor Flats
Nant-y-felin
1423
Cerrig
Garnedd-wen
Tanralt
Henryd

E

Garth
Port
Penrhyn
Madryn
Gwynion
Merchlyn

i
Hirael
Abercegin
Gorddinog
Garreg Fawr
Cammarnaint
S N O W D O N

Maes y
1168
Cefn Maen Amor
Glyn Isaf

Abergwyngregyn
Gaer
Aber Ddu

Bangor
Ogwen
A55
Wig
Bont Newydd
Foel
Lwyd
Tal y Fan
Rhiw
Rowen
ROWEN

Maesgeirchen
PENRHYN CASTLE
Crymlyn
Foel-ganol
1750
Bwlch y
Ddeufaen
Cae-coch

Llandyga
Tal-y-bont
Ty'n-y-hendre
Ffridd
Ddu
A. Rhaeadr-fawr
Drosgl
2037
A. Tafolog
Gorswen
Pontwgan

Bryn
GWYNEDD
Bronydd Isaf
Plas Maes-y-groes
N A T I O N A L

Minffordd
Pen-y-bryn
ABER FALLS
Afon Anafon
Hafoty Gwyn
Cefn

F

BANGOR
SERVICES
60
70 SH
Moel Wnion
1903
L. Anafon
Drum
2529
Penygadair
Llanbedr-y-cennin
Castell

A55
S
OCHWILLAN OLD HALL
Bryn Hall
Pen y Castell
2035
Pen-y-gaer

en
Glasinfryn
Halfway Bri.
Gyrn
1778
Llwytmor
Waterfall
Tal-y-Bont

vlas
Tal-y-cae
Llanllechid
Afon Goch
Foel-fras
3092

Cegin
Felin-hen
Rachub
Moel Faban
1340
Bera Mawr
2588
Foel-fras
Rowlyn
Afon Dulyn

5½
Drosgl
2484
Bera Bach
Garnedd
Uchaf
Bont-newydd

Tregarth
Gyrn Wigau
2019
Yr Aryg
2876
Coedty Res.

Sling
Parc
Dolgarrog

nyd-y-groes
Bryn
Eglwys
Coed-y-parc
Bethesda
15
Afon Caseg
16
Clogwynyreryri
Pont Dalgarrog

Waen-pentir
Braichmelyn
Gwaun-y-gwiail
Foel
Grach
Mountain
Refuge Hut
Du
A. Porth-llwyd
Moel Eilio

Carreg-y-Garth
Ogwen Bank
Foel
Ganol
Yr Elen
Melynllyn
Llyn
Eigiau Res.
Tyddyn-Wilym

1 2 3 4 5

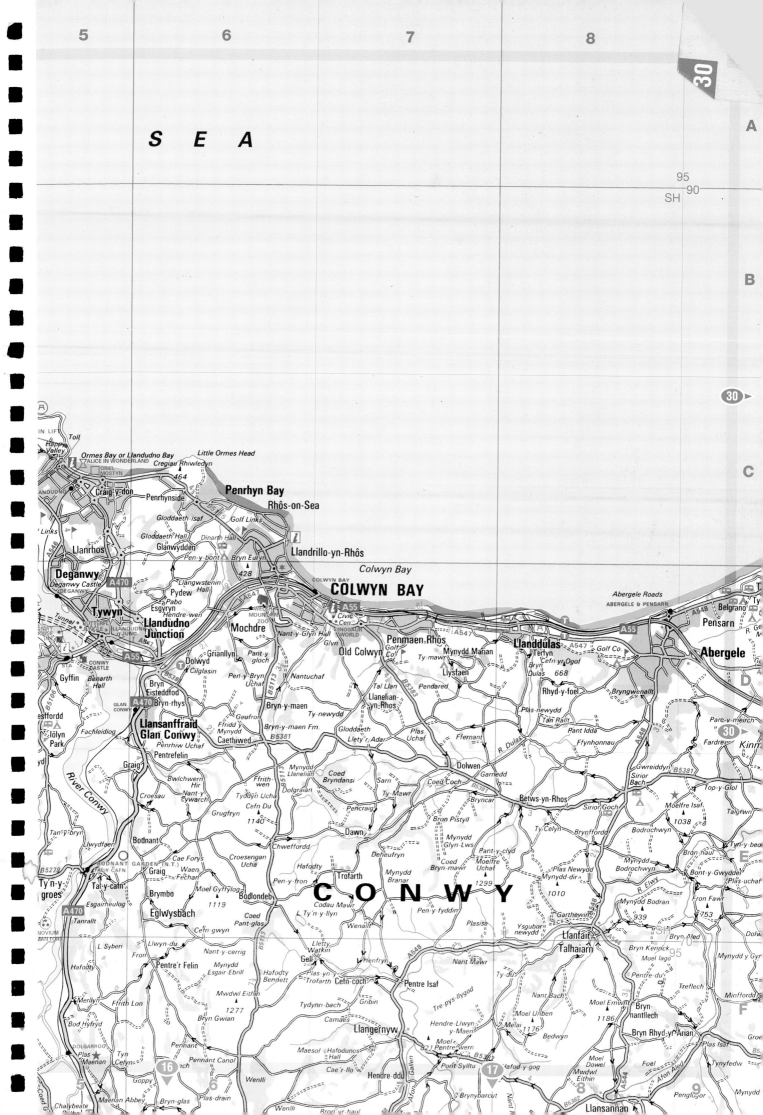

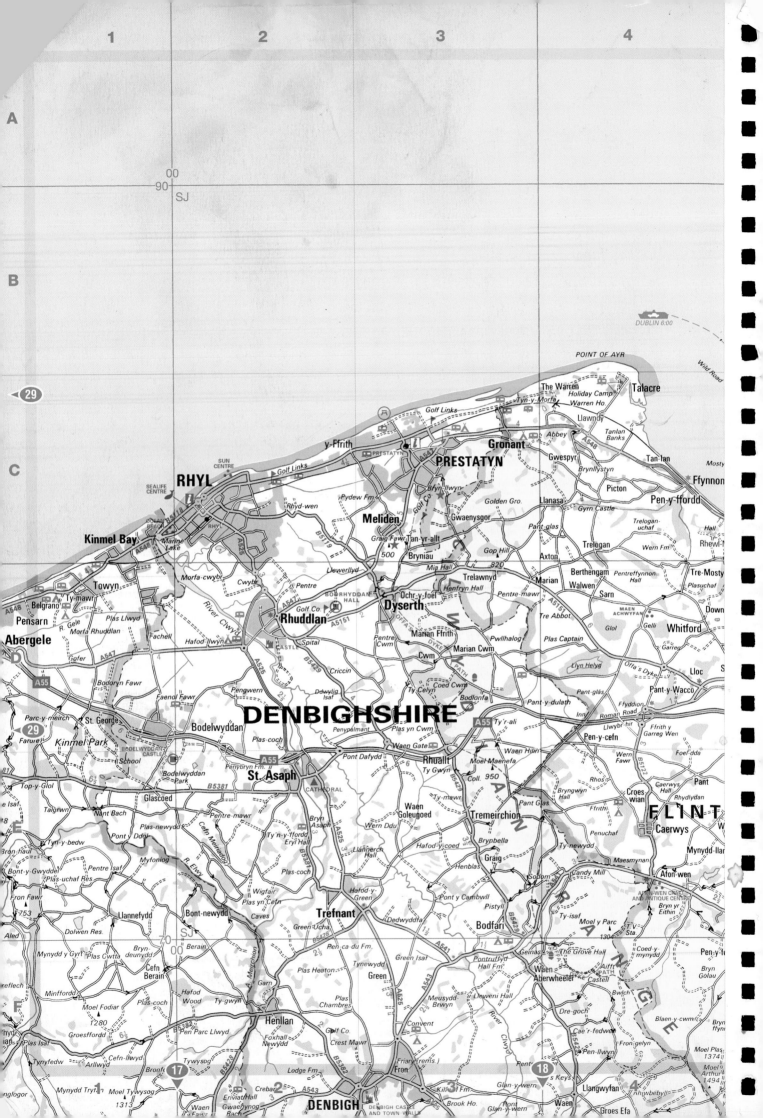

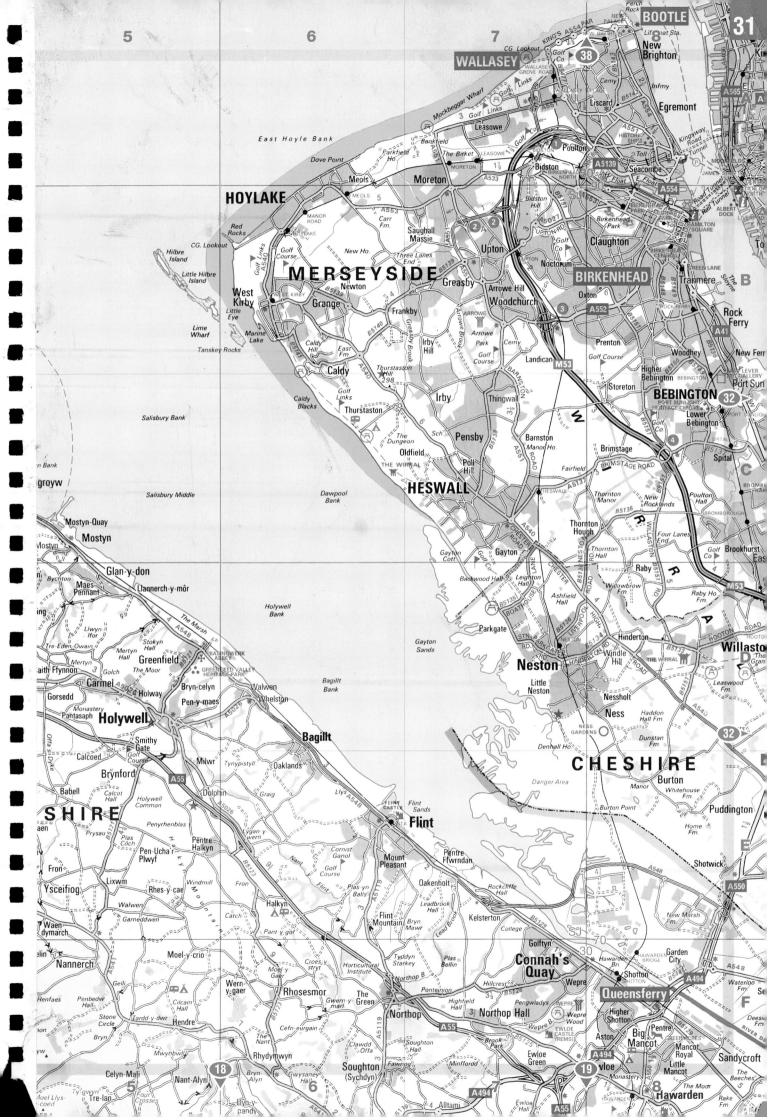

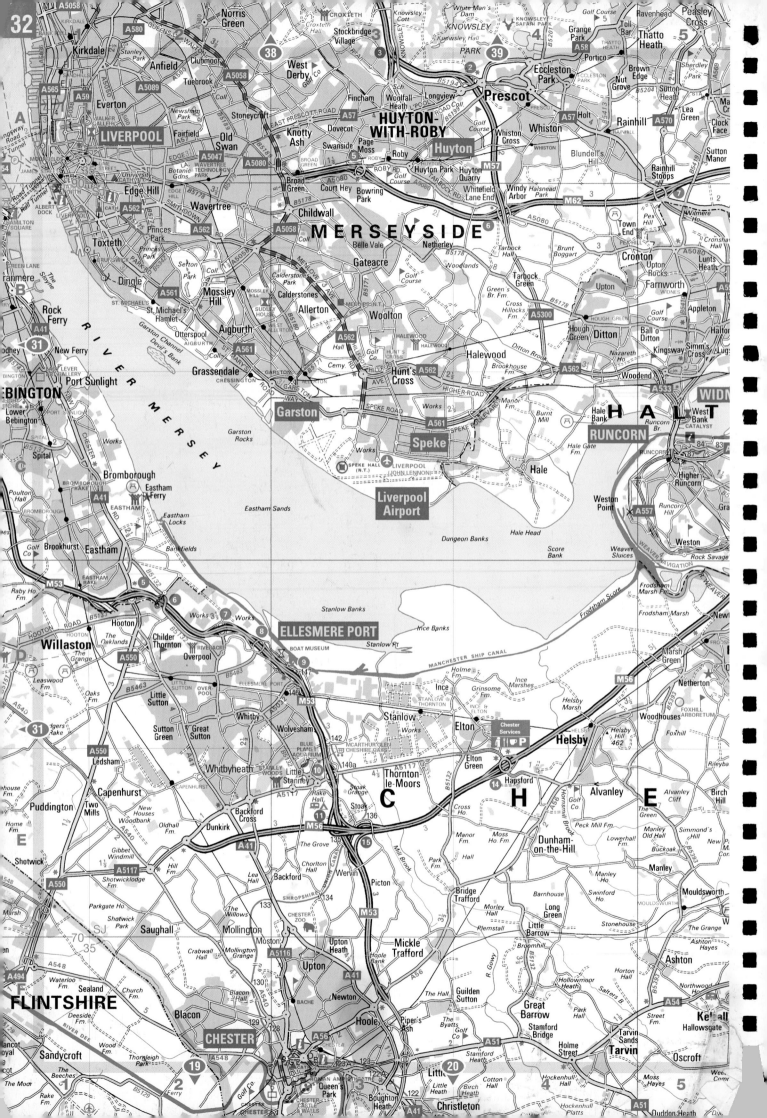

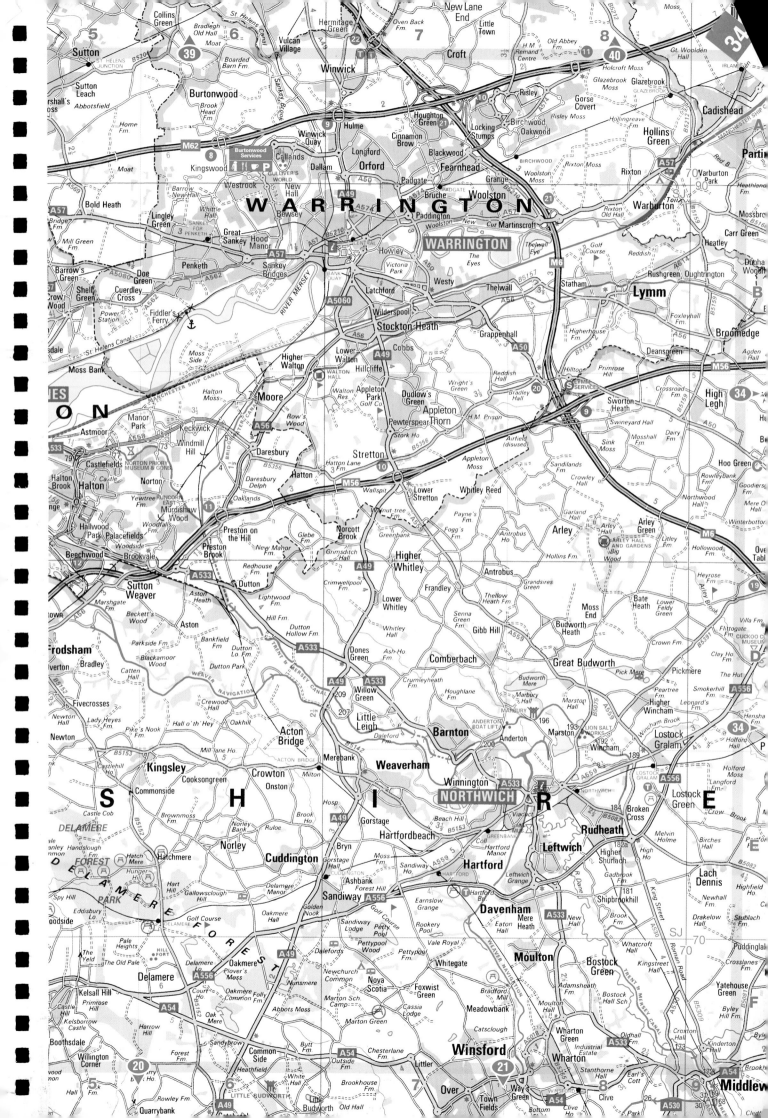

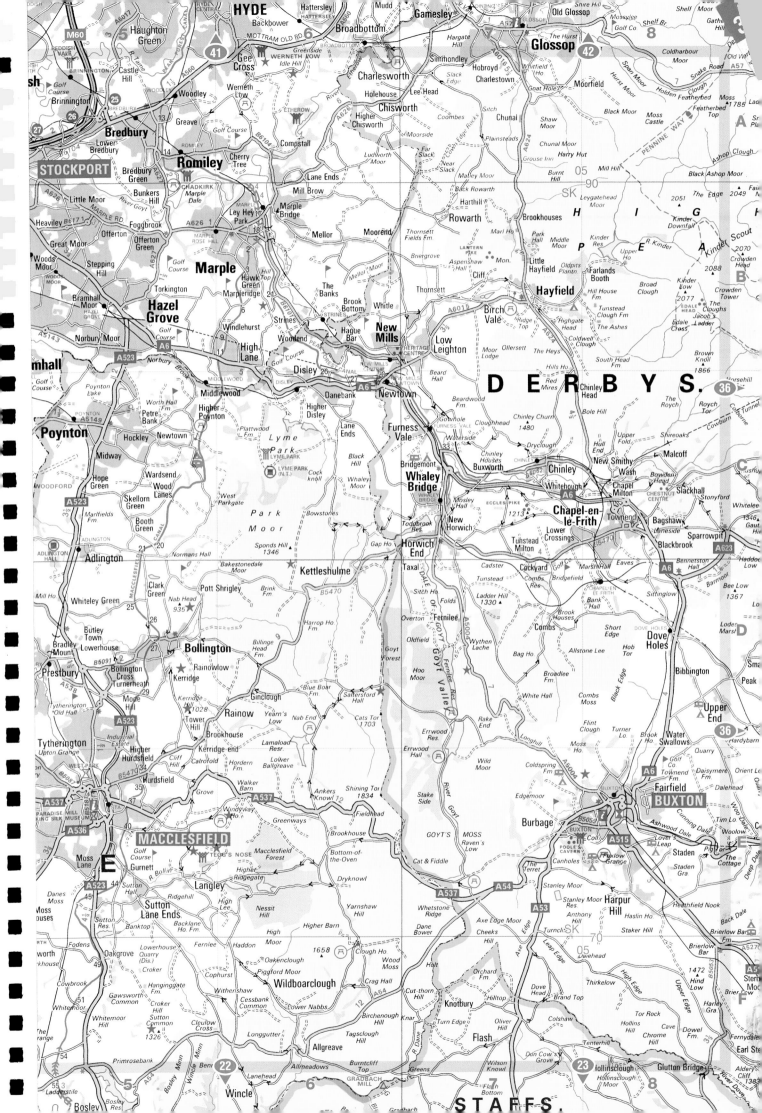

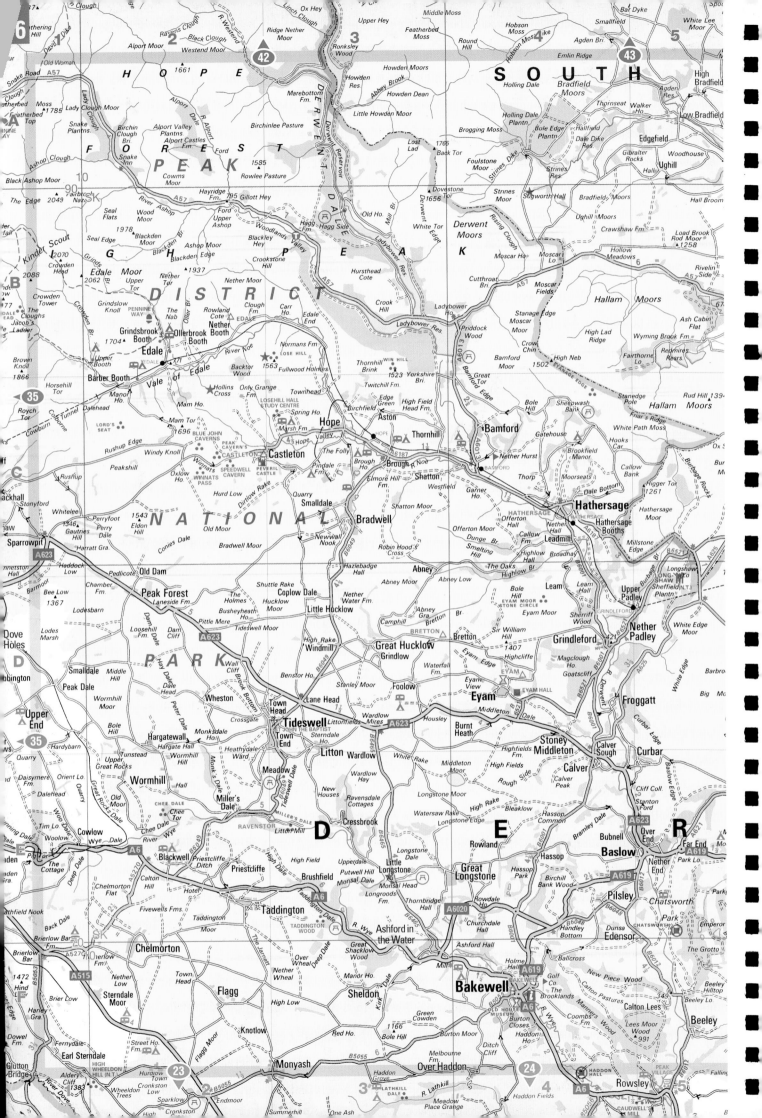

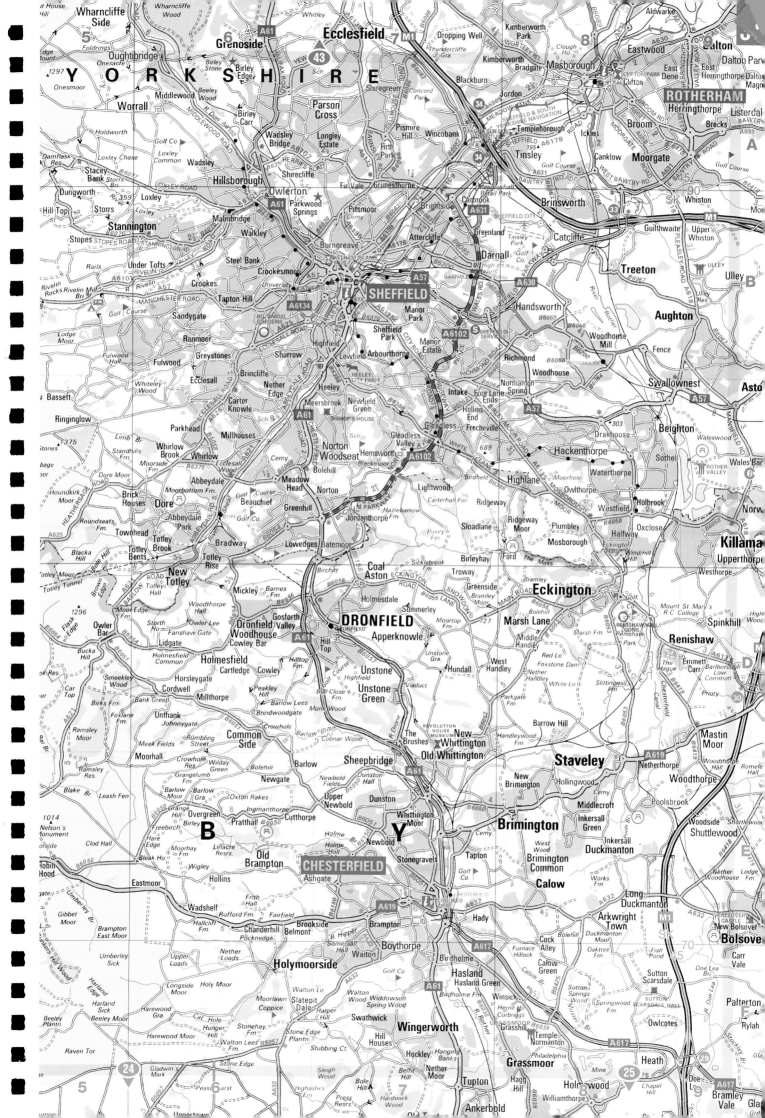

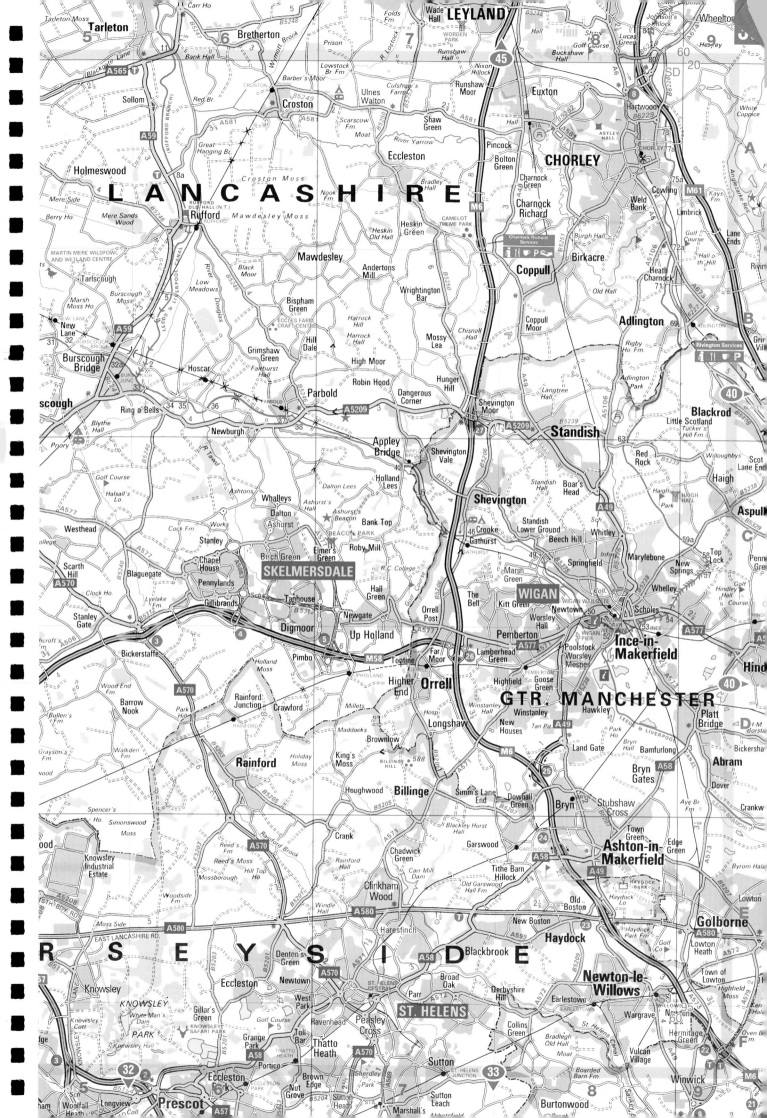

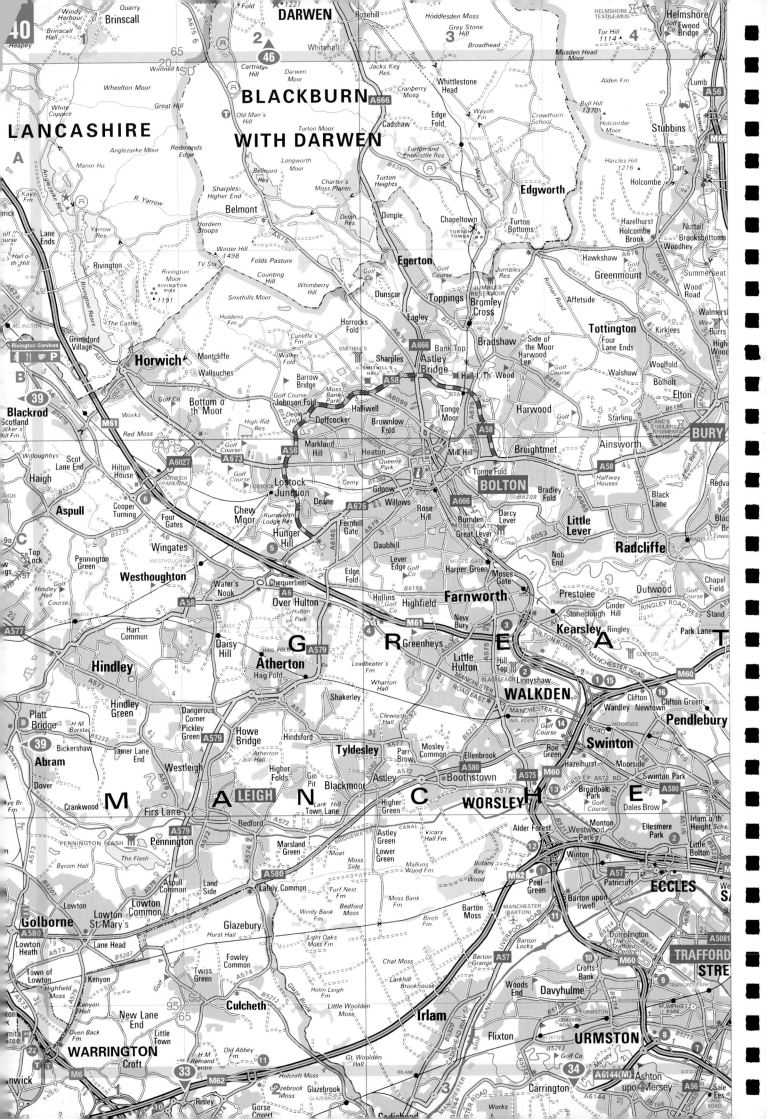

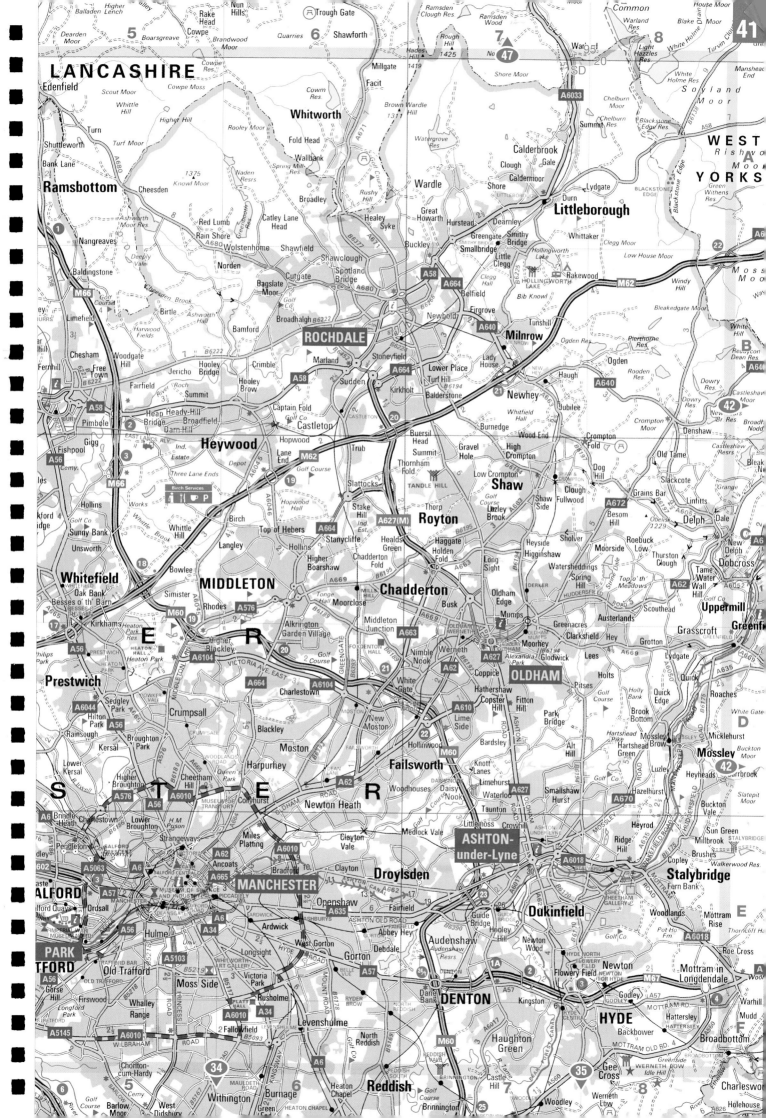

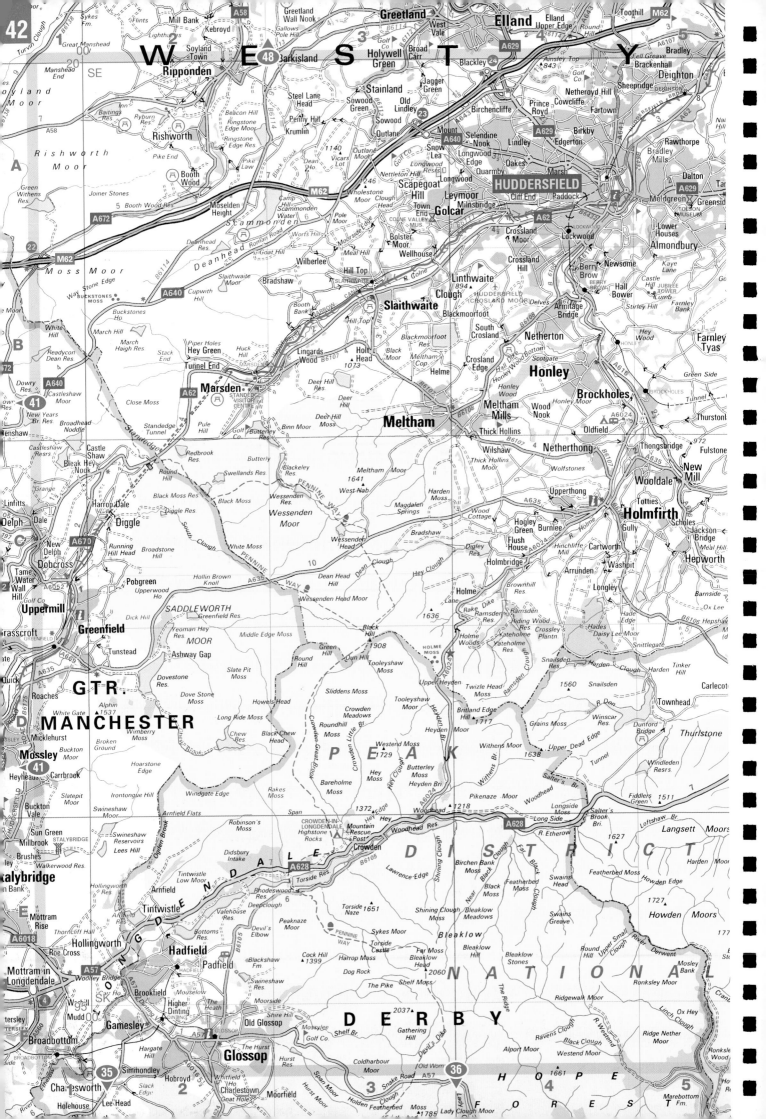

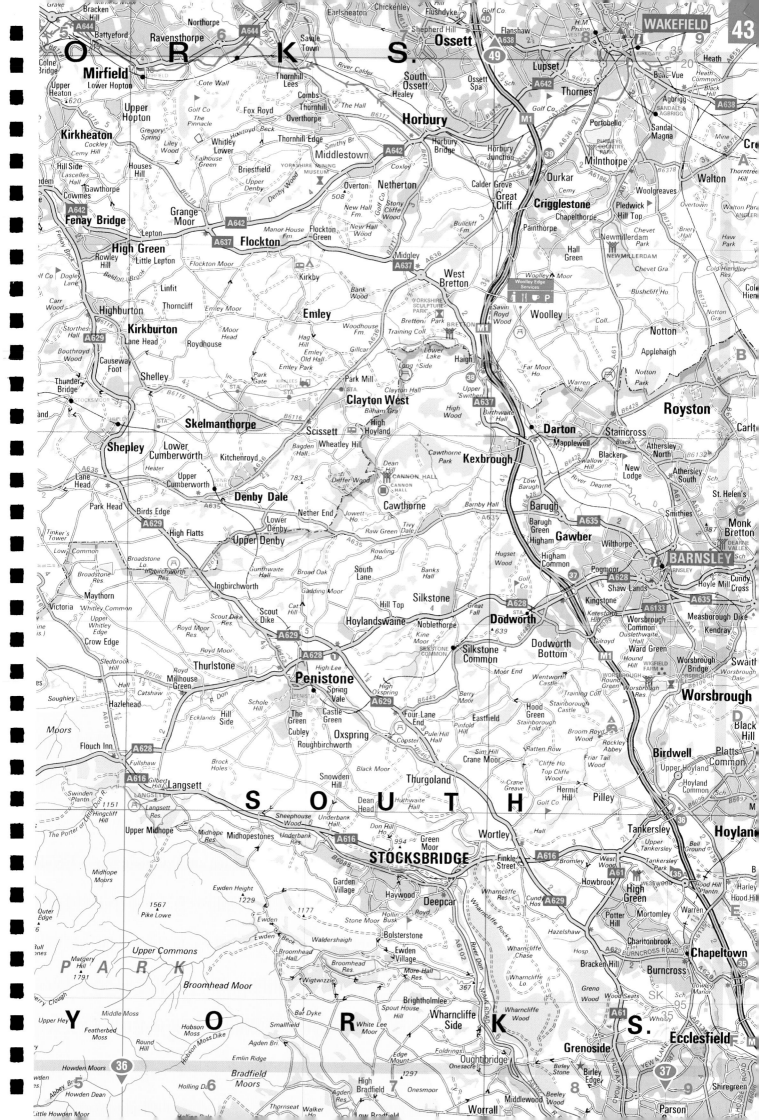

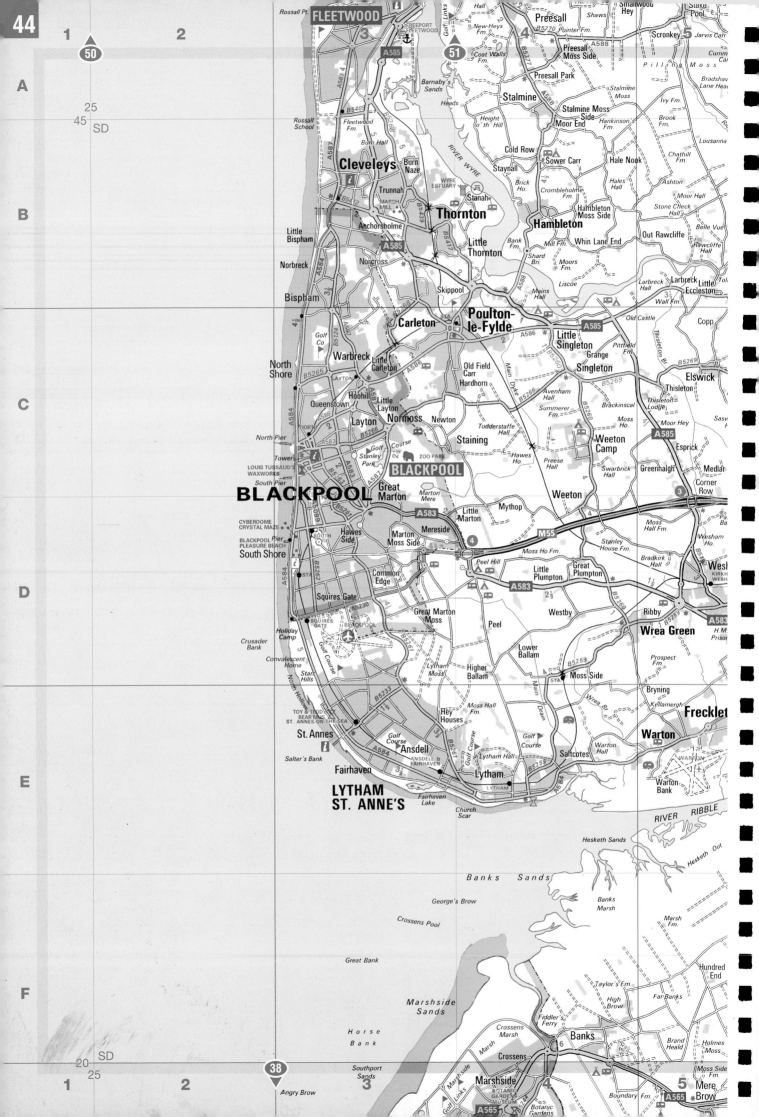

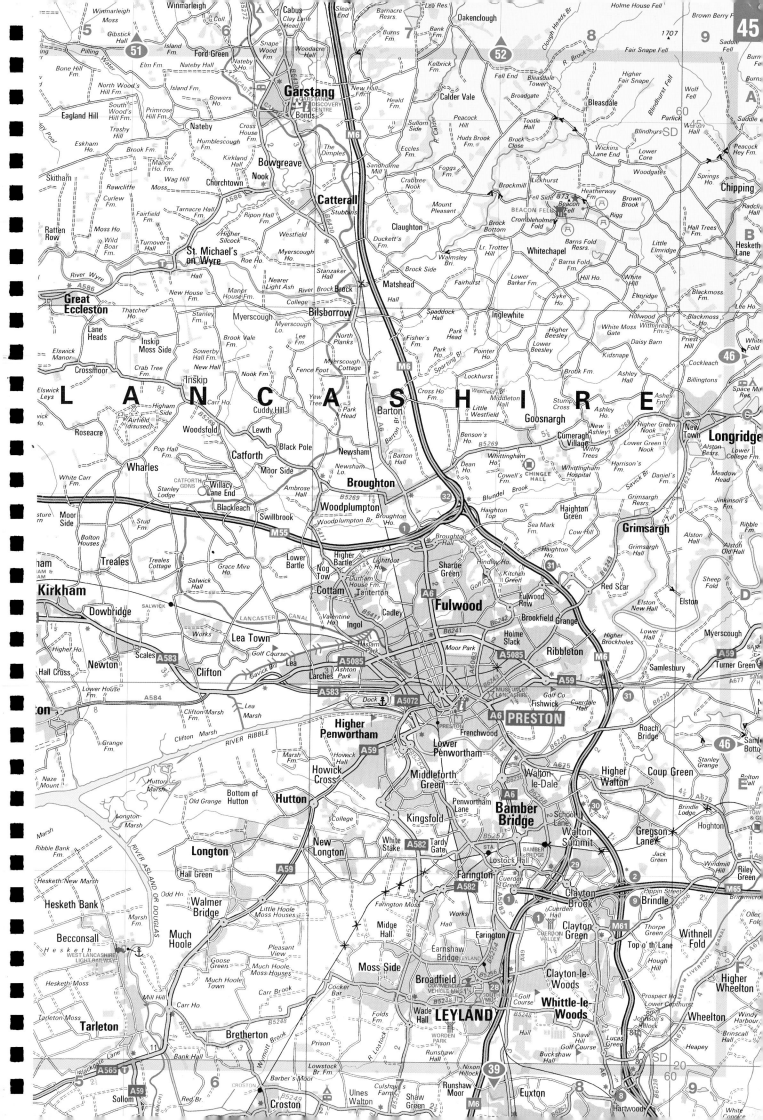

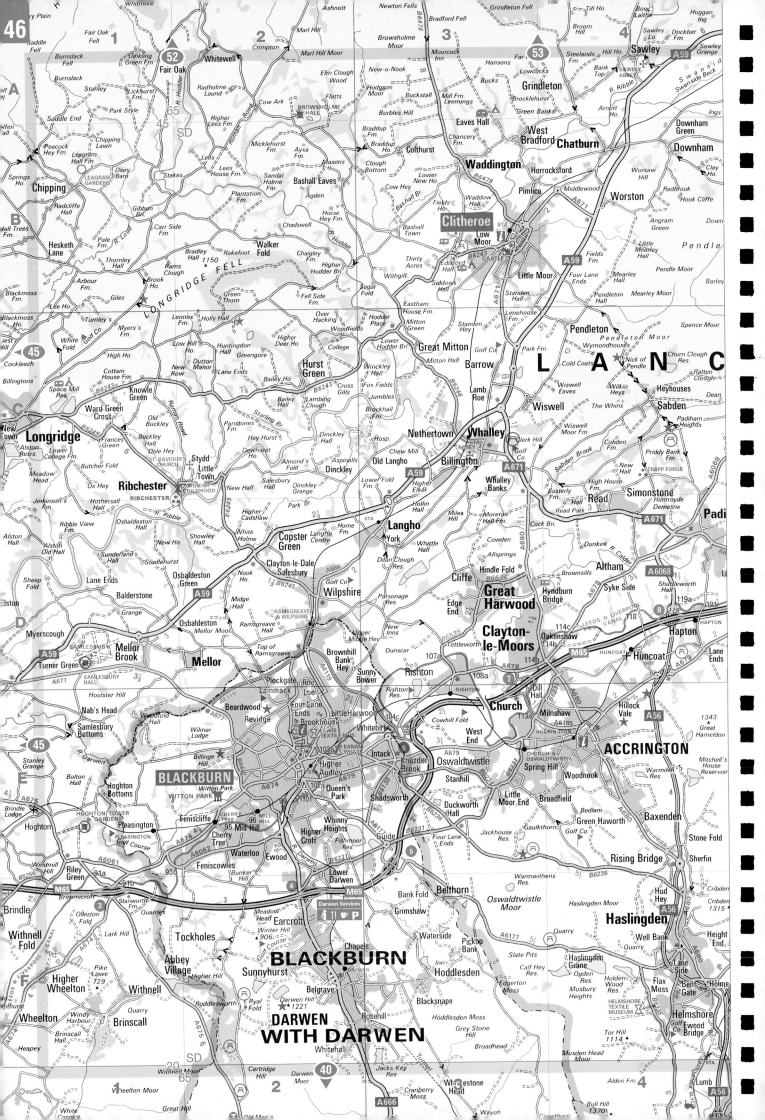

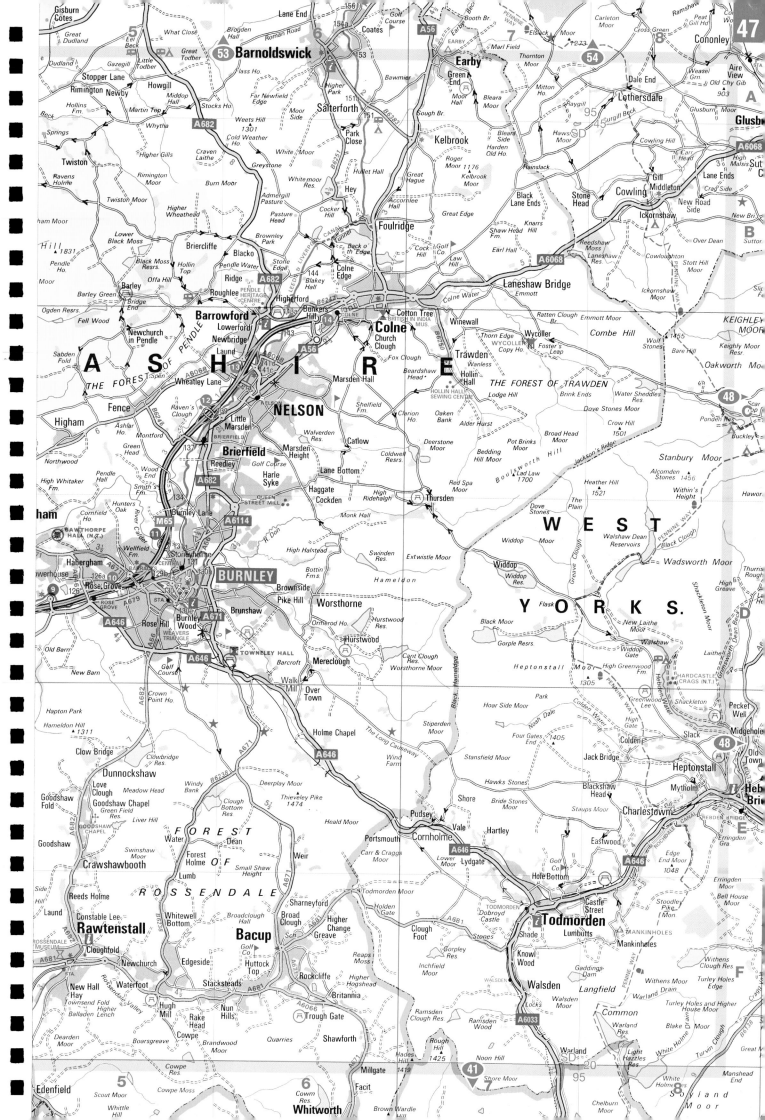

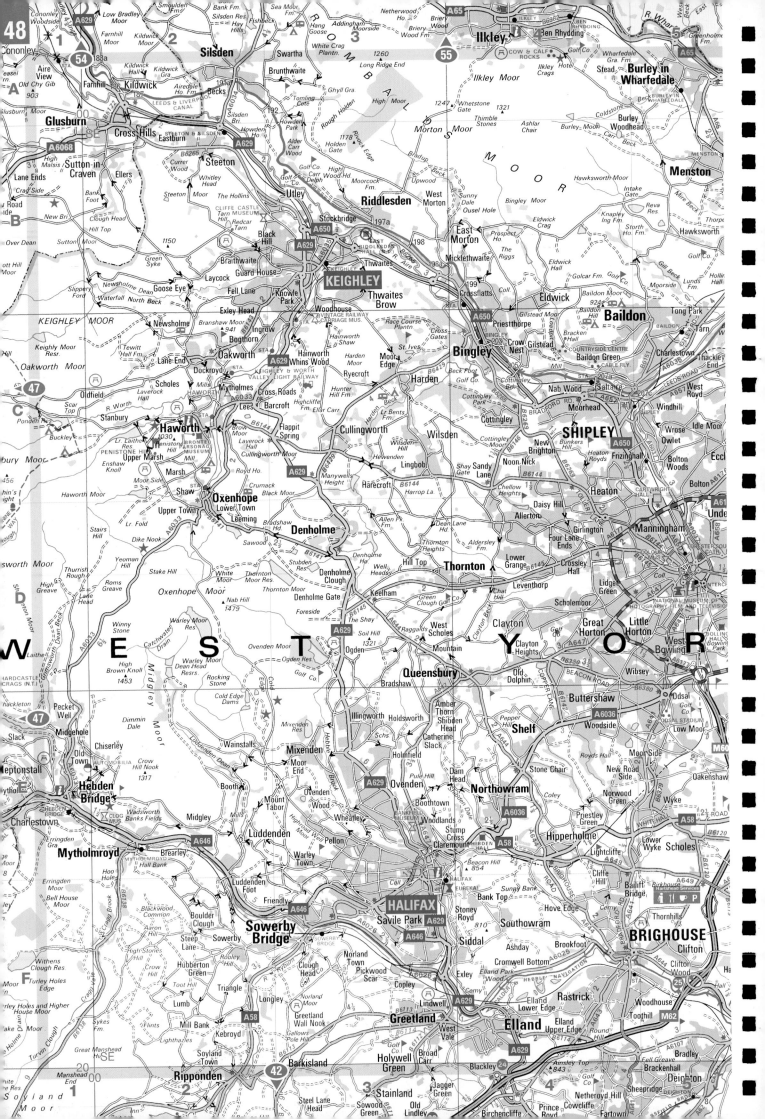

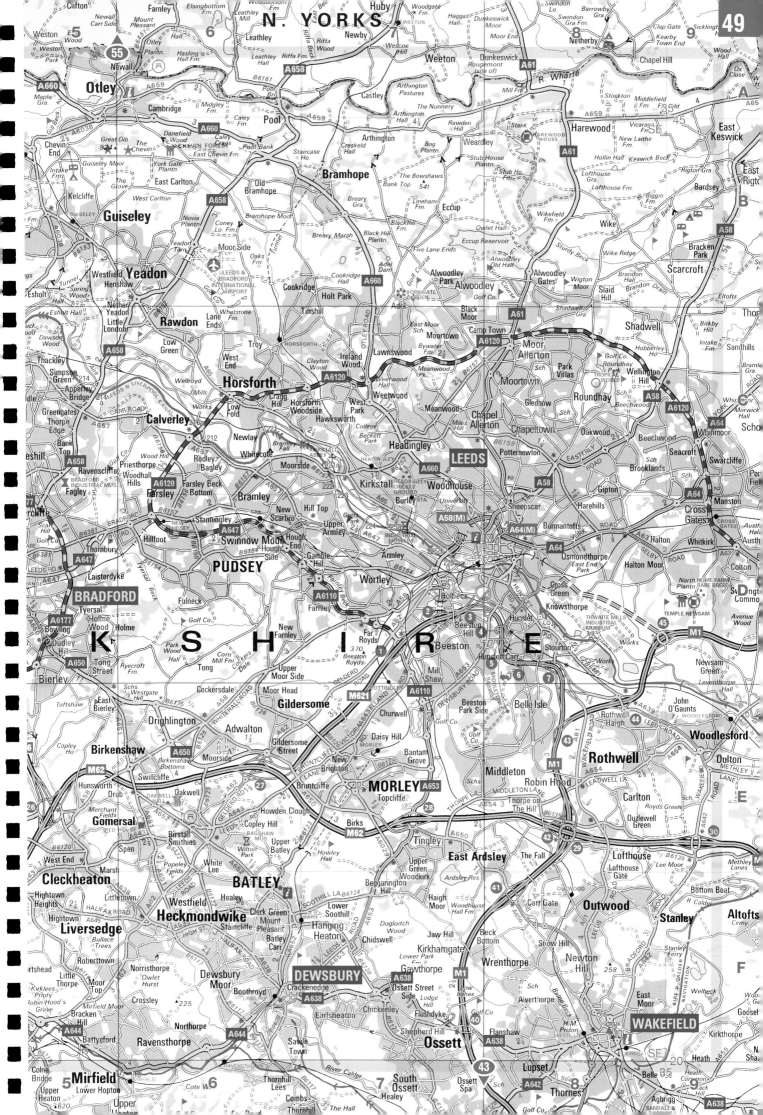

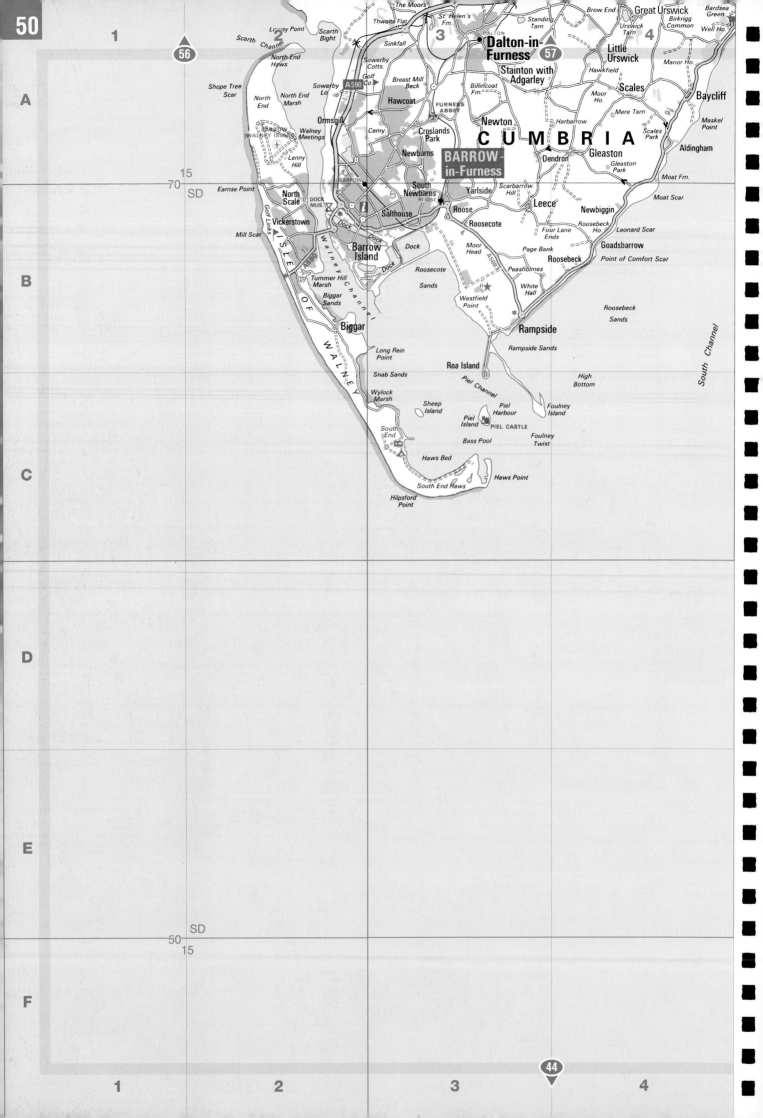

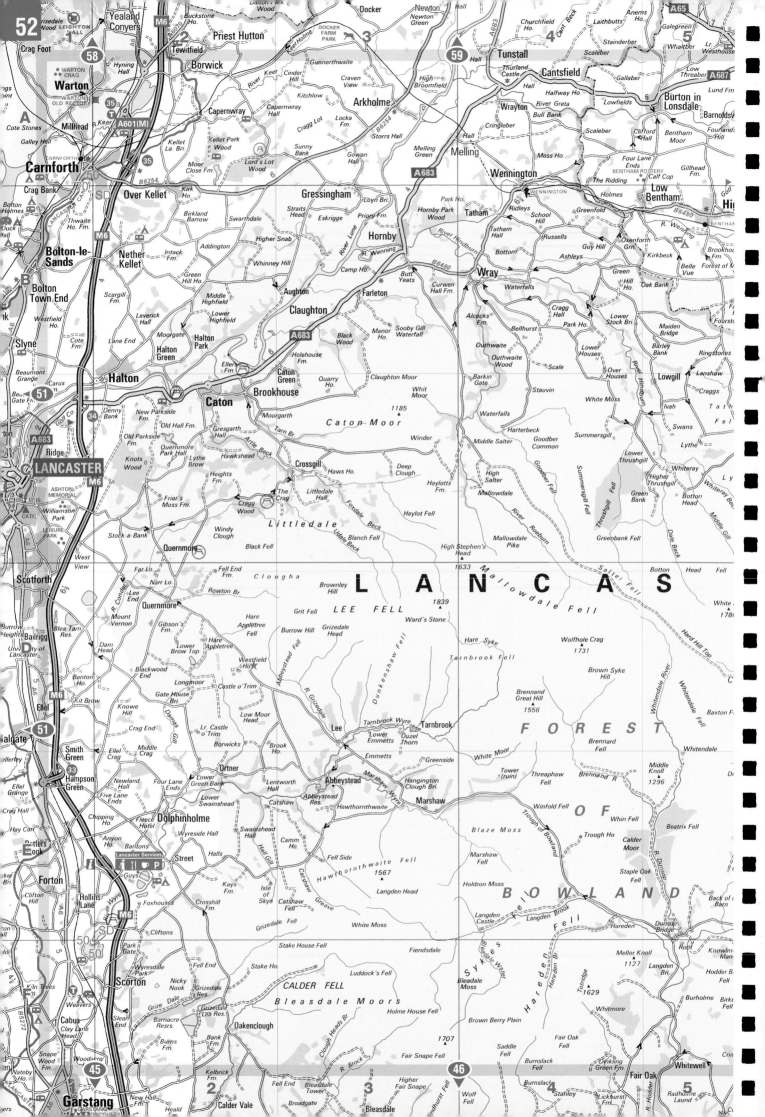

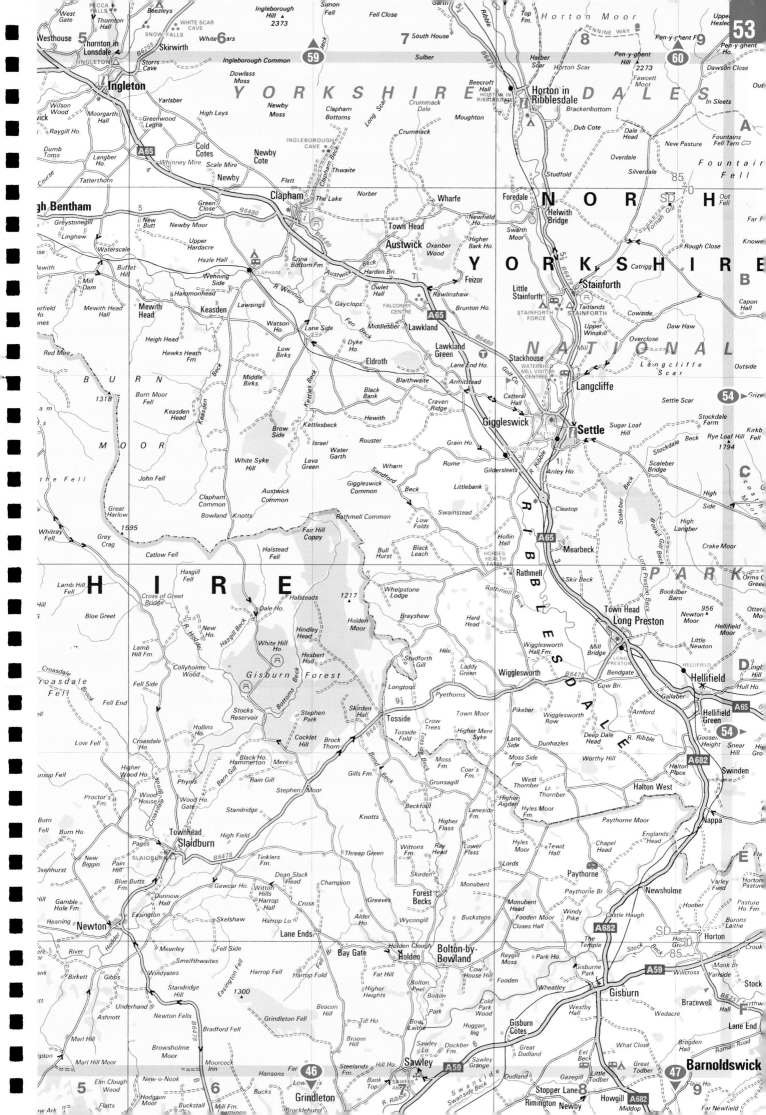

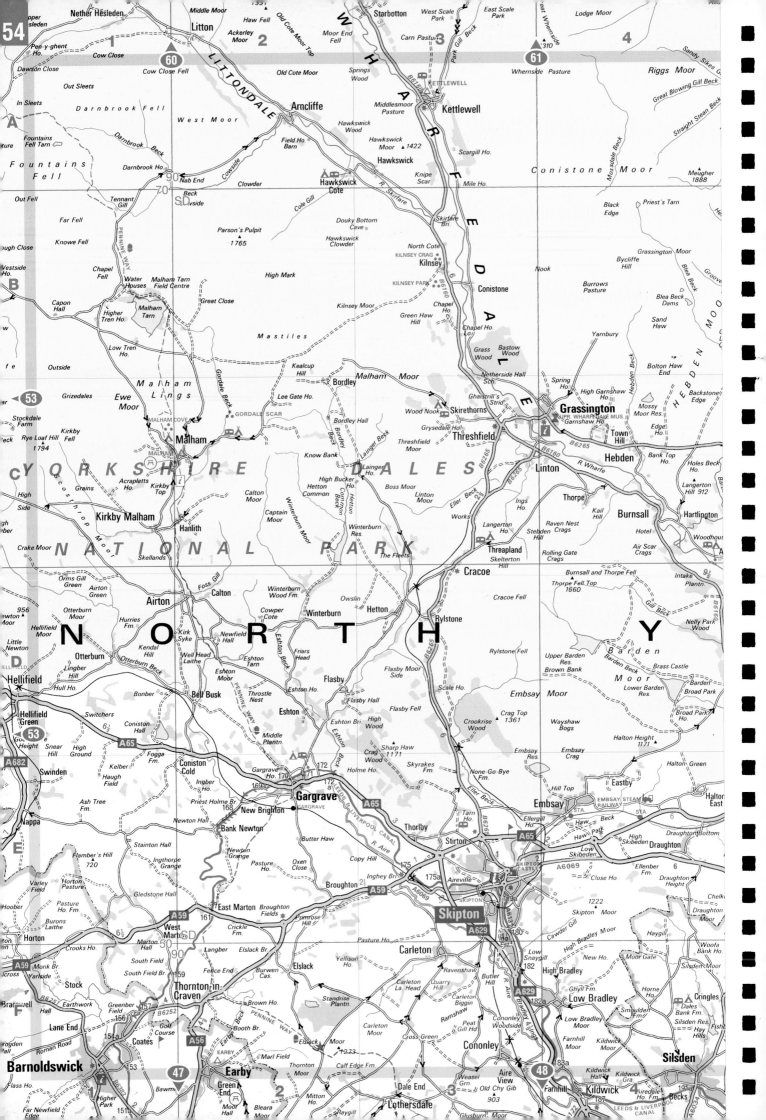

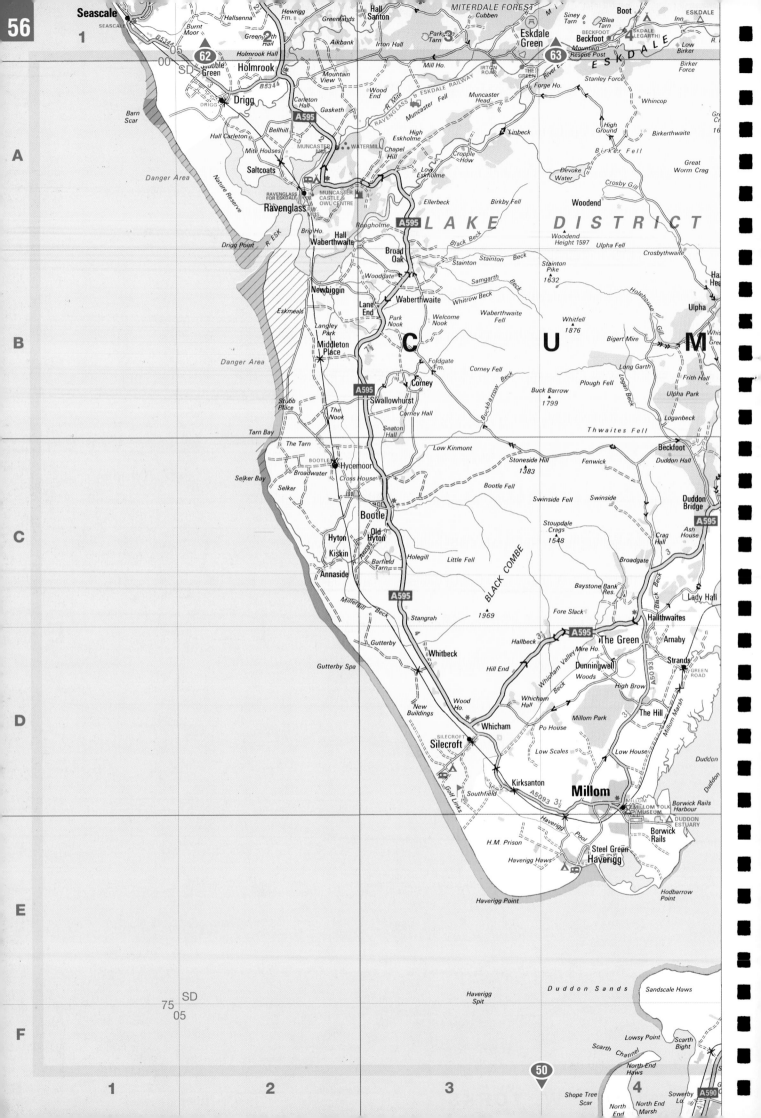

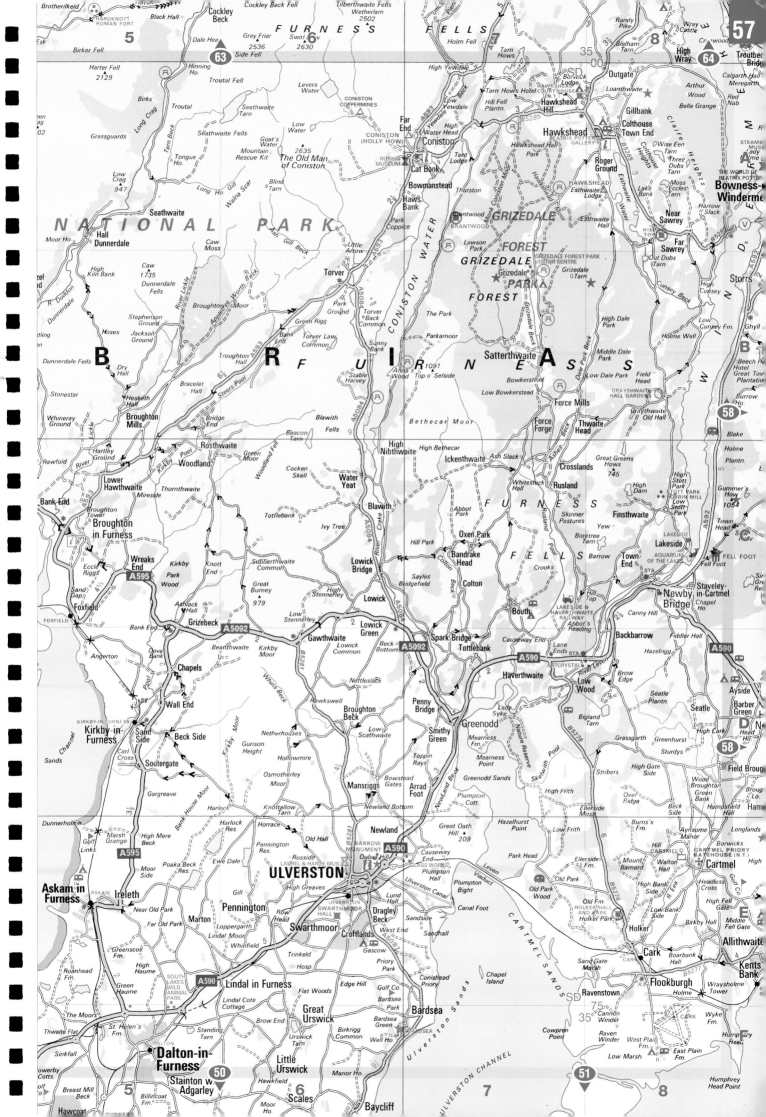

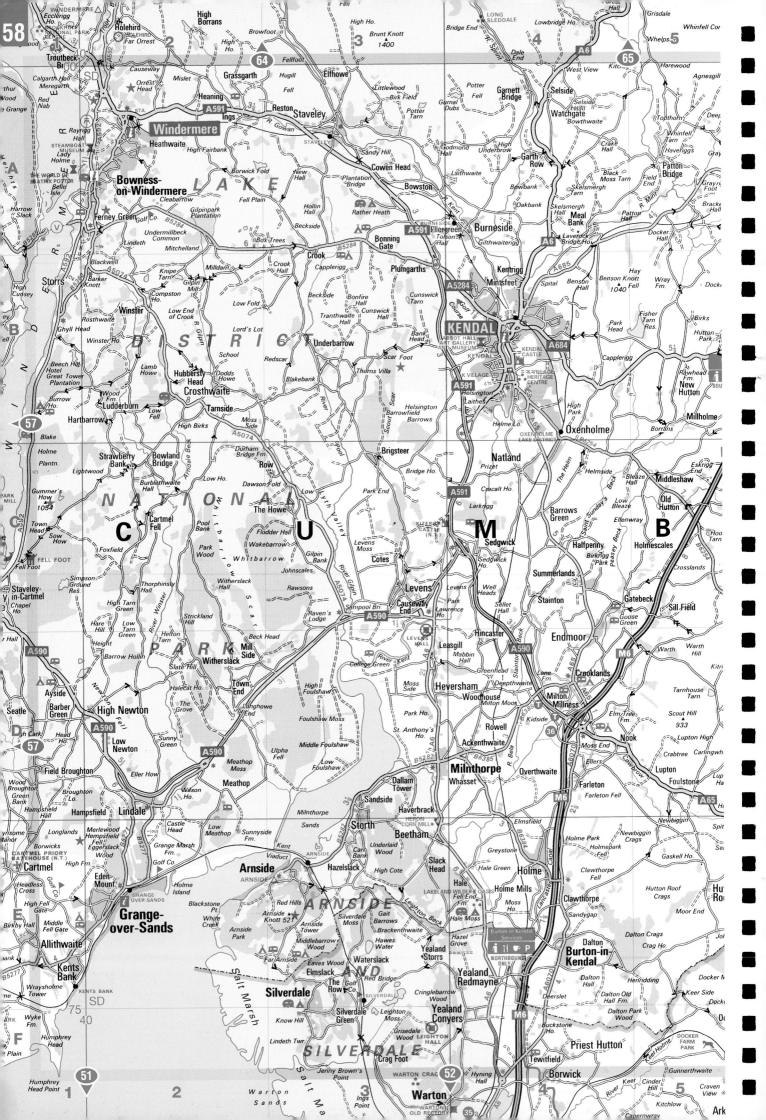

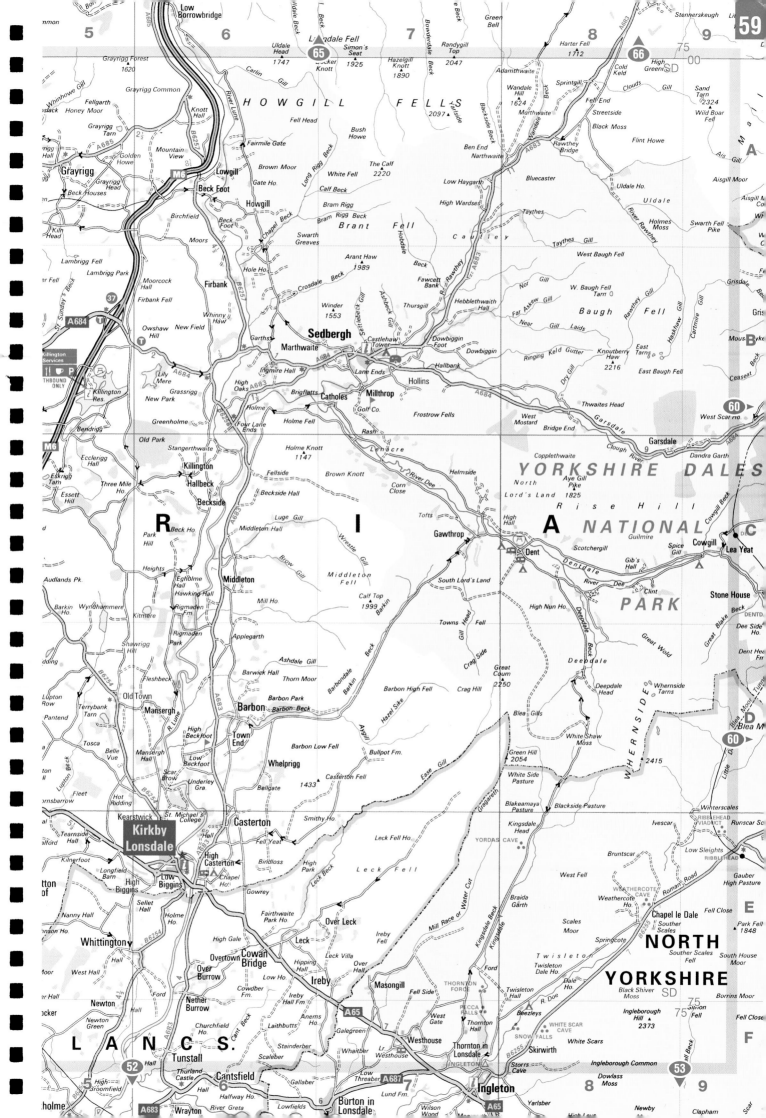

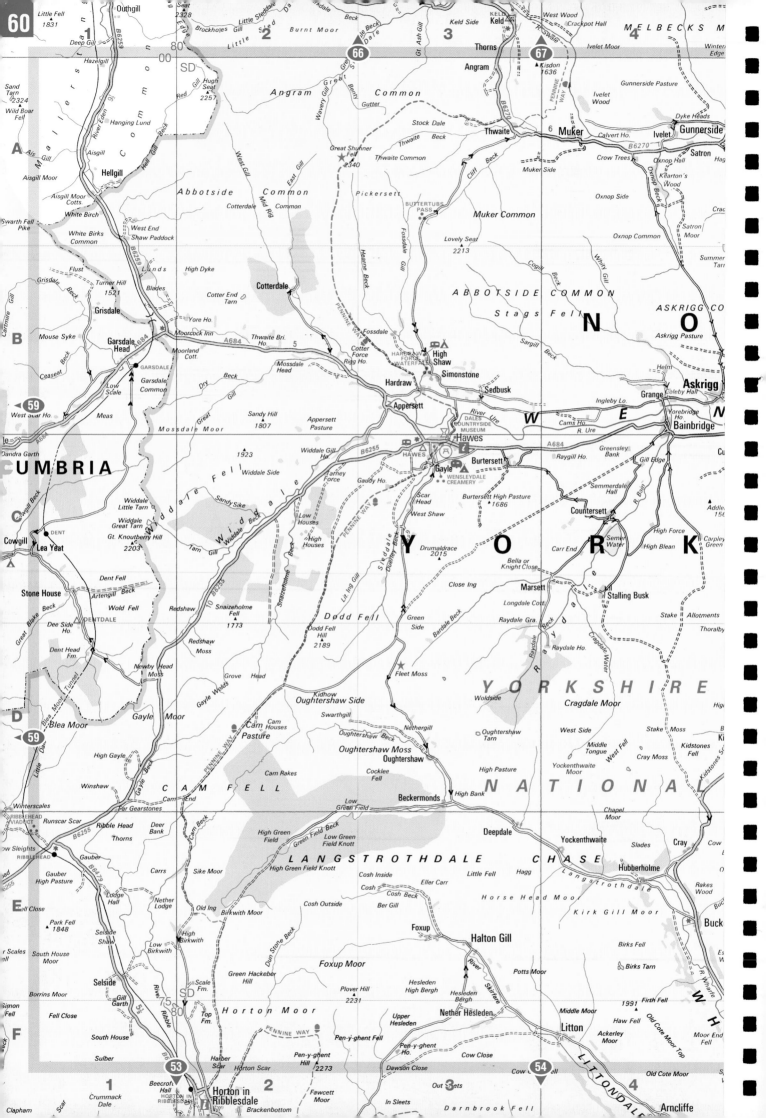

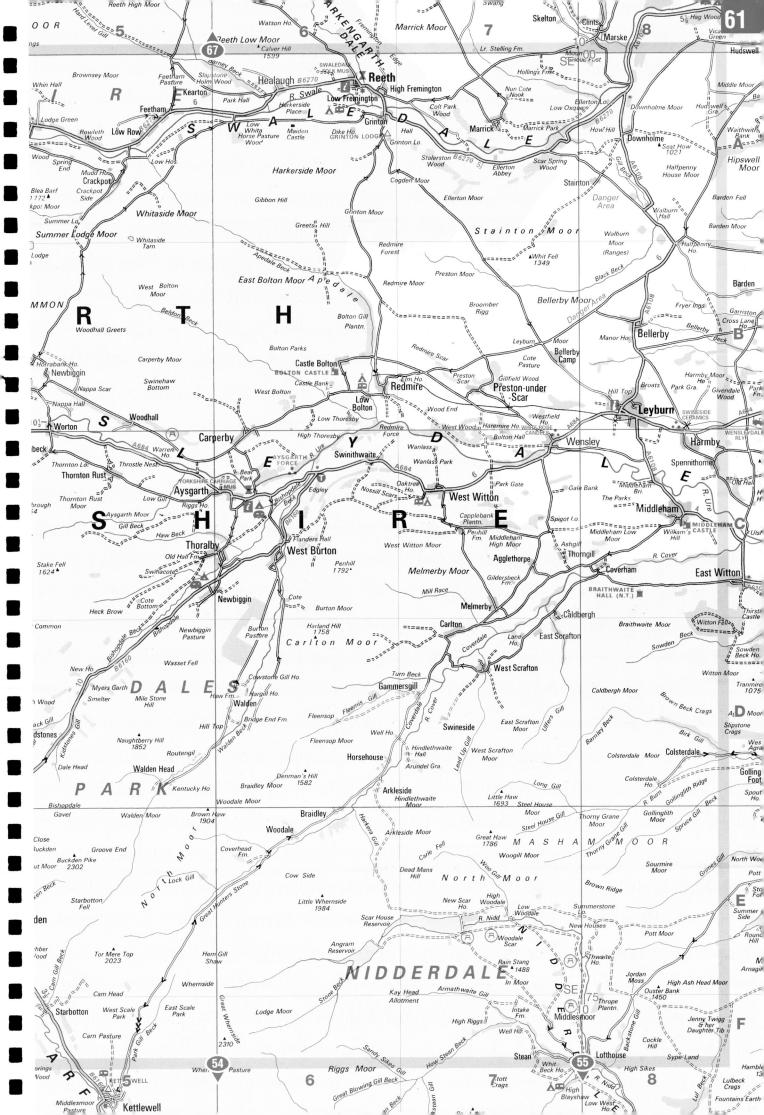

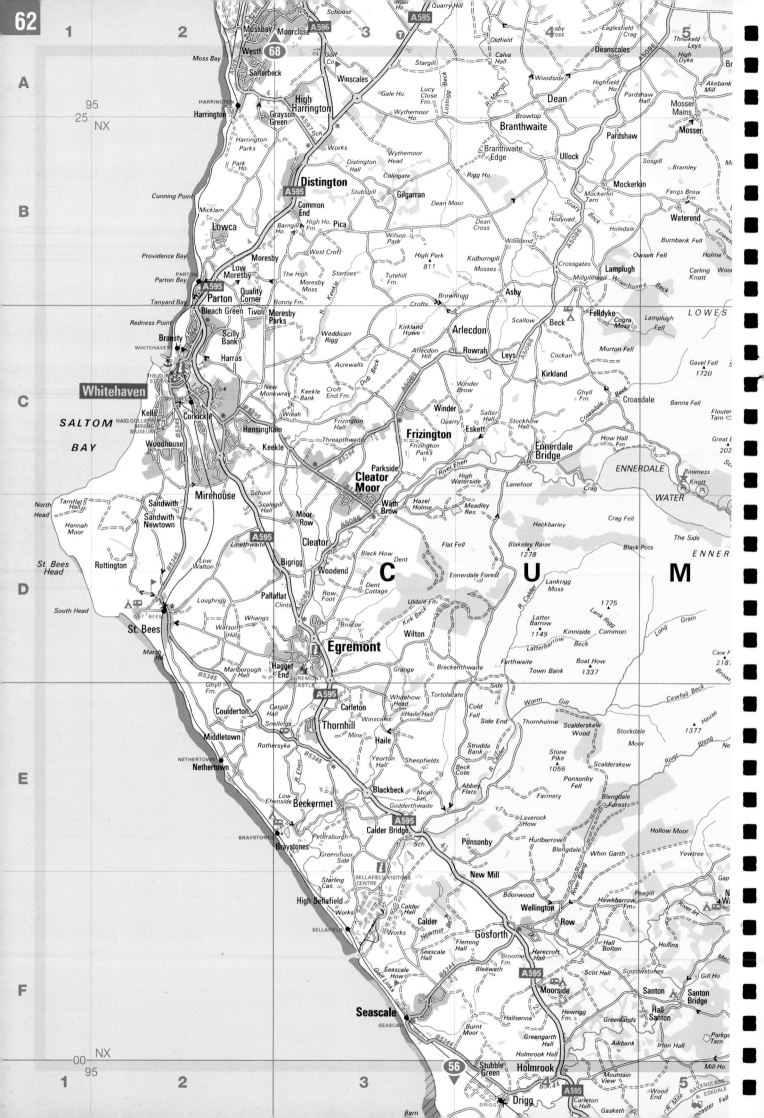

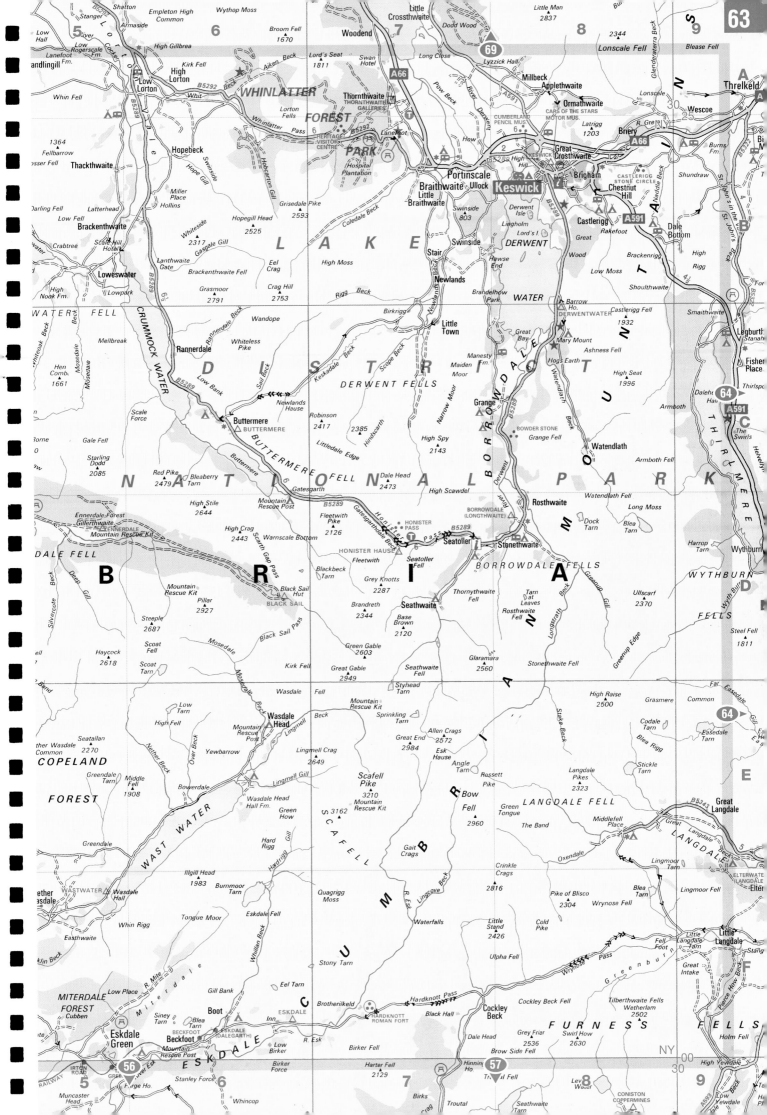

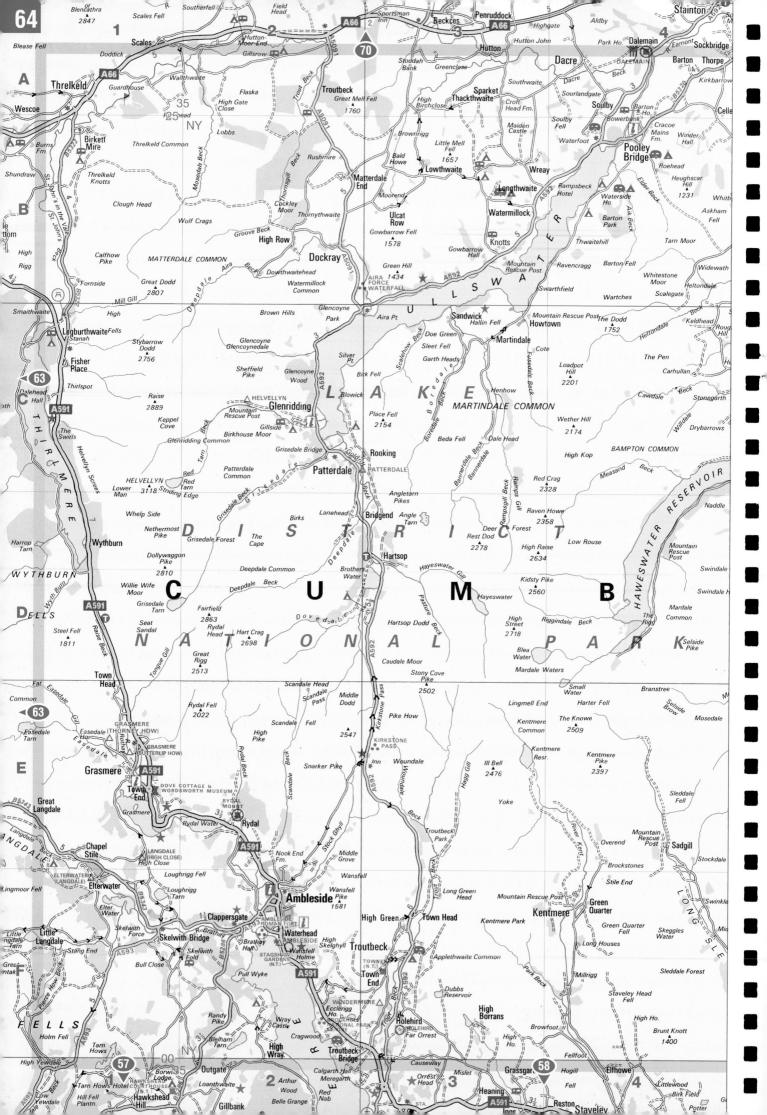

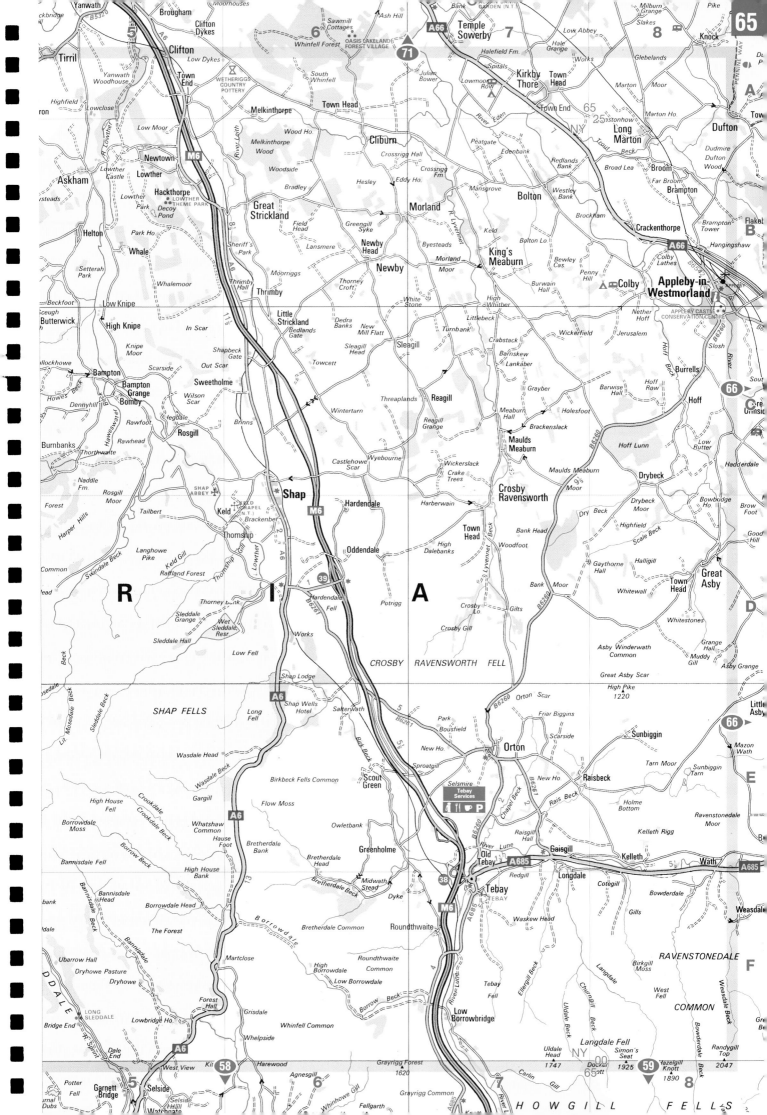

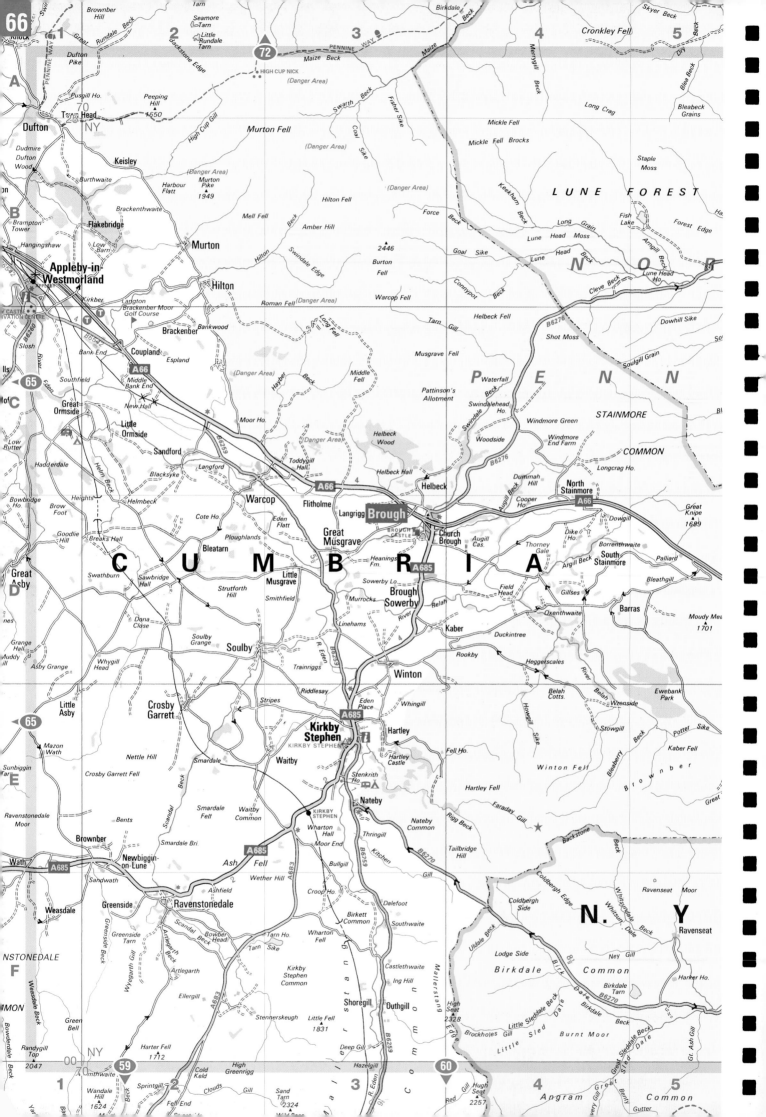

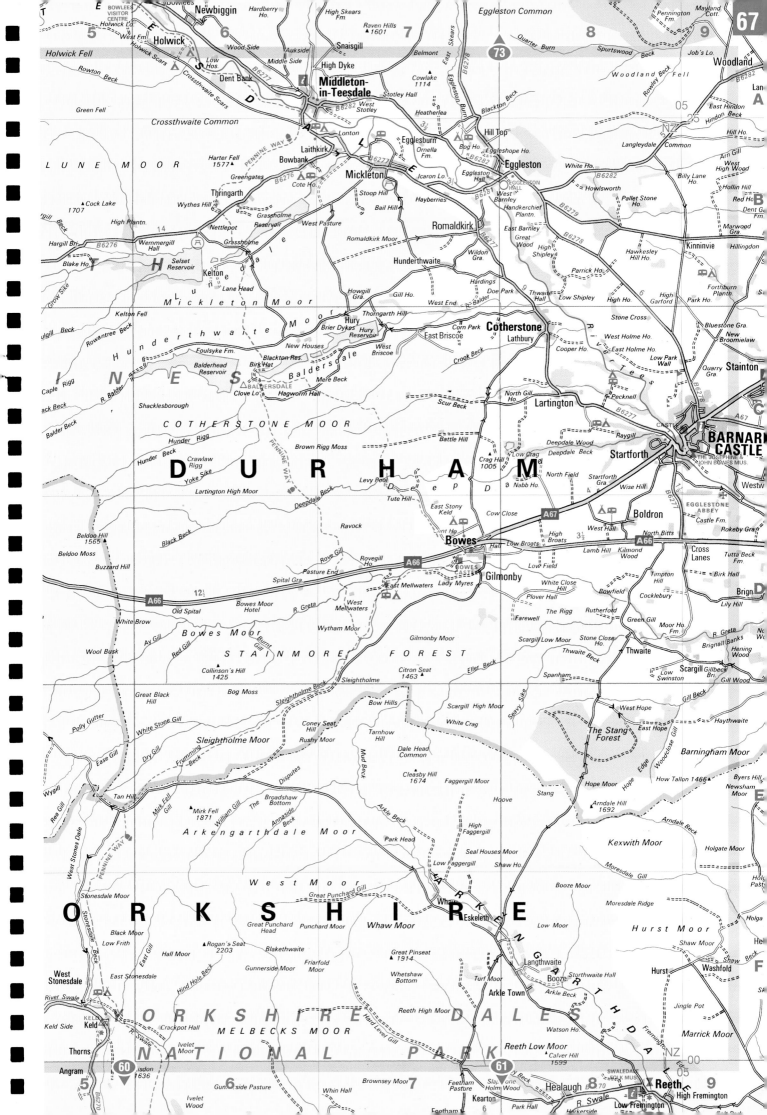

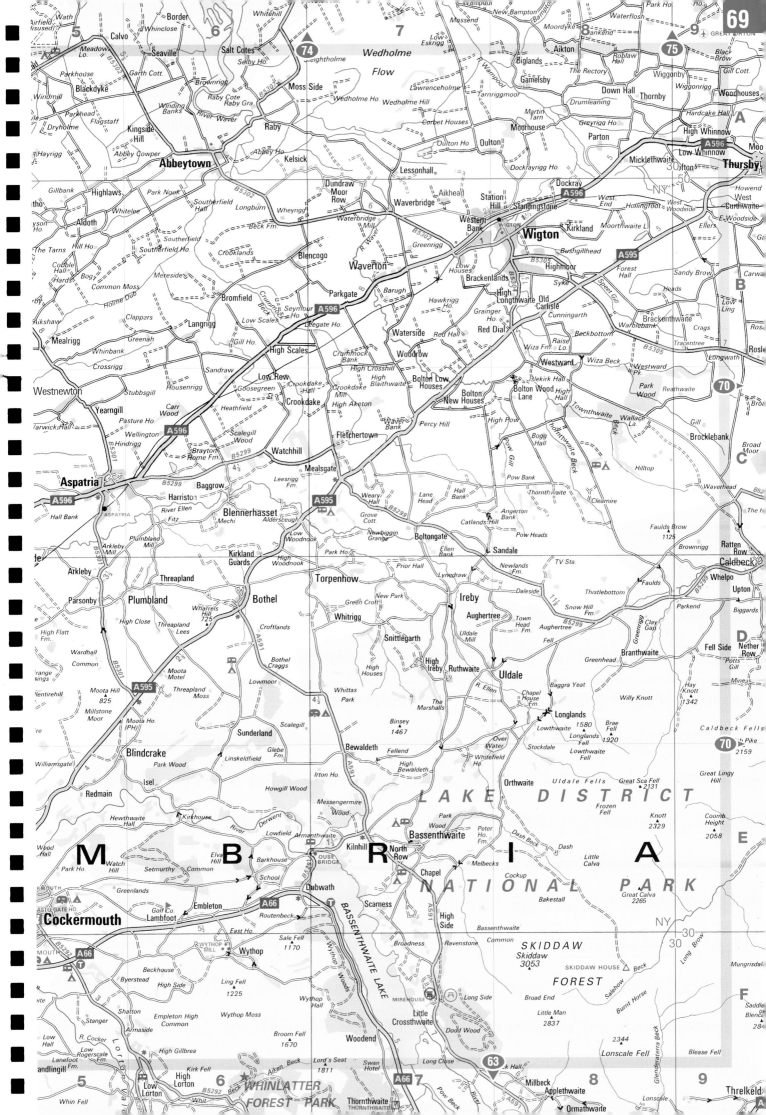

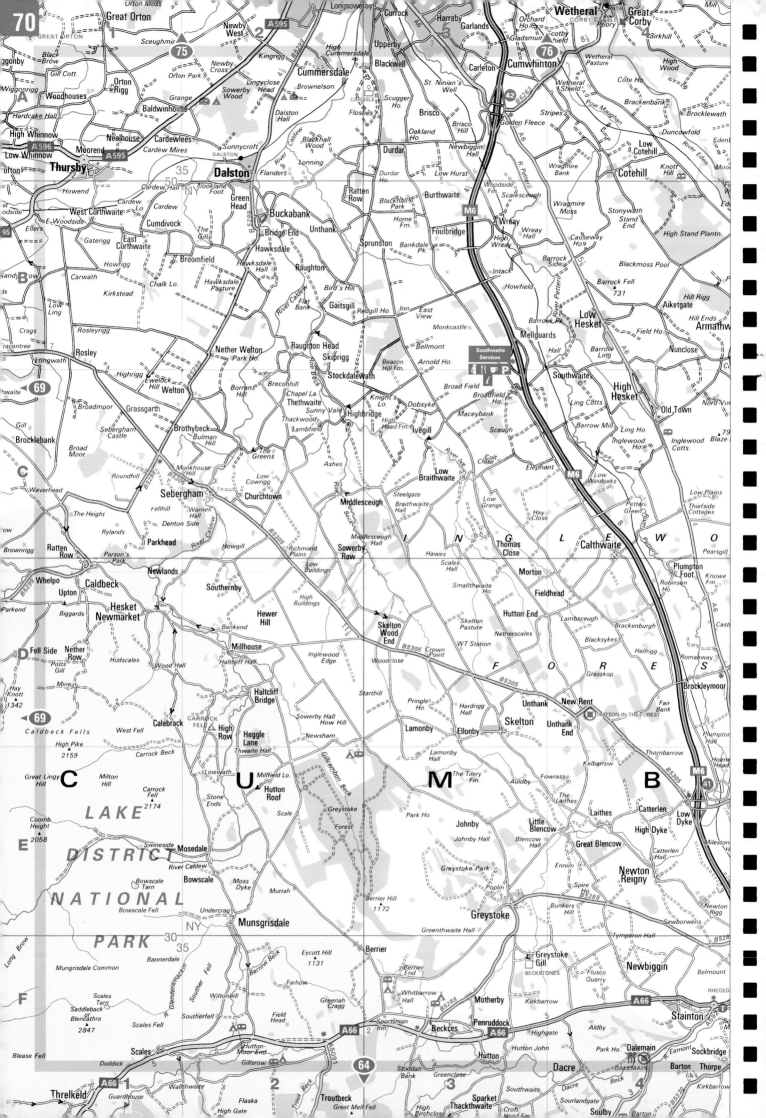

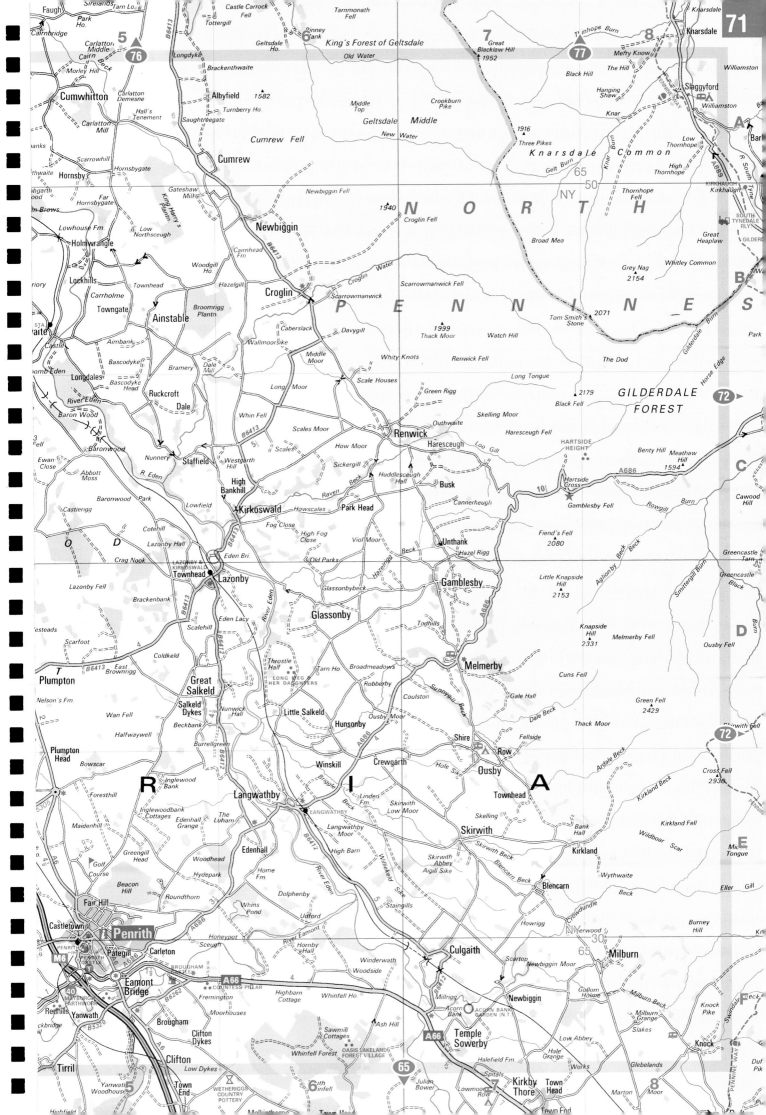

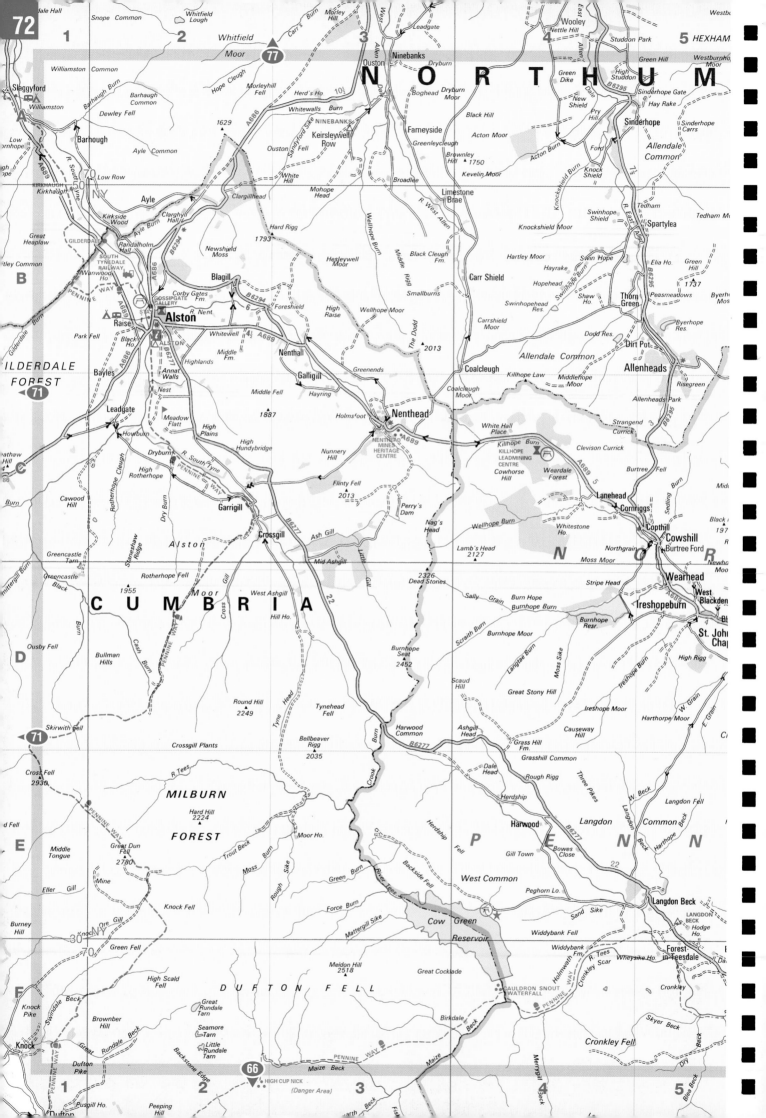

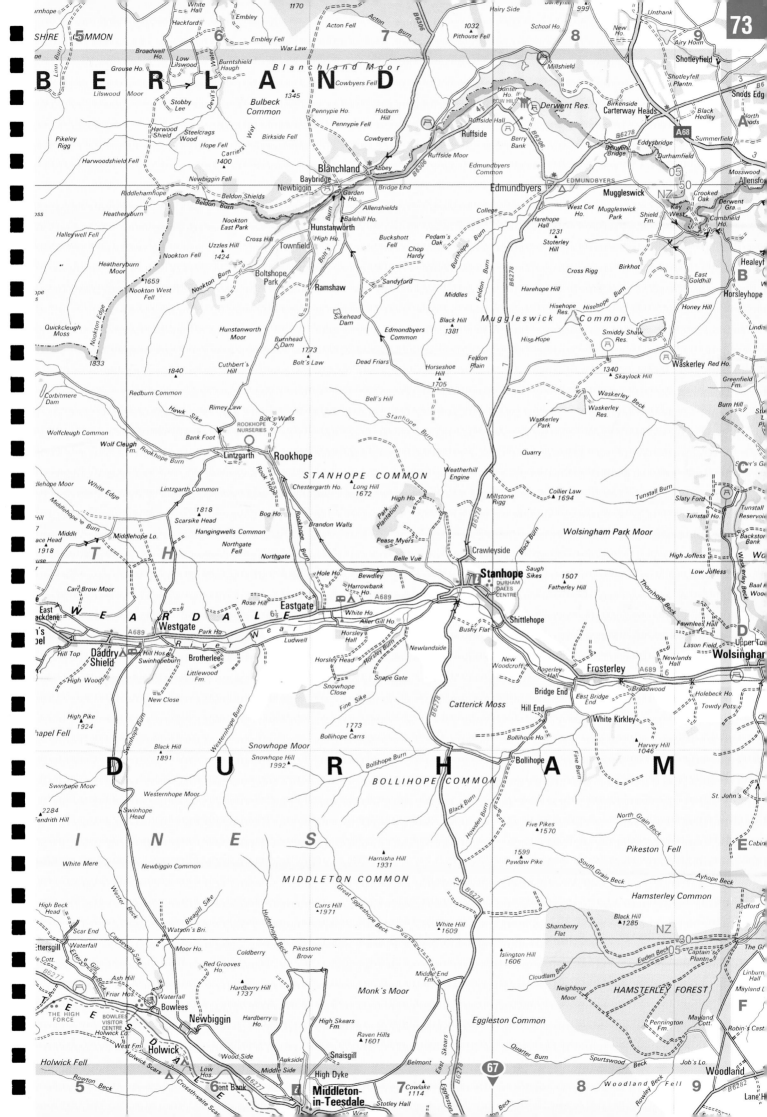

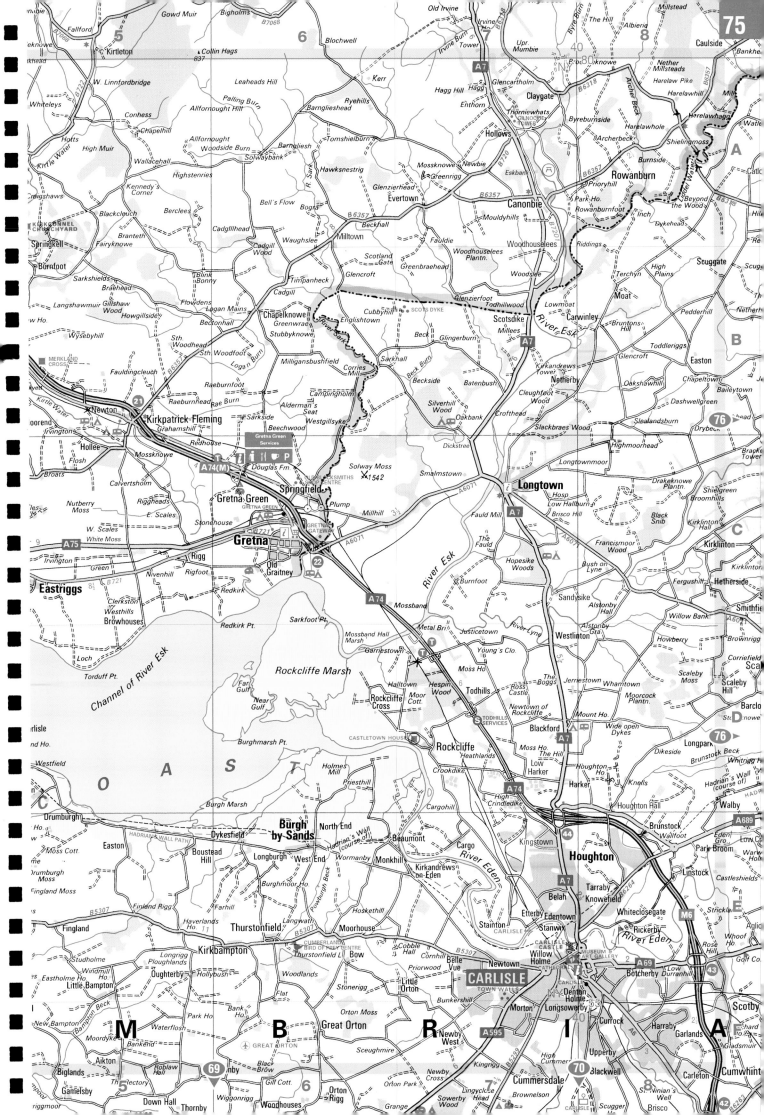

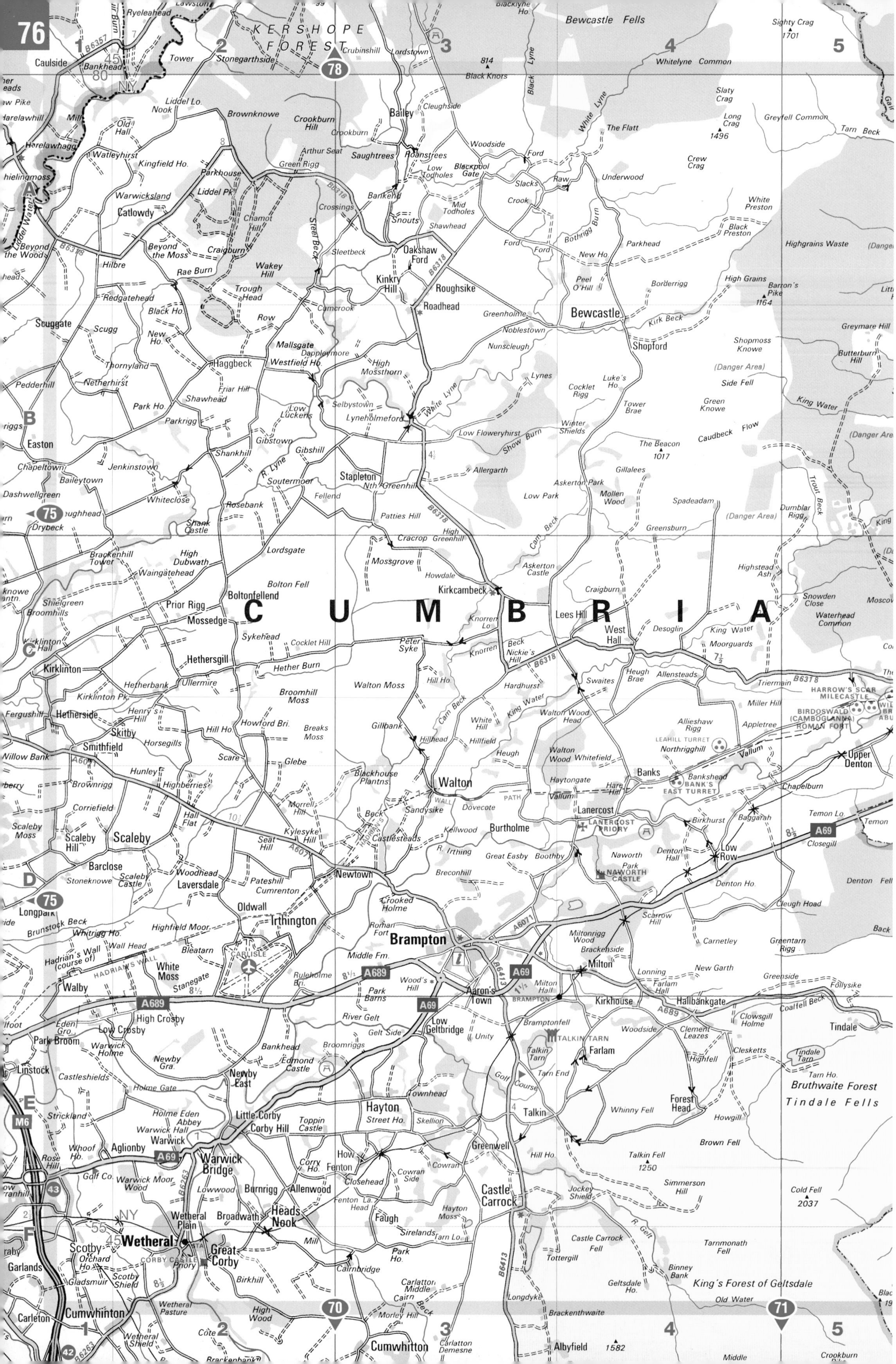

KERSHOPE FOREST
78
Bewcastle Fells
Sighty Crag 1701
Whitelyne Common
Caulside
Bankhead
Tower
Stonegarthside
Crubinshill
Lordstown
814 Black Knors
Slaty Crag
Long Crag 1496
Greyfell Common
Tarn Beck
Liddel Lo.
Nook
Brownknowe
Crookburn Hill
Crookburn
Bailey
Cleughside
The Flatt
Old Hall
Harelawhill
Harelawhagg
Watleyhirst
Kingfield Ho.
Arthur Seat
Green Rigg
Saughtrees
Roanstrees
Woodside
Ford
Crew Crag
Parkhouse
Low Todholes
Blackpool Gate
Raw
Underwood
Warwicksland
Liddel Pk.
Catlowdy
Crossings
Bankend
Slacks
Crook
Mid Todholes
Snouts
Shawhead
White Preston
Black Preston
Chamot Hill
Steel Beck
Bothrigg Burn
Parkhead
Highgrains Waste
Beyond the Wood
Beyond the Moss
Craigburn
Sleetbeck
Oakshaw Ford
Ford
New Ho.
Hilbre
Wakey Hill
Rae Burn
Kinkry Hill
Roughsike
Peel O'Hill
Borderrigg
High Grains
Barron's Pike 1164
Redgatehead
Trough Head
Roadhead
Greenholme
Bewcastle
Kirk Beck
Greymare Hill
Black Ho.
Camcrook
Row
Noblestown
Scuggate
Scugg
New Ho.
Mallsgate
Dappleymore
Nunscleugh
Shopford
Shopmoss Knowe
Butterburn Hill
Thornyland
Haggbeck
Westfield Ho.
High Mossthorn
Pedderhill
Netherhirst
Friar Hill
Lynes
Cocklet Rigg
Luke's Ho.
Side Fell
King Water
Park Ho.
Shawhead
Selbystown
Low Luckens
Lyneholmeford
White Lyne
Tower Brae
Green Knowe
Easton
Parkrigg
Gibstown
Low Flowerhirst
Show Burn
Winter Shields
Caudbeck Flow
The Beacon 1017
Shankhill
Gibshill
Chapeltown
Jenkinstown
R. Lyne
Allergarth
Gillalees
Baileytown
Stapleton
Nth Greenhill
Askerton Park
Soutermoor
Dashwellgreen
Whiteclose
Fellend
Low Park
Mollen Wood
Spadeadam
Rosebank
Trout Beck
75
Drybeck
Shank Castle
Patties Hill
Cam Beck
Greensburn
(Danger Area)
Dumblar Rigg
Cracrop
High Greenhill
Brackenhill Tower
High Dubwath
Lordsgate
Mossgrove
Howdale
Askerton Castle
Highstead Ash
Waingatehead
Bolton Fell
Kirkcambeck
Craigburn
Shielgreen
Broomhills
Prior Rigg
Boltonfellend
Snowden Close
CUMBRIA
Mossedge
Knorren Lo.
Lees Hill
West Hall
Desoglin
King Water
Waterhead Common
Kirklinton Hall
Sykehead
Cocklet Hill
Peter Syke
Beck
Nickie's Hill
Knorren
Moorguards
Hethersgill
Hether Burn
B6318
Heugh Brae
Allensteads
Kirklinton
Hill Ho.
Swaites
Triermain
Hetherbank
Ullermire
Walton Moss
Hardhurst
HARROW'S SCAR MILECASTLE
Kirklinton Pk.
Broomhill Moss
Miller Hill
BIRDOSWALD (CAMBOGLANNA) ROMAN FORT
Fergushill
Hetherside
Henry's Hill
White Hill
King Water
Walton Wood Head
Allieshaw Rigg
Appletree
Skitby
Hill Ho.
Howford Bri.
Breaks Moss
Gillbank
Hillhead
Hillfield
LEAHILL TURRET
Northrigghill
Smithfield
Horsegills
Heugh
Walton Wood
Whitefield
Vallum
Upper Denton
Willow Bank
A6071
Scare
Glebe
Blackhouse Plantns.
Banks
Bankshead
BANK'S EAST TURRET
Hunley
Haytongate
Hare Hill
Chapelburn
Brownrigg
Highberries
Walton
Vallum
Corriefield
Morrell Hill
WALL
Sandysike
Dovecote
PATH
Lanercost
Temon Lo.
Temon
Hall Flat
Beck
LANERCOST PRIORY
Birkhurst
Baggarah
Scaleby Moss
Scaleby Hill
Scaleby
Seat Hill
Kylesyke Hill
HADRIAN'S WALL
Castlesteads
Kellwood
Burtholme
A69
Closegill
R. Irthing
Low Row
Great Easby
Boothby
Naworth Park
Denton Hall
Barclose
A6071
Breconhill
NAWORTH CASTLE
Newtown
Denton Ho.
Denton Fell
Stoneknowe
Scaleby Castle
Woodhead
Laversdale
Pateshill
Crooked Holme
Currenton
Cleugh Head
Longpark
Oldwall
Scarrow Hill
Brunstock Beck
Irthington
Roman Fort
Back
Whitrigg Ho.
Highfield Moor
Brampton
Miltonrigg Wood
Carnetley
Greentarn Rigg
Hadrian's Wall (course of)
Wall Head
Bleatarn
CARLISLE
Brackenside
Middle Fm.
HADRIAN'S WALL
White Moss
Ruleholme Bri.
A689
Milton
New Garth
Stanegate
Wood's Hill
A69
Milton Hall
Lonning
Walby
Park Barns
Aaron's Town
BRAMPTON
Farlam Hall
Greenside
Follysike
A689
Kirkhouse
Hallbankgate
High Crosby
A69
Coalfell Beck
Eden Gro.
River Gelt
Low Crosby
Low Geltbridge
Bramptonfell
Woodside
Clement Leazes
Clowsgill Holme
Tindale
Park Broom
Warwick Holme
Gelt Side
Unity
TALKIN TARN
Farlam
Clesketts
Tindale Tarn
Bankhead
Broomriggs
Talkin Tarn
Highfell
Newby Gra.
Edmond Castle
Golf Course
Tarn End
Tarn Ho.
Linstock
Castlesheilds
Newby East
Bruthwaite Forest
Tindale Fells
Holme Gate
Townhead
Forest Head
Strickland
Holme Eden Abbey
Little Corby
Hayton
Whinny Fell
Warwick Hall
Corby Hill
Toppin Castle
Street Ho.
Skellion
Talkin
Howgill
M6
Warwick
Whoof Ho.
Aglionby
How
Greenwell
Brown Fell
Rose Hill
A69
Warwick Bridge
Corry Ho.
Fenton
Cowran
Hill Ho.
Talkin Fell 1250
Golf Co.
Warwick Moor
Wood
Cowran Side
Closehead
Simmerson Hill
Lowwood
Burnrigg
Allenwood
Castle Carrock
Jockey Shield
Cold Fell 2037
43
Fenton La. Head
Hayton Moss
R. Gelt
Wetheral Plain
Broadwath
Heads Nook
Faugh
Sirelands
Tarn Lo.
Castle Carrock Fell
Tarnmonath Fell
Scotby
Wetheral
Mill
Orchard Ho.
CORBY CASTLE
Great Corby
Park Ho.
Tottergill
Priory
Binney Bank
Garlands
Gladsmuir
Scotby Shield
Birkhill
Cairnbridge
Carlatton Middle
King's Forest of Geltsdale
Cairn Beck
Geltsdale Ho.
B6413
Longdyke
Old Water
Wetheral Pasture
High Wood
70
Morley Hill
Brackenthwaite
71
Carleton
Cumwhinton
Cote
Wetheral Shield
Cumwhitton
Carlatton Demesne
Albyfield
1582
Middle
Crookburn
42
B6263
Brackenbank
1
2
3
4
5
A
B
C
D
E
F

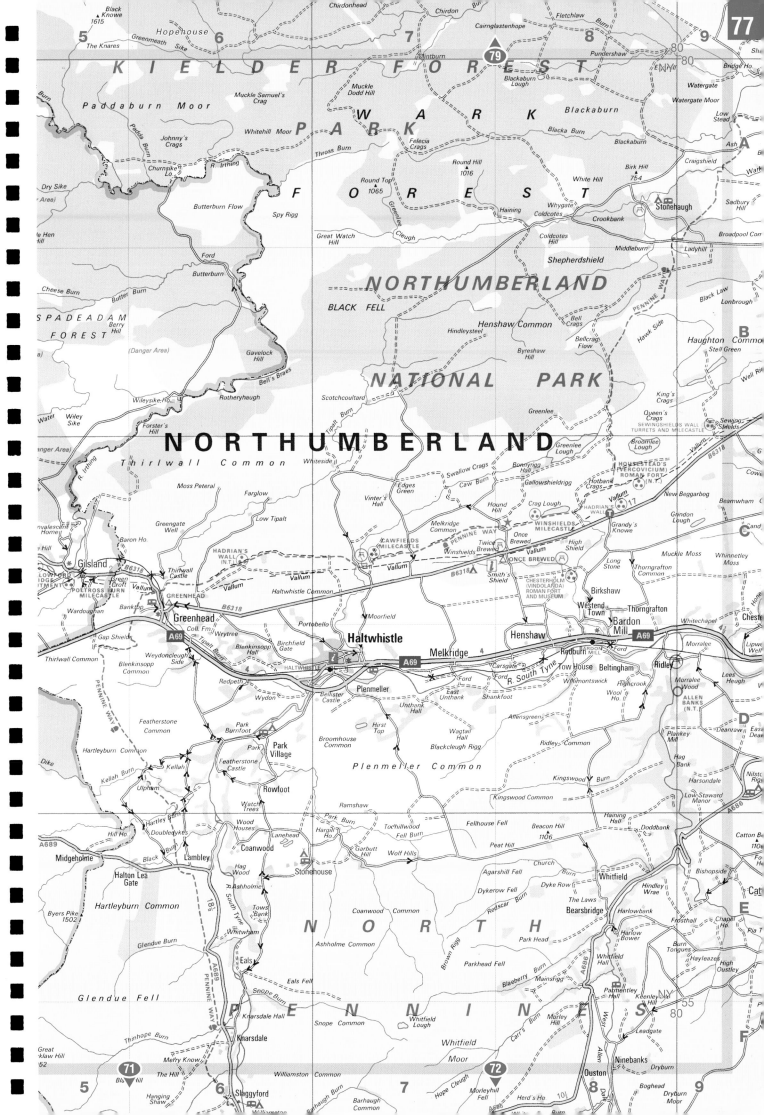

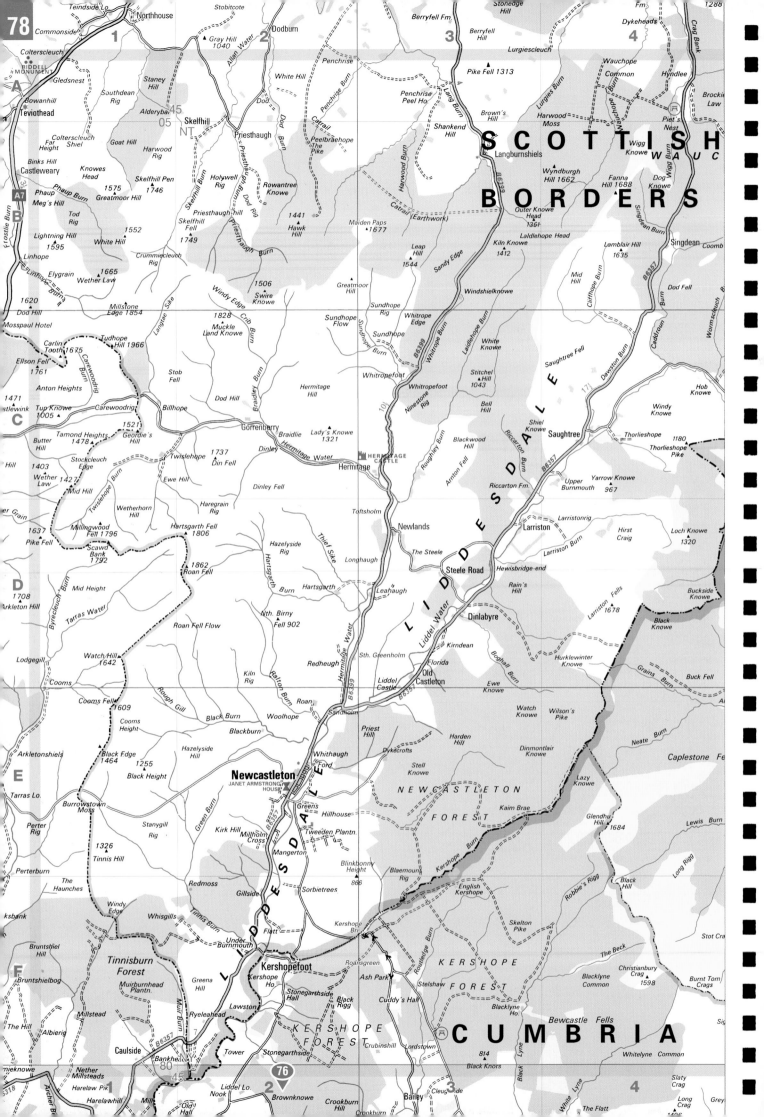

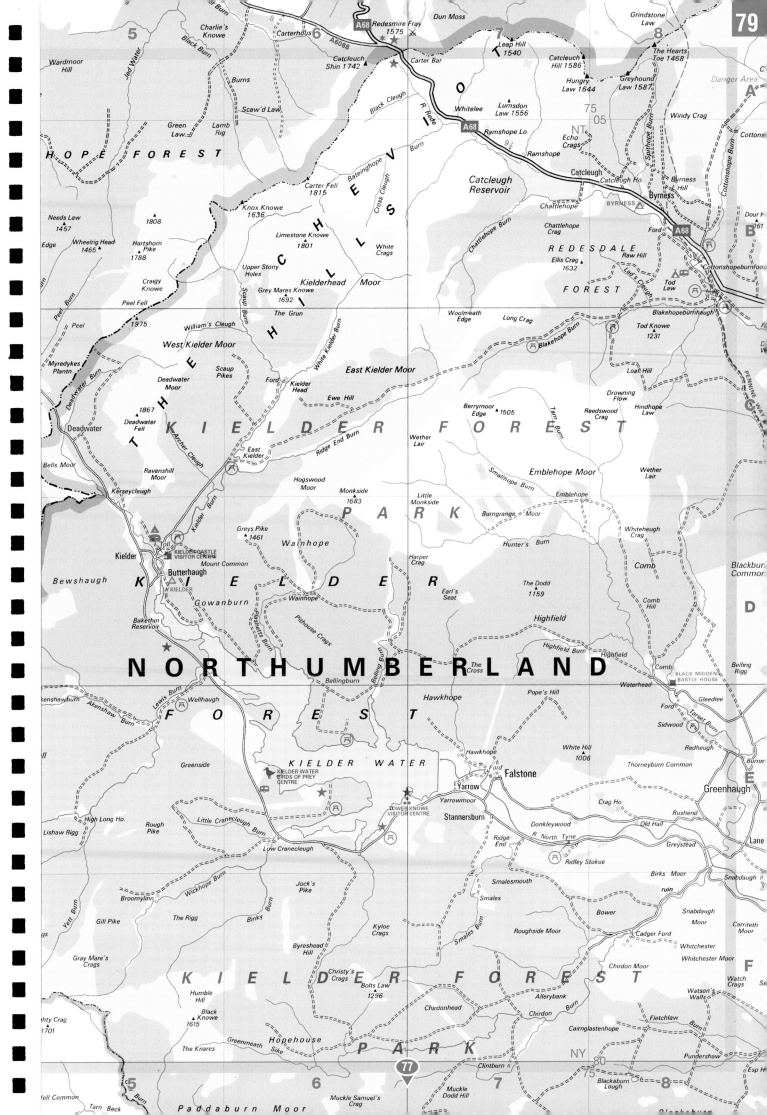

ISLE OF MAN

Scale 1:200,000

POINT OF AYRE

NX

NX

0   2   4   6   8   10 miles

0   2   4   6   8   10   12   14   16 kilometres

A

B

C

D

E

Rue Pt.

The Ayres

Glentruan

Cranstal

The Lhen

Dhowin

Bride

A10   A19   B6   A17   A16

MANX CROSSES

Andreas

Jurby Head

Jurby West

Jurby East

St. Judes

Regaby

JURBY SOUTH

Ballasalla

Sandygate

MANX CROSSES

Dhoor

The Cronk

CURRAGHS WILDLIFE PARK

Sulby

A14   A13

GROVE MUSEUM

RAMSEY BAY

Ramsey

Orrisdale

Ballaugh

Churchtown

MANX ELECTRIC RAILWAY

Port e Vullen

T.T. Course

9

A3

Glen Auldyn

Rhencullen

Ravensdale

Sulby

Dreemskerry

Maughold Head

Kirk Michael

565

Ballajora

MANX CROSSES

CELTIC CRAFT CENTRE

NORTH BARRULE

MANX CROSSES

I   **s**   **l**   **e**

Ballaleigh

SNAEFELL

Corrany

Cornaa

Barregarrow

Res.

621

Druidale

Glen Mona

9

o   **f**

MURRAYS MOTORCYCLE MUSEUM

Dhoon

544

Agneash

LAXEY WHEEL AND MINES

Bulgham Bay

Knocksharry

MANX TRANSPORT MUSEUM

Cronk-y-Voddy

487 COLDEN

SNAEFELL MOUNTAIN RAILWAY

Ballaquine

Laxey

St. Patrick's I.

PEEL

LAXEY WOOLLEN MILLS

C

Peel

HOUSE OF MANANNAN

A20

TYNWALD CRAFT CENTRE

M   **a**   **n**

BALLALHEANNAGH GARDENS

Old Laxey

Laxey Head

Contrary Head

KIPPER MUSEUM

A1

3

Greeba

Baldwin

Creg-ny-Baa

Fairy Cottage

Laxey Bay

Patrick

A30

St. John's

B22

Ballacannel

Glenmaye

333

T.T. Course

8

A23

B21

Baldrine

Clay Head

Dalby Pt.

Lower Foxdale

Crosby

Glen Vine

Strang

B20

7

Dalby

A1

Onchan

MANX CROSSES

Niarbyl

Foxdale

Union Mills

Tromode

GROUDLE GLEN RAILWAY

HEYSHAM 3:30

Niarbyl Bay

A24

Eairy

Braaid

Spring Valley

ONCHAN PLEASURE PARK

HEYSHAM 2:00 (Summer Only)

483 SOUTH BARRULE

Cooil

Douglas

Close Clark

222

Douglas Bay

14

A26

St. Mark's

Ballaveare

Douglas Head

LIVERPOOL 2:30

Ballamodha

Newtown

11

A25

Little Ness

Ronague

B30

Santon Head

Lingague

Grenaby

A34

LIVERPOOL 4:00 (Winter Only)

Fleshwick Bay

Surby

Colby

Ballabeg

RUSHEN ABBEY

B25

Port Greenaugh

Bradda Head

Bradda

A1

5

Port Erin

ISLE OF MAN STEAM RAILWAY

Four Roads

BILLOWN

Ballasalla

The Howe

Castletown

Derbyhaven

Cregneash

A31

Castle Rushen

Port St. Mary

SCARLETT VISITOR CENTRE

NAUTICAL MUS.

OLD HOUSE OF KEYS

St. Michael's I.

f of Man

128

CREGNEASH VILLAGE FOLK MUSEUM

Spanish Head

Scarlett Point

Dreswick Pt.

BELFAST 2:45 } (April-Sept)
DUBLIN 2:45 }

Chicken Rock

SC

SC

60

20

50

Key to Town Plan Symbols

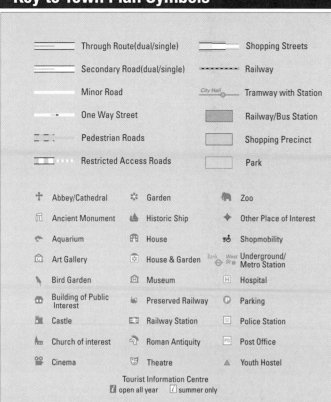

	Through Route(dual/single)
	Secondary Road(dual/single)
	Minor Road
	One Way Street
	Pedestrian Roads
	Restricted Access Roads
	Shopping Streets
	Railway
City Hall	Tramway with Station
	Railway/Bus Station
	Shopping Precinct
	Park

† Abbey/Cathedral
Ancient Monument
Aquarium
Art Gallery
Bird Garden
Building of Public Interest
Castle
Church of interest
Cinema

Garden
Historic Ship
House
House & Garden
Museum
Preserved Railway
Railway Station
Roman Antiquity
Theatre

Zoo
Other Place of Interest
Shopmobility
Underground/Metro Station
Hospital
Parking
Police Station
Post Office
Youth Hostel

Tourist Information Centre
open all year   summer only

Blackpool

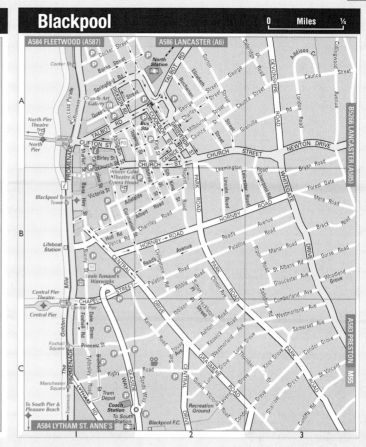

A584 FLEETWOOD (A587) A586 LANCASTER (A6)
A584 LYTHAM ST. ANNE'S

0 Miles ¼

Bradford

0 Miles ¼

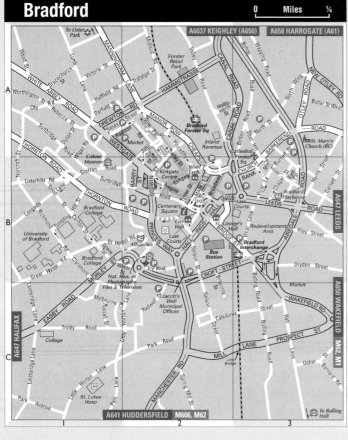

Carlisle

0 Miles ¼

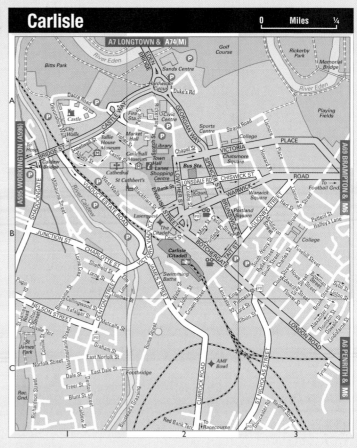

Bradford

Airedale Rd B3	Croft St B2	Little Horton La . . C1	Russell St. C1
Alhambra ☺ B2	Darfield St A1	Longside La B1	St George's
Barkerend Rd. . . . A3	Darley St A2	Lumb La. A1	Hall ☺ B2
Barnard Rd C3	Drewton Rd A1	Manchester Rd . . C2	St Lukes
Barry St B2	Dryden St B3	Manningham La . . A1	Hospital Ⓗ . . . C1
Bolling Rd C3	Dyson St A1	Manor Row A2	St Mary's
Bolton Rd. A3	Easby Rd. C1	Market A2/C3	Church ⛪ A3
Bradford College . B1	East Parade B3	Market St. B2	Simes St A1
Bradford Forster	Filey St. B3	Melbourne Place . C1	Smith St. B1
Sq ⛓ A2	Forster	Midland Rd A2	Spring Mill St . . . C2
Bradford	Retail Park . . . A2	Mill La C2	Stott Hill A3
Interchange ⛓.. B3	Forster Sq B3	Morley St B1	Sunbridge Rd. . . . A1
Bradford	Garnett St B3	Nat. Museum of	Thornton Rd. A1
Playhouse ☺ . . B3	Godwin St B2	Photography, Film	Trafalgar St. A2
Bridge St B2	Gracechurch St . . A1	& Television ☺.. B2	Trinity Rd C1
Britannia St B2	Grattan Rd. B1	Nelson St. B2	Tumbling Hill St . . B1
Broadway. B2	Great Horton Rd. . B1	New Otley Rd. . . . A3	Tyrrel St B2
Burnett St. B3	Grove Terr B1	Norcroft St. B1	University of
Bus Station B2	Hall Ings. B2	North Parade A2	Bradford. B1
Butler St West . . A2	Hall La C3	North St A3	Usher St A3
Caledonia St C2	Hallfield Rd A1	North Wing A3	Valley Rd A2
Canal Rd A2	Hammstrasse . . . A2	Otley Rd. A3	Vicar La B3
Carlton St A1	Harris St. B3	Park Ave C1	Victoria St A1
Cathedral ✝ . . . A3	Holdsworth St . . . A2	Park La C1	Wakefield Rd C3
Centenary Sq. . . . B2	Ice Rink ✦ B2	Park Rd C2	Wapping Rd A3
Chapel St. B3	Information Ctr ☑. B2	Peckover St B3	Westgate A1
Cheapside A2	Ivegate B2	Piccadilly A2	White Abbey Rd. . . A1
Church Bank . . . B3	James St A2	Police Station ☒ . B2	Wigan Rd. A1
City Hall ☺. . . . B2	John St A2	Post Office ☏. . . . B2	Wilton St B1
City Rd. A1	Kirkgate B2	Princes Way. . . . B2	Wood St A1
Claremont B1	Kirkgate Centre . B2	Prospect St C3	Wool
Colour	Laisteridge La . . . C1	Radwell Drive. . . . C2	Exchange ☺. . . . B2
Museum ☺ . . . B1	Law Courts B3	Rawson Rd A1	Worthington St. . . . A1
	Leeds Rd B3	Rebecca St A1	
	Listerhills Rd B1	Richmond Rd. . . . B1	

Carlisle

Abbey St A1	Close St B3	King St B2	Richardson St . . . C1
Aglionby St B3	Collingwood St . . C1	Lancaster St C2	Rickerby Park. . . . A3
Albion St C3	Colville St. C1	Lanes Shopping	Rickergate A2
Alexander St C3	Colville Terr C1	Centre. A2/B2	Rome St C2
AMF Bowl ✦ . . . C2	Court B2	Laserquest ✦ . . . B2	Rydal St B3
Annetwell St. . . . A1	Court St B2	Library A2	St Cuthbert's ✝ . . B2
Bank St B2	Crosby St. B2	Lime St B1	St James' Park . . C1
Bitts Park. A1	Crown St C2	Lindisfarne St . . . C3	St James' Rd C1
Blackfriars St B2	Currock Rd C2	Linton St A3	St Nicholas St . . . C3
Blencome St C1	Dacre Rd A1	Lismore Pl A3	Sands Centre A2
Blunt St C1	Dale St. C1	Lismore St. A3	Scotch St. A2
Botchergate B2	Denton St C1	London Rd. C3	Shaddongate B1
Boustead's	Devonshire Walk. . A1	Lonsdale Rd. B2	Sheffield St B1
Grassing ☺ . . . C2	Duke's Rd A2	Lord St. C1	South Henry St . . B3
Bowman St B3	East Dale St C1	Lorne Cres B1	South John St . . . C2
Broad St B3	East Norfolk St. . . C1	Lorne St. B1	South St. B3
Bridge St A1	Eden Bridge A2	Lowther St B2	Spencer St B2
Brook St C3	Edward St B3	Market Hall. A2	Sports Centre. . . . A2
Brunswick St C3	Elm St B1	Mary St B2	Strand Rd. A2
Bus Station B2	English St. B2	Memorial Bridge. . A1	Swimming Baths . B2
Caldew Bridge . . . A1	Fire Station A2	Metcalfe St C1	Sybil St B3
Caldew St B1	Fisher St A1	Milbourne St B1	Tait St B2
Carlisle (Citadel)	Flower St C3	Myddleton St B3	The Citadel B2
Station ⛓ B2	Freer St C1	Nelson St. C1	Thomas St B1
Castle ⛫ A1	Fusehill St B3	Norfolk St C1	Thomson St C3
Castle St A1	Georgian Way. . . . A2	Oswald St A3	Town Hall A2
Castle Way. A1	Gloucester Rd . . . C3	Peter St A2	Trafalgar St C1
Cathedral ✝ . . . A1	Golf Course A1	Petteril St. B3	Tullie House
Cecil St B2	Graham St C1	Police Station ☒ . A2	Museum ☺ . . . A1
Chapel St. A2	Grey St B3	Portland Pl. B2	Tyne St. C3
Charles St B3	Guildhall	Portland Sq B2	Viaduct
Charlotte St B1	Museum ☺ . . . A2	Post Office ☏. . . . A2	Estate Rd B1
Chatsmore	Halfey's La B3	Post Office ☏. . . . B3	Victoria Pl A2/A3
Square A2	Hardwicke Circus . A2	Post Office ☏. . . . C1	Victoria Viaduct . . B2
Chiswick St B2	Hart St. B3	Post Office ☏. . . . A2	Warwick Rd B3
City Walls A1	Howe St. B3	Princess St C3	Warwick Sq B3
Civic Centre A2	Information Ctr ☑. A2	Pugin St B1	Water St. B2
Clifton St C1	James St B2	Red Bank Terr . . . C2	West Walls B1
	Junction St. B1	Regent St. C3	Westmorland St . . C1

Chester

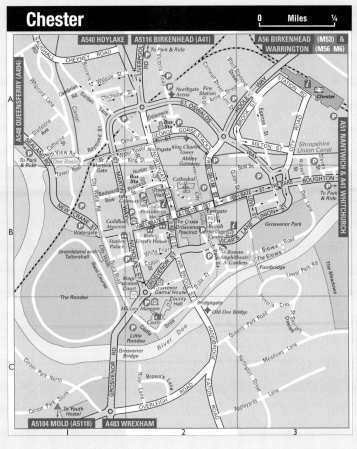

Lancaster

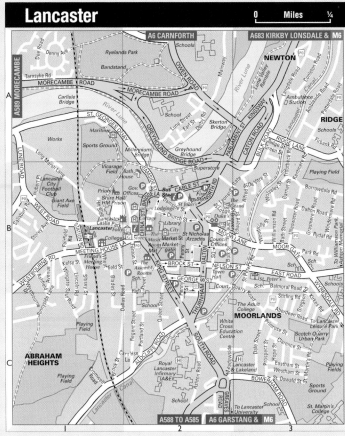

Chester

Abbey Gateway . . A2
Appleyards La . . . C3
Bedward Row B1
Bishop Lloyd's
    House 🏛 . . . B2
Black
    Diamond St A2
Bold Sq B3
Boughton B3
Bouverie St A1
Bridge St B2
Bridgegate C2
British Heritage
    Centre 🏛 B2
Brook St. A3
Brown's La. C2
Bus Station . . . A2/B2
Cambrian Rd A1
Canal St. A2
Castle 🏰 C2
Castle Dr C2
Cathedral ✝ B2
Catherine St. A1
Chester 🚉 A3
Cheyney Rd A1
Chichester St A1
City Rd A3
City Walls B1/B2
City Walls Rd B1
Cornwall St A1
County Hall C2
Cuppin St B2
Curzon Park
    North C1

Curzon Park
    South C1
Dee Basin A1
Dee La. B3
Delamere St A2
Duke St B2
Eastgate. B2
Eastgate St B2
Eaton Rd C2
Egerton St A3
Fire Station. A2
Foregate St B2
Frodsham St B2
Gamul House B2
Garden La A1
Gateway
    Theatre 🎭 . . . B2
George St A2
Gladstone Ave . . . A1
God's Providence
    House 🏛 B2
Gorse Stacks A2
Grandstand and
    Tattershall. B1
Grosvenor Bridge. C1
Grosvenor
    Museum 🏛 . . . B2
Grosvenor Park . . B3
Grosvenor
    Precinct B2
Grosvenor Rd. . . . C1
Grosvenor St B2
Groves Rd B3
Guildhall
    Museum 🏛 . . . B1
Handbridge C2

Hartington St C3
Hoole Way A2
Hunter St B2
Information Ctr 🛈 . A3
Information Ctr 🛈 . B2
King Charles'
    Tower ♦ A2
King St A2
Library B2
Little Roodee C2
Liverpool Rd A2
Love St B3
Lower Bridge St . . B2
Lower Park Rd . . . B3
Lyon St A2
Magistrates
    Court B2
Meadows La C3
Military
    Museum 🏛 . . . C2
Milton St A3
New Crane St B1
Nicholas St B2
Northgate. A2
Northgate
    Arena ♦ A2
Northgate St. A2
Nun's Rd B2
Old Dee Bridge ♦ . C2
Overleigh Rd C2
Park St. B2
Police Station 🏛 . . B2
Post Office 🏤 . . . B2
Princess St. B2
Queen St B2
Queen's Park Rd . C3

Race Course B1
Raymond St A1
River La C2
Roman
    Amphitheatre &
    Gardens 🏛 . . . B2
Russell St A3
St Anne St A2
St George's Cr . . . C3
St Martin's Gate . . A1
St Martin's Way . . A1
St Oswalds Way. . A2
Saughall Rd A1
Sealand Rd A1
South View Rd . . . A1
Stanley Palace 🏛 . B1
Station Rd A3
Steven St A3
The Bars B3
The Cross B2
The Groves B3
The Meadows B3
The Roodee B1
Tower Rd B1
Town Hall B2
Union St. B3
Vicar's La B2
Victoria Cr C3
Victoria Rd A2
Walpole St A1
Water Tower St. . . A1
Watergate B1
Watergate St B2
Whipcord La. A1
White Friars B2

Lancaster

Aberdeen Rd C3
Aldcliffe Rd C2
Alfred St. B3
Ambleside Rd. . . . A3
Ambulance
    Station A3
Ashfield Ave B1
Ashton Rd C2
Balmoral Rd. B3
Bath House 🏛 . . . B2
Bath St. B3
Blades St. B1
Borrowdale Rd. . . B3
Bowerham Rd . . . C3
Brewery La. B3
Bridge La. B2
Brock St. C1
Brook St C1
Bulk Rd A3
Bulk St. B2
Bus Station B2
Cable St. B2
Carlisle Bridge . . . A1
Carr House La . . . C2
Castle 🏰 B1
Castle Park B1
Caton Rd A3
China St. B2
Church St. B2
City Museum 🏛 . . B2
Clarence St C3
Coniston Rd A3
Cottage
    Museum 🏛 . . . B2
Council Offices. . . B2
Court B2
Cromwell Rd C1
Dale St. C3
Dallas Rd B1/C1
Dalton Rd. B3
Dalton Sq. B2
Damside St B2
De Vitre St B3
Dee Rd. A1
Denny Ave A1
Derby Rd A2
Duke's 🎭🎬 B2

Earl St A2
East Rd B3
Eastham St C3
Edward St B3
Fairfield Rd B1
Fenton St. B2
Firbank Rd A3
Fire Station B2
Folly Gallery 🏛 . . B2
Friend's Meeting
    House 🏛 B1
Garnet St. B3
George St B2
Giant Axe Field. . . B1
Gov. Offices B2
Grasmere Rd B3
Greaves Rd C2
Green St. A3
Gregson Rd C3
Greyhound
    Bridge Rd. A2
Greyhound Bridge A2
High St. B2
Hill Side B1
Hope St. C3
Hubert Pl B1
Information Ctr 🛈 . B2
Judges
    Lodgings 🏛 . . . B2
Kelsy St B1
Kentmere Rd B3
King St. B2
Kingsway A3
Kirkes Rd C2
Lancaster &
    Lakeland 🏥 . . . C3
Lancaster City
    Football Club. . . B1
Lancaster
    Station 🚉 B1
Langdale Rd. A3
Library B2
Lincoln Rd B1
Lodge St B2
Long Marsh La. . . B1
Lune Rd A1
Lune St A2
Lune Valley
    Ramble. A3

Mainway. A2
Maritime
    Museum 🏛 . . . A1
Market St. B2
Marketgate Shopping
    Centre B2
Meadowside C2
Meeting
    House La B1
Millennium
    Bridge A2
Moor Gate B3
Moor La. B3
Morecambe
    Rd. A1/A2
Nelson St B2
North Rd B2
Owen Rd A2
Park Rd B3
Parliament St A3
Patterdale Rd. . . . A3
Penny St B2
Police Station 🏛 . . B2
Portland St. C2
Post Office 🏤 . . . A3
Post Office 🏤 . . . B1
Post Office 🏤 . . . B2
Post Office 🏤 . . . B3
Post Office 🏤 . . . C3
Primrose St C3
Priory 🏛 B1
Prospect St C3
Quarry Rd B3
Queen St B2
Regent St. C2
Ridge La A3
Ridge St A3
Royal Lancaster
    Infirmary
    (A&E) 🏥 C2
Rydal Rd B3
Ryelands Park . . . A1
St. John's 🏛 B2
St. Nicholas Arcades
    Shopping
    Centre B2
St. Peter's Rd B3
St. Georges Quay. A1

St. Leonard's
    Gate. B2
St. Martin's
    College. C3
St. Martin's Rd . . . C3
St. Oswald St. . . . C3
St. Peter's ✝ B3
Salisbury Rd. B1
Scotch Quarry
    Urban Park. C3
Shire Hall/
    HM Prison B1
Sibsey St B1
Skerton Bridge . . . A2
South Rd C2
Station Rd B1
Stirling Rd C3
Storey Ave B1
Storey Gallery 🏛 . B2
Sunnyside La C1
Tarnsyke Rd A1
The Adult
    College. C3
The Assembly
    Rooms B2
The Grand 🎭 . . . B2
The Music
    Room 🎭 B2
Thurnham St C2
Town Hall B2
Troutbeck Rd B3
Ulleswater Rd. . . . B3
Vicarage Field . . . B1
West Rd B1
Westbourne Dr. . . C1
Westbourne Rd . . B1
Westham St C3
Wheatfield St B1
White Cross
    Education
    Centre C2
Williamson Rd . . . B3
Windermere Rd . . B3
Wingate-Saul Rd . B1
Wolseley St B3
Woodville St B3
Wyresdale Rd . . . C3

Leeds

0   Miles   ¼

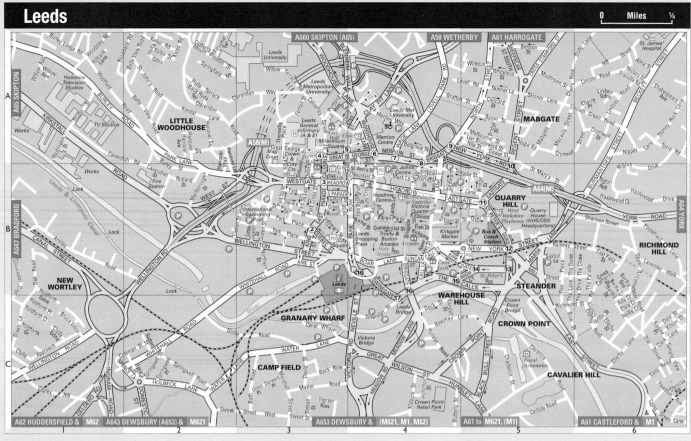

Liverpool

0 Miles ¼

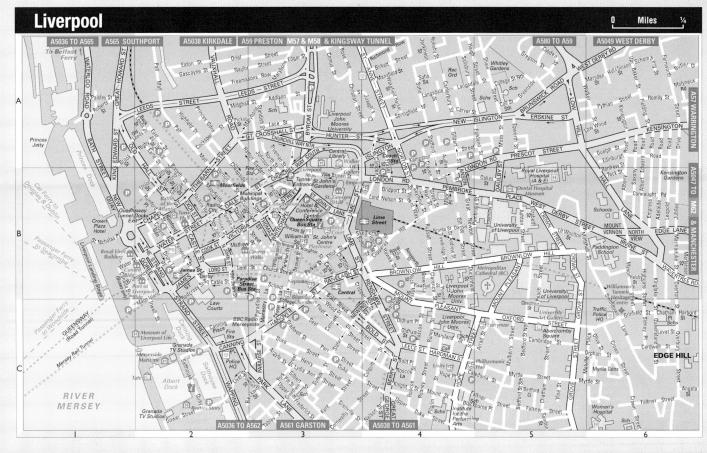

A5036 TO A565 | A565 SOUTHPORT | A5038 KIRKDALE | A59 PRESTON | M57 & M58 & KINGSWAY TUNNEL | A580 TO A59 | A5049 WEST DERBY

A57 WARRINGTON
A5047 TO M62 & MANCHESTER

EDGE HILL

RIVER MERSEY

A5036 TO A562 | A561 GARSTON | A5038 TO A561

Manchester

0   Miles   ¼

Manchester

Preston

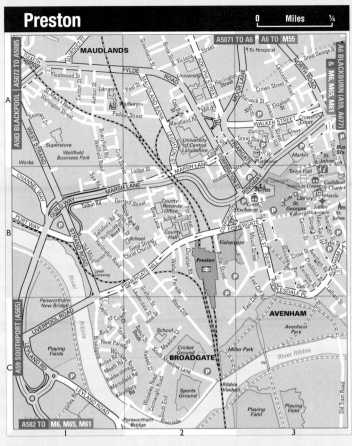

Miles 0 – ¼

Stoke-on-Trent (Hanley)

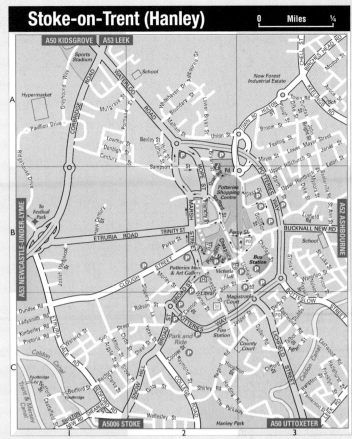

Miles 0 – ¼

Preston

Stoke-on-Trent (Hanley)

Sheffield

0   Miles   ¼

Sheffield

A

Aaron's Town Cumb 76 D3
Abbey Green Staffs 23 C5
Abbey Hey Gtr Man 41 E6
Abbey Hulton Stoke 22 E4
Abbey Village Lancs 46 F1
Abbeydale S Yorks 37 C6
Abbeydale Park S Yorks 37 C6
Abbeystead Lancs 52 E3
Abbeytown Cumb 69 A6
Aber-Cywarch Gwyn 8 E2
Aber-oer Wrex 19 F6
Aber-Tafol Gwyn 2 D3
Aberangell Powys 3 B7
Abercegir Powys 3 C7
Abercregan Denbs 19 F6
Aberdaron Gwyn 4 C3
Aberdesach Gwyn 14 D4
Aberdovey = Aberdyfi Gwyn 2 D3
Aberdyfi Gwyn 2 D3
Abererch Gwyn 5 A7
Aberffraw Angl 26 F4
Abergele Conwy 29 D9
Abergwyngregyn Gwyn 28 E2
Abergynolwyn Gwyn 2 B4
Aberhosan Powys 3 D7
Aberllefenni Gwyn 3 B6
Abermorddu Flints 19 C7
Abersoch Gwyn 5 C6
Abertridwr Powys 9 E5
Abney Derby 36 D3
Abraham Heights Lancs 51 C8
Abram Gtr Man 39 D9
Accrington Lancs 46 E4
Ackenthwaite Cumb 58 D4
Acrefair Wrex 19 F6
Acton Ches 21 D5
Acton Staffs 22 F2
Acton Wrex 19 D7
Acton Bridge Ches 33 D6
Acton Park Wrex 19 D7
Acton Trussell Staffs 13 E8
Adbaston Staffs 12 C5
Adderley Shrops 12 A5
Adderley Green Stoke 22 F4
Addingham W Yorks 55 F5
Adel W Yorks 49 C7
Adeney Telford 12 E4
Adlington Ches 35 C5
Adlington Lancs 39 B8
Admaston Telford 12 F2
Adswood Gtr Man 34 B4
Adwalton W Yorks 49 A6
Affetside Gtr Man 40 B4
Afon Eltha Wrex 19 F6
Afon-wen Flints 30 E4
Agbrigg W Yorks 43 A8
Agglethorpe N Yorks 61 C7
Aglionby Cumb 76 E1
Agneash I/Man 80 C4
Aigburth Mersey 32 B2
Aiketgate Cumb 70 B4
Aikhead Cumb 69 B7
Aikton Cumb 75 F5
Ainsdale Mersey 38 B3
Ainsdale-on-Sea Mersey 38 B2
Ainstable Cumb 71 B5
Ainsworth Gtr Man 40 C4
Aintree Mersey 38 E4
Aire View N Yorks 48 A1
Airton N Yorks 54 D1
Alberbury Shrops 10 F4
Albrighton Shrops 11 E6
Albyfield Cumb 71 A5
Aldcliffe Lancs 51 C8
Alder Forest Gtr Man 40 E3
Aldercar Derby 25 E6
Alderley Edge Ches 34 E3
Aldersey Green Ches 20 C2
Alderwasley Derby 24 D4
Aldford Ches 20 C1
Aldingham Cumb 50 A4
Aldoth Cumb 69 B5
Aldwark Derby 24 C2
Alfreton Derby 25 C6
Alkington Shrops 11 A7
Alkrington Garden Village Gtr Man 41 D6
Allenheads Northum 72 B5
Allensford Durham 73 B9
Allenwood Cumb 76 E2
Allerby Cumb 68 D4
Allerton Mersey 32 B3
Allerton W Yorks 48 D4
Allgreave Ches 35 F6
Allithwaite Cumb 58 E1
Allmore Green Staffs 13 E7
Allonby Cumb 68 C4
Allostock Ches 34 E1
Allscott Telford 12 F2
Alltami Flints 18 A5
Almagill Dumf/Gal 74 A1
Almington Staffs 12 B4
Almondbury W Yorks 42 A5
Alport Derby 24 B2
Alpraham Ches 20 C4
Alsager Ches 22 D2
Alsagers Bank Staffs 22 E2
Alsop en le Dale Derby 23 C9
Alston Cumb 72 B2
Alstonefield Staffs 23 C8
Alt Hill Gtr Man 41 D7
Altham Lancs 46 D4
Altofts W Yorks 49 F9
Alton Derby 25 B5
Alton Staffs 23 F7
Altrincham Gtr Man 34 B2
Alvanley Ches 32 E4
Alverthorpe W Yorks 49 F8
Alwoodley W Yorks 49 B7
Alwoodley Gates W Yorks 49 B8
Alwoodley Park W Yorks 49 B7
Ambergate Derby 25 D5
Ambler Thorn W Yorks 48 E3
Ambleside Cumb 64 F2
Amlwch Angl 27 A5
Amlwch Port Angl 27 A6
Anchorsholme Blackp'l 44 B3
Ancoats Gtr Man 41 E6
Anderton Ches 33 D7
Anderton's Mill Lancs 39 B7
Andreas I/Man 80 B4
Anfield Mersey 32 A2
Angerton Cumb 74 E4
Angram N Yorks 60 A3
Ankerbold Derby 25 A5
Annan Dumf/Gal 74 C3
Annaside Cumb 56 C2
Annesley Notts 25 D8
Annesley Woodhouse Notts 25 D7
Ansdell Lancs 44 E3
Anthorn Cumb 74 E3
Antrobus Ches 33 D7
Apeton Staffs 13 E7
Apperknowle Derby 37 D7
Apperley Bridge W Yorks 49 C5
Appersett N Yorks 60 B3
Appleby-in-Westmorland Cumb 65 B8
Applehaigh W Yorks 43 B8
Applethwaite Cumb 63 A8
Appleton Halton 32 B5
Appleton Park Warrington 33 C7
Appleton Thorn Warrington 33 C7
Appletreewick N Yorks 55 C5
Appley Bridge Lancs 39 C7
Arbourthorne S Yorks 37 B7
Arddleen Powys 10 E2
Ardwick Gtr Man 41 E6
Arkholme Lancs 52 A3
Arkle Town N Yorks 67 F8
Arkleby Cumb 69 D5
Arkleside N Yorks 61 D6
Arkwright Town Derby 37 E8
Arlecdon Cumb 62 C3
Arley Ches 33 C8
Arley Green Ches 33 C8
Armathwaite Cumb 71 B5
Armitage Bridge W Yorks 42 B4
Armley W Yorks 49 D7
Arnaby Cumb 56 D4
Arncliffe N Yorks 54 A2
Arnfield Derby 42 E2
Arnside Cumb 58 E3
Arowry Wrex 11 A6
Arrad Foot Cumb 57 D7
Arrowe Hill Mersey 31 B7
Arrunden W Yorks 42 C4
Arthill Ches 34 B1
Arthington W Yorks 49 B7
Arthog Gwyn 6 F4
Asby Cumb 62 B4
Ash Bank Staffs 22 E4
Ash Magna Shrops 11 A8
Ash Parva Shrops 11 A8
Ashbank Ches 21 C6
Ashbank Ches 33 E7
Ashbourne Derby 24 E1
Ashday W Yorks 48 F4
Ashford in the water Derby 36 F3
Ashgate Derby 37 E7
Ashley Ches 41 E7
Ashley Staffs 12 A5
Ashley Dale Staffs 12 A5
Ashley Heath Gtr Man 34 B2
Ashley Heath Staffs 12 B3
Ashover Derby 25 B5
Ashton Ches 32 F5
Ashton-in-Makerfield Gtr Man 39 E8
Ashton-under-Lyne Gtr Man 41 E7
Ashton upon Mersey Gtr Man 34 A2
Ashurst Mersey 39 C6
Ashway Gap Gtr Man 42 D2
Askham Cumb 65 B5
Askham in Furness Cumb 57 E5
Askrigg N Yorks 60 B4
Askwith N Yorks 55 F7
Aspatria Cumb 69 C5
Aspley Nott'ham 25 F8
Aspull Gtr Man 40 C1
Aspull Common Gtr Man 40 E1
Astbury Ches 22 B2
Astley Gtr Man 40 D3
Astley Shrops 11 E7
Astley Bridge Gtr Man 40 B3
Astley Green Gtr Man 40 E3
Astmoor Halton 33 C5
Aston Ches 21 E5
Aston Ches 33 D6
Aston Derby 36 C3
Aston Flints 31 F8
Aston Shrops 11 C7
Aston S Yorks 37 C9
Aston Staffs 21 F8
Aston-by-Stone Staffs 13 B8
Aston Juxta Mondrum Ches 21 C5
Aston Square Shrops 10 C3
Astwith Derby 25 B6
Athersley North S Yorks 43 C8
Athersley South S Yorks 43 C9
Atherton Gtr Man 40 D2
Atlow Derby 24 E2
Attercliffe S Yorks 37 B7
Audenshaw Gtr Man 41 E7
Audlem Ches 21 F6
Audley Staffs 22 D1
Audmore Staffs 13 D6
Aughertree Cumb 69 D8
Aughton Lancs 38 C4
Aughton Lancs 52 B3
Aughton S Yorks 37 B9
Aughton Park Lancs 38 C5
Ault Hucknall Derby 25 A7
Austerlands Gtr Man 41 C8
Austwick N Yorks 53 B7
Awsworth Notts 25 F7
Axton Flints 30 C4
Ayle Northum 72 B2
Aysgarth N Yorks 61 C6
Ayside Cumb 58 D1

B

Babbinswood Shrops 10 B3
Babell Flints 31 E5
Babylon Flints 19 B7
Bachau Angl 27 C5
Back o' th' Brook Staffs 23 D7
Backbarrow Cumb 57 D8
Backbower Gtr Man 41 F8
Backford Ches 32 E3
Backford Cross Ches 32 E2
Bacup Lancs 47 F6
Baddeley Green Stoke 22 D4
Baggrow Cumb 69 C6
Bagillt Flints 31 D6
Bagley Shrops 11 C5
Bagley W Yorks 49 C6
Bagnall Staffs 22 D4
Bagshaw Derby 35 C8
Bagslate Moor Gtr Man 41 B6
Bagthorpe Notts 25 D7
Baguley Gtr Man 34 B3
Baildon W Yorks 48 C5
Baildon Green W Yorks 48 C4
Bailey Cumb 76 A3
Bailiff Bridge W Yorks 48 F4
Bailrigg Lancs 51 D8
Bainbridge N Yorks 60 B4
Bakewell Derby 36 F4
Bala Gwyn 8 A3
Balderstone Gtr Man 41 B7
Balderstone Lancs 46 D1
Balderton Ches 19 B8
Baldingstone Gtr Man 41 B5
Baldrine I/Man 80 C4
Baldwin I/Man 80 C3
Baldwinholme Cumb 70 A1
Baldwin's Gate Staffs 13 A5
Ball Shrops 10 C3
Ball Green Stoke 22 D3
Ball Haye Green Staffs 23 C5
Ball o' Ditton Halton 32 B5
Ballabeg I/Man 80 D2
Ballacannel I/Man 80 C4
Ballajora I/Man 80 B4
Ballaleigh I/Man 80 C3
Ballamodha I/Man 80 D2
Ballaquine I/Man 80 C4
Ballasalla I/Man 80 B3
Ballasalla I/Man 80 D2
Ballaugh I/Man 80 B3
Ballaveare I/Man 80 D3
Ballidon Derby 24 D2
Balmer Heath Shrops 11 B5
Balterley Staffs 21 D8
Balterley Heath Staffs 21 D7
Bamber Bridge Lancs 45 E8
Bamford Derby 36 C4
Bamford Gtr Man 41 B6
Bamfurlong Gtr Man 39 D8
Bampton Cumb 65 C5
Bampton Grange Cumb 65 C5
Bandrake Head Cumb 57 C7
Bangor Gwyn 27 E8
Bangor-is-y-coed Wrex 19 F7
Bangor's Green Lancs 38 C4
Bank End Cumb 57 C5
Bank Fold Blackb'n 46 F3
Bank Hey Blackb'n 46 D2
Bank Lane Gtr Man 41 A5
Bank Newton N Yorks 54 E2
Bank Top Gtr Man 40 B3
Bank Top Lancs 39 C7
Bank Top W Yorks 48 F4
Bank Top W Yorks 49 C5
Banks Cumb 76 D4
Banks Lancs 44 F4
Bantam Grove W Yorks 49 E7
Barber Booth Derby 36 C2
Barber Green Cumb 58 D1
Barbon Cumb 59 D6
Barbridge Ches 21 C5
Barclose Cumb 76 D1
Barcroft W Yorks 48 C2
Barden N Yorks 55 D5
Barden N Yorks 61 B8
Bardon Mill Northum 77 D8
Bardsea Cumb 57 F7
Bardsey W Yorks 49 B9
Bardsley Gtr Man 41 D7
Bare Lancs 51 C8
Barepot Cumb 68 F3
Barhough Northum 72 A1
Barkers Green Shrops 11 C7
Barkisland W Yorks 42 A3
Barlaston Staffs 13 A7
Barley Lancs 47 B5
Barlow Derby 37 E6
Barlow Moor Gtr Man 34 A3
Barmouth Gwyn 6 E4
Barnard Castle Durham 67 C9
Barnoldswick Lancs 54 F1
Barnoldswick N Yorks 53 A5
Barnsley S Yorks 43 C9
Barnston Mersey 31 C7
Barnton Ches 33 D7
Barras Cumb 66 D4
Barregarrow I/Man 80 C3
Barrow Lancs 46 C3
Barrow Bridge Gtr Man 40 B2
Barrow Hill Derby 37 D8
Barrow-in-Furness Cumb 50 A3
Barrow Island Cumb 50 B2
Barrow Nook Lancs 39 D5
Barrowford Lancs 47 C6
Barrows Green Ches 21 C6
Barrows Green Cumb 58 C4
Barrow's Green Halton 33 B5
Barrows Green Notts 25 D6
Barthomley Ches 21 D8
Barton Ches 20 D1
Barton Cumb 64 A4
Barton Lancs 38 C4
Barton Lancs 45 C7
Barton Moss Gtr Man 40 E3
Barton upon Irwell Gtr Man 40 E4
Barugh S Yorks 43 C8
Barugh Green S Yorks 43 C8
Baschurch Shrops 11 D5
Basford Staffs 22 E3
Bashall Eaves Lancs 46 B2
Baslow Derby 36 E4
Bassenthwaite Cumb 69 E7
Baswich Staffs 13 D8
Bate Heath Ches 33 D8
Batemoor S Yorks 37 C7
Batley W Yorks 49 F6
Batley Carr W Yorks 49 F6
Battlefield Shrops 11 E7
Battyeford W Yorks 49 F5
Baxenden Lancs 46 E4
Bay Gate Lancs 53 F7
Baybridge Northum 73 A7
Baycliff Cumb 50 A4
Bayles Cumb 72 B2
Beaconside Staffs 13 D8
Beamsley N Yorks 55 E5
Beardwood Blackb'n 46 E2
Bearsbridge Northum 77 E8
Bearstone Shrops 12 B3
Beau Vale Notts 25 E8
Beauchief S Yorks 37 C6
Beaumaris Angl 28 D2
Beaumont Cumb 75 E6
Beauvale Notts 25 E7
Bebington Mersey 32 C1
Becconsall Lancs 45 F5
Beck Cumb 62 C4
Beck Bottom W Yorks 49 F7
Beck Foot Cumb 59 A6
Beck Side Cumb 57 D5
Beckermet Cumb 62 E3
Beckermonds N Yorks 60 D3
Beckfoot Cumb 56 C4
Beckfoot Cumb 63 F6
Beckfoot Cumb 68 B4
Beckoes Cumb 70 F3
Becks W Yorks 48 A2
Beckside Cumb 59 C6
Beddgelert Gwyn 15 E7
Bedford Gtr Man 40 E2
Bedford Gtr Man 40 E2
Bednall Staffs 13 E9
Beech Staffs 13 A7
Beech Hill Gtr Man 39 C8
Beechwood Halton 33 C5
Beechwood W Yorks 49 C8
Beeley Derby 36 F5
Beeston Ches 20 C3
Beeston W Yorks 49 D7
Beeston Hill W Yorks 49 D7
Beeston Park Side W Yorks 49 E7
Beetham Cumb 58 E3
Beffcote Staffs 13 E6
Beggarington Hill W Yorks 49 F7
Beighton S Yorks 37 C8
Belah Cumb 75 E7
Belfield Gtr Man 41 B7
Belgrano Conwy 29 D9
Belgrave Blackb'n 46 F2
Bell Busk N Yorks 54 D2
Bell o'th'Hill Ches 20 E3
Belle Isle W Yorks 49 E8
Belle Vale Mersey 32 B3
Belle Vue Cumb 68 E5
Belle Vue Cumb 75 E7
Belle Vue W Yorks 43 A8
Bellerby N Yorks 61 B8
Bellerby Camp N Yorks 61 B7
Belmont Blackb'n 40 A2
Belmont Derby 37 E6
Belper Derby 25 E5
Belper Lane End Derby 24 E4
Belthorn Lancs 46 F3
Beltingham Northum 77 D8
Ben Rhydding W Yorks 55 F6
Benchill Gtr Man 34 B3
Benllech Angl 27 C7
Bent Gate Lancs 46 F4
Bentilee Stoke 22 E4
Berkeley Towers Ches 21 D6
Berrier Cumb 70 F2
Berry Brow W Yorks 42 B4
Berry Hill Stoke 22 E3
Bersham Wrex 19 E7
Berthengam Flints 30 D4
Berwyn Denbs 18 F4
Bescar Lancs 38 B4
Besom Hill Gtr Man 41 C8
Besses o'th' Barn Gtr Man 41 C5
Bethania Gwyn 15 D8
Bethania Gwyn 16 E2
Bethel Angl 26 E4
Bethel Gwyn 15 A6
Bethel Gwyn 8 A4
Bethesda Gwyn 28 F2
Betley Staffs 21 E8
Bettisfield Wrex 11 A6
Betton Shrops 12 A3
Bettws Gwerfil Goch Denbs 17 E8
Betws Garmon Gwyn 15 C6
Betws-y-coed Conwy 16 C3
Betws-yn-Rhos Conwy 29 E8
Bewaldeth Cumb 69 E7
Bewcastle Cumb 76 B4
Bewerley N Yorks 55 C7
Bewsey Warrington 33 B6
Bibbington Derby 35 D8
Bickershaw Gtr Man 40 D1
Bickerstaffe Lancs 39 D5
Bickerton Ches 20 D3
Bickley Moss Ches 20 E3
Bickley Town Ches 20 E3
Bicton Shrops 11 E5
Bicton Heath Shrops 11 F6
Biddulph Staffs 22 C3
Biddulph Moor Staffs 22 C4
Bidston Mersey 31 A7
Bierley W Yorks 49 D5
Big Mancot Flints 31 F8
Biggar Cumb 50 B2
Biggin Derby 23 C9
Biggin Derby 24 E3
Biglands Cumb 69 A8
Bigrigg Cumb 62 D3
Bilborough Nott'ham 25 F8
Billinge Mersey 39 D7
Billington Lancs 46 C3
Bilsborrow Lancs 45 C7
Bingley W Yorks 48 C4
Birch Gtr Man 41 C6
Birch Green Lancs 39 C6
Birch Heath Ches 20 B3
Birch Hill Ches 32 E5
Birch Vale Derby 35 B7
Birchall Staffs 23 D5
Birchencliffe W Yorks 42 A4
Birchover Derby 24 B2
Birchwood Warrington 33 A8
Birdholme Derby 37 E7
Birds Edge W Yorks 43 C6
Birdwell S Yorks 43 D8
Birkacre Lancs 39 B8
Birkby Cumb 68 D4
Birkby W Yorks 42 A4
Birkdale Mersey 38 B3
Birkenhead Mersey 31 B8
Birkenshaw W Yorks 49 E6
Birkett Mire Cumb 64 B1
Birks W Yorks 49 E7
Birkshaw Northum 77 C8
Birley Carr S Yorks 37 A6
Birley Edge S Yorks 37 A6
Birleyhay Derby 37 C7
Birstall Smithies W Yorks 49 E6
Birstwith N Yorks 55 D8
Birtle Gtr Man 41 B5
Bishop's Offley Staffs 13 C5
Bispham Blackp'l 44 B3
Bispham Green Lancs 39 B6
Black Hill W Yorks 48 B3
Black Lane Gtr Man 40 C4
Black Lane Ends Lancs 47 B7
Black Moor W Yorks 49 C7
Black Pole Lancs 45 D6
Blackbeck Cumb 62 E3
Blackbrook Derby 24 E4
Blackbrook Derby 35 C8
Blackbrook Mersey 39 E7
Blackbrook Staffs 12 A5
Blackburn Blackb'n 46 E2
Blackburn S Yorks 37 A7
Blackden Heath Ches 34 E2
Blackdyke Cumb 69 A5
Blackenhall Ches 21 E7
Blacker S Yorks 43 C8
Blacker Hill S Yorks 43 D9
Blackford Cumb 75 D7
Blackford Bridge Gtr Man 40 C4
Blackleach Lancs 45 D6
Blackley Gtr Man 41 D6
Blackley W Yorks 42 A4
Blackmoor Gtr Man 40 D2
Blackmoorfoot W Yorks 42 B4
Blacko Lancs 47 B6
Blackpool Blackp'l 44 C3
Blackrod Gtr Man 39 B9
Blackshaw Dumf/Gal 74 C1
Blackshaw Head W Yorks 47 F7
Blacksnape Blackb'n 46 F3
Blackwell Cumb 70 A3
Blackwell Derby 25 C6
Blackwell Derby 36 E2
Blackwood Warrington 33 A7
Blackwood Hill Staffs 22 C4
Blacon Ches 32 F2
Blaenau Dolwyddelan Conwy 16 D2
Blaenau Ffestiniog Gwyn 16 E2
Blaenau Uchaf Wrex 19 F6
Blagill Cumb 72 B2
Blaguegate Lancs 39 C6
Blakeley Lane Staffs 23 E5
Blakelow Ches 21 D6
Blanchland Northum 73 A7
Bland Hill N Yorks 55 E8
Blawith Cumb 57 D5
Blazefield N Yorks 55 B7
Bleach Green Cumb 62 C2
Bleak Hey Nook Gtr Man 42 C2
Bleasdale Lancs 45 A8
Bleatarn Cumb 66 D2
Blencarn Cumb 71 E7
Blencogo Cumb 69 B6
Blennerhasset Cumb 69 C6
Bletchley Shrops 12 B2
Blindcrake Cumb 69 E6
Blitterlees Cumb 68 A5
Blore Staffs 23 E8
Blowick Mersey 38 A4
Blubberhouses N Yorks 55 D7
Blundell's Hill Mersey 32 A4
Blundellsands Mersey 38 E3
Blurton Stoke 22 F3
Blychau Conwy 17 B7
Blymhill Staffs 13 F6
Blymhill Common Staffs 13 F5
Blythe Bridge Staffs 22 F5
Blythe Marsh Staffs 22 F5
Boar's Head Gtr Man 39 C8
Bodedern Angl 26 C3
Bodelwyddan Denbs 30 D2
Bodewryd Angl 26 A4
Bodfari Denbs 30 E3
Bodffordd Angl 27 D5
Bodlith Powys 9 C9
Bodlondeb Conwy 29 E6
Bodnant Conwy 29 E6
Boduan Gwyn 5 A6
Bogend Notts 25 E7
Bogthorn W Yorks 48 C2
Boholt Gtr Man 40 B4
Bold Heath Mersey 33 B5
Boldron Durham 67 D8
Bolehill Derby 24 C3
Bolehill S Yorks 37 C7
Bollihope Durham 73 E8
Bollington Ches 35 D5
Bollington Cross Ches 35 D5
Bolsover Derby 37 E9
Bolster Moor W Yorks 42 A3
Bolsterstone S Yorks 43 E7
Bolton Cumb 65 B8
Bolton Gtr Man 40 C3
Bolton W Yorks 48 C5
Bolton Abbey N Yorks 55 E5
Bolton Bridge N Yorks 55 E5
Bolton by Bowland Lancs 53 F7
Bolton Green Lancs 39 A8
Bolton-le-Sands Lancs 51 B8
Bolton Low Houses Cumb 69 C7
Bolton New Houses Cumb 69 C7
Bolton Town End Lancs 51 B8
Bolton Wood Lane Cumb 69 C8
Bolton Woods W Yorks 48 C5
Boltonfellend Cumb 76 C2
Boltongate Cumb 69 C7
Boltshope Park Durham 73 B6
Bomby Cumb 65 C5
Bomere Heath Shrops 11 E6
Bonc Wrex 9 A8
Bonds Lancs 45 A6
Bonning Gate Cumb 58 A3
Bonsall Derby 24 C3
Bont Dolgadfan Powys 3 C8
Bont-goch Ceredig'n 2 F4
Bont-newydd Conwy 30 E2
Bont Newydd Gwyn 16 F2
Bontddu Gwyn 6 E5
Bontnewydd Gwyn 15 C5
Bontuchel Denbs 18 C2
Bonwm Denbs 18 F3
Boon Hill Staffs 22 D2
Boot Cumb 63 F6
Booth W Yorks 48 E2
Booth Bank Ches 34 B1
Booth Green Ches 35 C5
Booth Wood W Yorks 42 A2
Boothen Stoke 22 F3
Boothroyd W Yorks 49 F6
Boothsdale Ches 33 F5
Boothstown Gtr Man 40 D3
Boothtown W Yorks 48 E3
Bootle Cumb 56 C3
Bootle Mersey 38 F3
Boots Green Ches 34 E2
Booze N Yorks 67 F8
Border Cumb 74 F3
Bordley N Yorks 54 C2
Borras Wrex 19 D7
Borth Ceredig'n 2 E3
Borth-y-Gest Gwyn 6 A3
Borthwnog Gwyn 6 E5
Borwick Lancs 52 A2
Borwick Rails Cumb 56 E4
Boscomoor Staffs 13 F8
Bosley Ches 22 A4
Bostock Green Ches 33 F8
Botcherby Cumb 75 E8
Bothel Cumb 69 D6
Bottom Boat W Yorks 49 F9
Bottom House Staffs 23 D6
Bottom of Hutton Lancs 45 E6
Bottom o'th'Moor Gtr Man 40 B2
Botwnnog Gwyn 4 B5
Boughton Heath Ches 20 A1
Boulder Clough W Yorks 48 F2
Boundary Staffs 23 F5
Boustead Hill Cumb 75 E5
Bouth Cumb 57 C7
Bouthwaite N Yorks 55 A6
Bow Cumb 75 E6
Bowbank Durham 66 B6
Bowbrook Shrops 11 F6
Bowdon Gtr Man 34 B2
Bowers Staffs 13 A6
Bowes Durham 67 D7
Bowe's Gate Ches 20 C4
Bowgreave Lancs 45 B6
Bowgreen Gtr Man 34 B2
Bowker's Green Lancs 38 D5
Bowland Bridge Cumb 58 C2
Bowlee Gtr Man 41 C5
Bowlees Durham 73 F6
Bowling W Yorks 49 D5
Bowling Bank Wrex 19 E9
Bowmanstead Cumb 57 A7
Bowness-on-Solway Cumb 78 D4
Bowness-on-Windermere Cumb 58 A2
Bowring Park Mersey 32 B3
Bowscale Cumb 70 E2
Bowston Cumb 58 A3
Boythorpe Derby 37 E7
Braaid I/Man 80 D3
Bracewell Lancs 53 F9
Bracken Hall W Yorks 42 A5
Bracken Hill S Yorks 43 E8
Bracken Hill W Yorks 49 F5
Bracken Park W Yorks 49 B9
Brackenber Cumb 66 C2
Brackenfield Derby 25 C5
Brackenlands Cumb 69 B8
Brackenthwaite Cumb 63 B6
Brackenthwaite Cumb 69 B8
Bradbourne Derby 24 D2
Bradda I/Man 80 E1
Braddocks Hay Staffs 22 C3
Bradeley Stoke 22 D3
Bradfield Green Ches 21 C6
Bradford Gtr Man 41 E6
Bradford W Yorks 49 D5
Bradgate S Yorks 37 A8
Bradley Ches 33 D5
Bradley Derby 24 E2
Bradley Staffs 13 E7
Bradley W Yorks 48 F5
Bradley Wrex 19 D7
Bradley Fold Gtr Man 40 C4
Bradley Green Ches 20 E3
Bradley in the Moors Staffs 23 F7
Bradley Mills W Yorks 42 A5
Bradley Mount Ches 35 D5
Bradnop Staffs 23 C6
Bradshaw Gtr Man 40 B3
Bradshaw W Yorks 42 B3
Bradshaw W Yorks 48 D3
Bradwall Green Ches 21 B8
Bradway S Yorks 37 C6
Bradwell Derby 36 C3
Bradwell Staffs 22 E2
Braichmelyn Gwyn 15 A8
Braidley N Yorks 61 E6
Brailsford Derby 24 F3
Brailsford Green Derby 24 F2
Braithwaite Cumb 63 B7
Braithwaite W Yorks 48 B2
Bramelane N Yorks 55 E8
Bramhall Gtr Man 34 B4
Bramhall Moor Gtr Man 35 B5
Bramhall Park Gtr Man 34 B4
Bramhope W Yorks 49 B7
Bramley W Yorks 49 D6
Bramley Head N Yorks 55 D6
Bramley Vale Derby 25 A7
Brampton Cumb 65 B8
Brampton Cumb 76 D3
Brampton Derby 37 D7
Brandingill Cumb 62 A5
Bransty Cumb 62 C2
Branthwaite Cumb 62 B4
Branthwaite Cumb 69 D8
Branthwaite Edge Cumb 62 B4
Brassey Green Ches 20 B3
Brassington Derby 24 D2
Braystones Cumb 62 E3
Breaden Heath Shrops 11 A5
Brearley W Yorks 48 E2
Brecks S Yorks 37 A9
Bredbury Gtr Man 35 A5
Bredbury Green Gtr Man 35 A5
Breightmet Gtr Man 40 C3
Brereton Green Ches 21 B8
Brereton Heath Ches 22 B2
Bretherton Lancs 45 F6
Bretton Derby 36 D4
Bretton Flints 19 B8
Brick Houses S Yorks 37 C6
Bride I/Man 80 A4
Bridekirk Cumb 68 E5
Bridge End Cumb 70 B2
Bridge End Durham 73 D8
Bridge End Flints 19 C7
Bridge Trafford Ches 32 E4
Bridgefoot Cumb 68 F4
Bridgehouse Gate N Yorks 55 B7
Bridgemont Derby 35 C7
Bridgend Cumb 64 D3
Briercliffe Lancs 47 B5
Brierfield Lancs 47 C6
Briery Cumb 63 B8
Briestfield W Yorks 43 A6
Brigham Cumb 63 B8
Brigham Cumb 68 E4
Brighouse W Yorks 48 F4
Brightgate Derby 24 C3
Brightholmlee S Yorks 43 F7
Brighton le Sands Mersey 38 E3
Brightside S Yorks 37 B7
Brignall Durham 67 D9
Brigsteer Cumb 58 C3
Brimington Derby 37 E8
Brimington Common Derby 37 E8
Brimstage Mersey 31 C8
Brincliffe S Yorks 37 B6
Brindle Lancs 45 F8
Brindle Heath Gtr Man 41 E5
Brindley Ches 20 D4
Brindley Ford Stoke 22 D3
Brineton Staffs 13 F6
Brinnington Gtr Man 35 A5
Brinscall Lancs 46 F1
Brinsley Notts 25 E7
Brinsworth S Yorks 37 B8
Brisco Cumb 70 A3
Britannia Lancs 47 F6
Brithdir Denbs 7 E7
Broad Carr W Yorks 42 A3
Broad Clough Lancs 47 F6
Broad Green Mersey 32 B3
Broad Meadow Staffs 22 E2
Broad Oak Cumb 56 B3
Broad Oak Mersey 39 E7
Broadbottom Gtr Man 41 F8
Broadfield Gtr Man 41 B5
Broadfield Lancs 45 F8
Broadfield Lancs 46 E3
Broadhalgh Gtr Man 41 B6
Broadheath Gtr Man 34 B2
Broadholm Derby 25 E5
Broadley Gtr Man 41 A6
Broadoak Park Gtr Man 40 D4
Broadwath Cumb 76 E2
Brock Lancs 45 B7
Brockholes W Yorks 42 B4
Brockhurst Derby 24 B4
Brocklebank Cumb 69 C9
Brocklehirst Dumf/Gal 74 B1
Brockleymoor Cumb 70 D4
Brockton Staffs 13 B6
Brockton Telford 12 E4
Brocton Staffs 13 E9
Broken Cross Ches 33 E8
Broken Cross Ches 34 D4
Bromborough Mersey 32 C2
Bromfield Cumb 69 B6
Bromley Cross Gtr Man 40 B3
Bromstead Heath Staffs 13 E5
Bron-y-main Powys 9 F8
Bronaber Gwyn 7 B6
Bronington Wrex 11 A6
Bronygarth Shrops 10 A2
Brook Bottom Derby 35 B6
Brook Bottom Gtr Man 41 D8
Brookbottoms Gtr Man 40 A4
Brookfield Derby 42 E2
Brookfield Lancs 45 D8
Brookfoot W Yorks 48 F4
Brookhouse Blackb'n 46 E2
Brookhouse Ches 35 D5
Brookhouse Lancs 52 C2
Brookhouse Green Ches 22 B2
Brookhouses Derby 35 B7
Brookhouses Staffs 23 F5
Brookhurst Mersey 32 C1
Brooklands Gtr Man 34 A2
Brooklands Shrops 20 F3
Brooklands W Yorks 49 C8
Brookside Derby 37 E6
Brookvale Halton 33 C5
Broom Cumb 65 B8
Broom S Yorks 37 A8
Broomedge Warrington 33 B9
Broomfield Cumb 70 B1
Broomfields Shrops 11 E5
Broomhill Notts 25 E8
Brotherlee Durham 73 D7
Brothybeck Cumb 70 C2
Brough Cumb 66 D3
Brough Derby 36 C3
Brough Sowerby Cumb 66 D3
Broughall Shrops 20 F4
Brougham Cumb 71 F5
Broughton Flints 19 B7
Broughton Lancs 45 C7
Broughton N Yorks 54 E2
Broughton Beck Cumb 57 D6
Broughton Cross Cumb 68 E4
Broughton in Furness Cumb 57 C5
Broughton Mills Cumb 57 B5
Broughton Moor Cumb 68 E4
Broughton Park Gtr Man 41 D5
Browhouses Dumf/Gal 75 D5
Brown Edge Lancs 38 B4
Brown Edge Mersey 32 A4
Brown Edge Staffs 22 D4
Brown Heath Ches 20 A2
Brown Knowl Ches 20 D2
Brown Lees Staffs 22 C3
Brownber Cumb 66 E2
Brownheath Shrops 11 C6
Brownhill Blackb'n 46 D2
Brownhill Shrops 11 D5
Brownlow Gtr Man 39 D7
Brownlow Fold Gtr Man 40 B3
Brown's Bank Ches 21 F5
Brownside Lancs 47 D6
Broxstowe Nott'ham 25 F8

N

Nab Wood W Yorks 48 C4
Nab's Head Lancs 46 E1
Nangreaves Lancs 41 A5
Nanhoron Gwyn 5 B5
Nannerch Flints 31 F5
Nant Denbs 18 C4
Nant Alyn Flints 18 A4
Nant Mawr Flints 19 B6
Nant Peris Gwyn 15 C7
Nant-y-Caws Shrops 10 C2
Nant-y-felin Conwy 28 E3
Nant-y-gollen Shrops 10 A1
Nant-y-pandy Conwy 28 E3
Nantglyn Denbs 17 B8
Nantlle Gwyn 15 D6
Nantmawr Shrops 10 D2
Nantmor Gwyn 15 E8
Nantwich Ches 21 D6
Nappa N Yorks 53 E9
Nasareth Gwyn 14 D5
Nateby Cumb 66 E3
Nateby Lancs 45 B6
Natland Cumb 58 C4
Nealhouse Cumb 70 A1
Near Sawrey Cumb 57 A8
Nebo Angl 27 A6
Nebo Conwy 16 C4
Nebo Gwyn 15 D5
Nefyn Gwyn 14 F2
Nelson Lancs 47 C6
Nenthall Cumb 72 B3
Nenthead Cumb 72 C3
Nepgill Cumb 68 F4
Nercwys Flints 18 B5
Nesfield N Yorks 55 F5
Ness Ches 31 D8
Nesscliffe Shrops 10 E4
Nessholt Ches 31 D8
Neston Ches 31 D7
Nether Alderley Ches 34 D3
Nether Booth Derby 36 B2
Nether Burrow Lancs 59 E6
Nether Edge S Yorks 37 C6
Nether End Derby 36 E5
Nether End W Yorks 43 C7
Nether Heage Derby 25 D5
Nether Hesleden N Yorks 60 F3
Nether Kellet Lancs 52 B2
Nether Moor Derby 25 A5
Nether Padley Derby 36 D4
Nether Row Cumb 70 D1
Nether Wasdale Cumb 62 F5
Nether Welton Cumb 70 B2
Nether Yeadon W Yorks 49 C5
Netherby Cumb 75 B7
Netherby N Yorks 49 A8
Netherley Mersey 32 B3
Netheroyd Hill W Yorks 42 A4
Netherthong W Yorks 42 C4
Netherthorpe Derby 37 E8
Netherton Ches 32 D5
Netherton Cumb 68 D3
Netherton Mersey 38 D4
Netherton W Yorks 42 B4
Netherton W Yorks 43 A7
Nethertown Cumb 62 E2
Nethertown Lancs 46 C3
New Bolsover Derby 37 E9
New Boston Mersey 39 E8
New Brighton Flints 18 A5
New Brighton Mersey 38 F3
New Brighton N Yorks 54 E2
New Brighton W Yorks 48 C4
New Brighton W Yorks 49 E7
New Brighton Wrex 19 D6
New Brimington Derby 37 E8
New Brinsley Notts 25 D7
New Broughton Wrex 19 D7
New Bury Gtr Man 40 C3
New Cowper Cumb 69 B5
New Delph Gtr Man 42 C1
New Eastwood Notts 25 E7
New Farnley W Yorks 49 D6
New Ferry Mersey 32 B1
New Hall Warrington 33 B6
New Hall Hey Lancs 47 F5
New Horwich Derby 35 C7
New Houghton Derby 25 A7
New Houghton Derby 25 A8
New Houses Gtr Man 39 D8
New Hutton Cumb 58 B5
New Lane Lancs 39 B5
New Lane End Warrington 40 F1
New Lodge S Yorks 43 C8
New Longton Lancs 45 E7
New Marton Shrops 10 B3
New Mill Cumb 62 F4
New Mill W Yorks 42 C5
New Mills Ches 34 C2
New Mills Derby 35 B6
New Mills Powys 9 E7
New Moston Gtr Man 41 D6
New Rent Cumb 70 D4
New Road Side N Yorks 47 B8
New Road Side W Yorks 48 E4
New Scarbro W Yorks 49 D6
New Smithy Derby 35 C8
New Springs Gtr Man 39 C9
New Street Staffs 23 D7
New Totley S Yorks 37 D6
New Town Lancs 45 C9
New Whittington Derby 37 D7
New Woodhouse Shrops 20 F4
New York N Yorks 55 C7
Newall W Yorks 49 A5
Newall Green Gtr Man 34 B3
Newbarns Cumb 50 A3
Newbiggin Cumb 50 B4
Newbiggin Cumb 56 B2
Newbiggin Cumb 70 F4
Newbiggin Cumb 71 B6
Newbiggin Cumb 71 F7
Newbiggin Durham 73 F6
Newbiggin N Yorks 61 B5
Newbiggin N Yorks 61 C6
Newbiggin Northum 73 B7
Newbiggin-on-Lune Cumb 66 E2
Newbold Derby 37 E7
Newbold Gtr Man 41 B7
Newborough Angl 14 A4
Newbridge Lancs 47 C6
Newbridge Wrex 19 F6
Newburgh Lancs 39 B6
Newby Cumb 65 B6
Newby Lancs 47 A5
Newby N Yorks 49 A7
Newby N Yorks 53 A6
Newby Bridge Cumb 57 C8
Newby Cote N Yorks 53 A6
Newby East Cumb 76 E2
Newby Head Cumb 65 B6
Newby West Cumb 75 F7
Newcastle-under-Lyme Stoke 22 E2
Newcastleton Scot Borders 78 E2
Newchapel Staffs 22 D3
Newchurch Lancs 47 F5
Newchurch in Pendle Lancs 47 C5
Newfield Green S Yorks 37 C7
Newgate Derby 37 E6
Newgate Lancs 39 C7
Newhall Ches 21 E5
Newhaven Derby 24 C1
Newhey Gtr Man 41 B7
Newland Cumb 57 E6
Newlands Cumb 63 B7
Newlands Cumb 70 D1
Newlands Derby 25 E6
Newlands Scot Borders 78 D3
Newlands Park Angl 26 C2
Newlay W Yorks 49 C6
Newmillerdam W Yorks 43 A8
Newpool Staffs 22 C3
Newport Telford 12 E4
Newsam Green W Yorks 49 D9
Newsbank Ches 22 A2
Newsham Lancs 45 C7
Newsholme Lancs 53 E8
Newsholme W Yorks 48 C2
Newsome W Yorks 42 B4
Newstead Notts 25 D8
Newstead Stoke 22 F3
Newstreet Lane Shrops 12 A2
Newthorpe Notts 25 E7
Newthorpe Common Notts 25 E7
Newton Ches 20 C3
Newton Ches 32 F3
Newton Ches 33 D5
Newton Cumb 50 A3
Newton Derby 25 C6
Newton Dumf/Gal 75 B5
Newton Gtr Man 41 E8
Newton Lancs 44 C3
Newton Lancs 45 D5
Newton Lancs 53 E5
Newton Lancs 59 F5
Newton Mersey 31 B6
Newton Arlosh Cumb 74 E3
Newton Heath Gtr Man 41 D6
Newton Hill W Yorks 49 F8
Newton-le-Willows Mersey 39 E8
Newton on the Hill Shrops 11 D6
Newton Park Mersey 39 F8
Newton Reigny Cumb 70 E4
Newton Wood Gtr Man 41 E7
Newtown Ches 21 E5
Newtown Ches 32 D5
Newtown Ches 35 C5
Newtown Cumb 65 B5
Newtown Cumb 68 B4
Newtown Cumb 75 E7
Newtown Cumb 76 D3
Newtown Derby 35 C6
Newtown Gtr Man 39 C8
Newtown Gtr Man 40 D4
Newtown I/Man 80 D3
Newtown Mersey 39 E6
Newtown Shrops 11 B6
Newtown Shrops 11 D5
Newtown Staffs 23 B7
Niarbyl I/Man 80 D2
Nib Heath Shrops 11 E5
Nimble Nook Gtr Man 41 D7
Ninebanks Northum 77 F8
Niwbwrch = Newborough Angl 14 A4
No Man's Heath Ches 20 E3
Nob End Gtr Man 40 C4
Noblethorpe S Yorks 43 D7
Noctorum Mersey 31 B7
Nog Tow Lancs 45 D7
Noneley Shrops 11 C6
Nook Cumb 58 D4
Nook Lancs 45 B6
Noon Nick W Yorks 48 C4
Norbreck Blackp'l 44 B3
Norbury Ches 20 E4
Norbury Derby 23 F8
Norbury Staffs 13 D5
Norbury Common Ches 20 E4
Norbury Junction Staffs 13 D5
Norbury Moor Gtr Man 35 B5
Norcott Brook Ches 33 C7
Norcross Blackp'l 44 B3
Norden Gtr Man 41 B6
Norland Town W Yorks 48 F3
Norley Ches 33 E6
Normacot Stoke 22 F4
Normanton Spring S Yorks 37 C8
Normos Blackp'l 44 C3
Norris Green Mersey 38 F4
Norristhorpe W Yorks 49 F6
North End Cumb 75 E6
North End Mersey 38 D3
North Reddish Gtr Man 41 F6
North Rode Ches 22 A3
North Row Cumb 69 E7
North Scale Cumb 50 B2
North Shore Blackp'l 44 C3
North Side Cumb 68 F3
North Stainmore Cumb 66 C4
North Wingfield Derby 25 B6
Northedge Derby 25 B5
Northenden Gtr Man 34 A3
Northern Moor Gtr Man 34 A3
Northhouse Scot Borders 78 A1
Northop Flints 31 F6
Northop Hall Flints 31 F7
Northorpe W Yorks 49 F6
Northowram W Yorks 48 E4
Northwich Ches 33 E8
Northwood Derby 24 B3
Northwood Mersey 38 E5
Northwood Shrops 11 B6
Northwood Staffs 22 F3
Northwood Stoke 22 E3
Norton Halton 33 C6
Norton S Yorks 37 C7
Norton Bridge Staffs 13 B7
Norton Green Stoke 22 D3
Norton in Hales Shrops 12 B3
Norton-in-the-Moors Stoke 22 D3
Norton Woodseats S Yorks 37 C7
Norwood Derby 37 C9
Norwood Green W Yorks 48 E4
Notton W Yorks 43 B8
Nova Scotia Ches 33 F7
Nun Hills Lancs 47 F6
Nuncargate Notts 25 D8
Nunclose Cumb 70 B4
Nut Grove Mersey 32 A4
Nuthall Notts 25 E8
Nuttall Gtr Man 40 A4

O

Oak Bank Gtr Man 41 C5
Oak Hill Stoke 22 F3
Oakamoor Staffs 23 F7
Oakenclough Lancs 52 F2
Oakenholt Flints 31 E7
Oakenshaw Lancs 46 D4
Oakenshaw W Yorks 48 E5
Oakerthorpe Derby 25 D5
Oakes W Yorks 42 A4
Oakgrove Ches 35 F5
Oaklands Flints 31 E6
Oakmere Ches 33 F6
Oakshaw Ford Cumb 76 E3
Oakwell W Yorks 49 E6
Oakwood Warrington 39 E9
Oakwood W Yorks 49 C8
Oakworth W Yorks 48 C2
Oat Hill Ches 20 E2
Ochr-y-foel Denbs 30 D3
Oddendale Cumb 65 D6
Odgen Gtr Man 41 B8
Odsal W Yorks 48 E5
Offerton Gtr Man 35 B5
Offerton Green Gtr Man 35 B5
Offleyhay Staffs 13 C5
Offleymarsh Staffs 13 C5
Offleyrock Staffs 13 C5
Ogden W Yorks 48 D3
Oker Derby 24 B3
Old Boston Mersey 39 E8
Old Bramhope W Yorks 49 B6
Old Brampton Derby 37 E6
Old Carlisle Cumb 69 B8
Old Castleton Scot Borders 78 D3
Old Colwyn Conwy 29 D7
Old Dam Derby 36 D2
Old Dolphin W Yorks 48 D4
Old Field Carr Lancs 44 C4
Old Glossop Derby 42 F2
Old Graitney Dumf/Gal 75 C6
Old Hutton Cumb 58 C5
Old Hyton Cumb 56 C3
Old Langho Lancs 46 C3
Old Laxey I/Man 80 C4
Old Lindley W Yorks 42 A3
Old Swan Mersey 32 A2
Old Tame Gtr Man 41 C8
Old Tebay Cumb 65 E7
Old Town Cumb 59 D5
Old Town Cumb 70 C4
Old Town W Yorks 48 E1
Old Trafford Gtr Man 41 E5
Old Tupton Derby 25 A5
Old Whittington Derby 37 E7
Old Woodhouse Shrops 20 F4
Old Woods Shrops 11 D6
Oldcastle Heath Ches 20 E2
Oldfield Mersey 31 C7
Oldfield W Yorks 42 B4
Oldfield W Yorks 48 C2
Oldfield Brow Gtr Man 34 B1
Oldfurnace Staffs 23 F6
Oldham Gtr Man 41 D7
Oldham Edge Gtr Man 41 C7
Oldwall Cumb 76 D2
Ollerbrook Booth Derby 36 C2
Ollerton Ches 34 D2
Ollerton Shrops 12 C3
Onchan I/Man 80 D3
Onecote Staffs 23 C6
Onneley Staffs 21 F8
Onston Ches 33 E6
Openshaw Gtr Man 41 F6
Openwoodgate Derby 25 E5
Ordsall Gtr Man 41 E5
Orford Warrington 33 A7
Ormathwaite Cumb 63 A8
Ormsgill Cumb 50 A2
Ormskirk Lancs 38 C5
Orrell Gtr Man 39 D7
Orrell Mersey 38 E3
Orrell Post Gtr Man 39 C7
Orrisdale I/Man 80 B3
Orslow Staffs 13 E6
Orthwaite Cumb 69 E8
Ortner Lancs 52 E2
Orton Cumb 65 E7
Orton Rigg Cumb 70 A1
Osbaldeston Lancs 46 D1
Osbaldeston Green Lancs 46 D1
Osbaston Telford 12 E2
Oscroft Ches 32 F5
Osmaston Derby 24 F1
Osmondthorpe W Yorks 49 D8
Ossett W Yorks 49 F7
Ossett Spa W Yorks 43 A7
Ossett Street Side W Yorks 49 F7
Oswaldtwistle Lancs 46 E3
Oswestry Shrops 10 C2
Otley W Yorks 49 B5
Otterburn N Yorks 54 D1
Otterspool Mersey 32 C1
Oughterby Cumb 75 E5
Oughtershaw N Yorks 60 D3
Oughterside Cumb 68 C5
Oughtibridge S Yorks 43 F8
Oughtrington Warrington 33 B8
Oulton Cumb 69 A7
Oulton Staffs 13 A8
Oulton W Yorks 49 E9
Oulton Heath Staffs 13 A8
Oultoncross Staffs 13 B8
Ousby Cumb 71 E7
Ouston Northum 72 A3
Out Gate Cumb 57 A8
Out Rawcliffe Lancs 44 B5
Outhgill Cumb 66 F3
Outlane W Yorks 42 A3
Outwood Gtr Man 40 C4
Outwood W Yorks 49 F8
Outwoods Staffs 13 E5
Ouzlewell Green W Yorks 49 E8
Ovenden W Yorks 48 E3
Ovenden Wood W Yorks 48 E3
Over Ches 21 A5
Over Burrow Lancs 59 E6
Over End Derby 36 E5
Over Haddon Derby 36 F4
Over Hulton Gtr Man 40 C2
Over Kellet Lancs 52 B2
Over Knutsford Ches 34 D2
Over Leck Lancs 59 E7
Over Tabley Ches 34 C1
Over Town Lancs 47 E6
Overgreen Derby 37 E6
Overpool Ches 32 D2
Overthorpe W Yorks 43 A6
Overthwaite Cumb 58 D4
Overton Ches 33 D5
Overton Lancs 51 D7
Overton W Yorks 43 A7
Overton Wrex 19 F8
Overtown Lancs 59 E6
Owlcotes Derby 37 F8
Owler Bar Derby 37 D5
Owlerton S Yorks 37 B6
Owlet W Yorks 48 C5
Owlthorpe S Yorks 37 C8
Oxclose S Yorks 37 C8
Oxen Park Cumb 57 C7
Oxenholme Cumb 58 B4
Oxenhope W Yorks 48 C2
Oxspring S Yorks 43 D7
Oxton Mersey 31 B7

P

Packmoor Stoke 22 D3
Paddington Warrington 33 B7
Paddock W Yorks 42 A4
Paddolgreen Shrops 11 B7
Padfield Derby 42 E2
Padgate Warrington 33 A7
Padiham Lancs 46 D4
Padog Conwy 16 D4
Padside N Yorks 55 D7
Padside Green N Yorks 55 D7
Page Moss Mersey 32 A3
Painthorpe W Yorks 43 A8
Palacefields Halton 33 C6
Pale Gwyn 8 A4
Palla Flat Cumb 62 D2
Palterton Derby 37 F9
Pandy Gwyn 2 C3
Pandy Gwyn 8 C2
Pandy Wrex 9 A8
Pandy Tudur Conwy 17 B5
Pandy'r Capel Denbs 18 D2
Pant Denbs 18 D5
Pant Flints 30 E4
Pant Gwyn 4 B4
Pant Shrops 10 D2
Pant Wrex 19 E6
Pant-Glas Gwyn 14 E5
Pant-glas Shrops 10 B2
Pant-pastynog Denbs 18 B1
Pant-y-mwyn Flints 18 B4
Pant-y-Wacco Flints 30 D4
Pantasaph Flints 31 D5
Papcastle Cumb 68 E5
Papplewick Notts 25 D8
Parbold Lancs 39 B6
Parc Gwyn 8 B2
Parciau Angl 27 C6
Pardshaw Cumb 62 B4
Park Bridge Gtr Man 41 D7
Park Broom Cumb 76 E1
Park Close Lancs 47 B6
Park Head Cumb 71 C6
Park Head W Yorks 43 C5
Park Lane Gtr Man 40 D4
Park Mill W Yorks 43 B7
Park Village Northum 77 D6
Park Villas W Yorks 49 C8
Parkgate Ches 31 D7
Parkgate Ches 34 E2
Parkgate Cumb 69 B7
Parkhead Cumb 70 C1
Parkhead S Yorks 37 C6
Parkhouse Green Derby 25 B6
Parkside Cumb 62 C3
Parkside Staffs 13 C8
Parkwood Springs S Yorks 37 B6
Parr Mersey 39 E7
Parr Brow Gtr Man 40 D3
Parson Cross S Yorks 37 A7
Parsonby Cumb 69 D5
Partington Gtr Man 34 A1
Parton Cumb 62 B2
Parton Cumb 69 A8
Parwich Derby 24 D1
Pategill Cumb 71 F5
Pateley Bridge N Yorks 55 B7
Patrick I/Man 80 C2
Patricroft Gtr Man 40 E4
Patterdale Cumb 64 C2
Patton Bridge Cumb 58 A5
Pave Lane Telford 12 E5
Paythorne Lancs 53 E8
Peak Dale Derby 36 D1
Peak Forest Derby 36 D2
Peasley Cross Mersey 39 F8
Pecket Well W Yorks 48 E1
Peckforton Ches 20 C3
Pedair-ffordd Powys 9 D7
Peel I/Man 80 C2
Peel Lancs 44 D4
Peel Green Gtr Man 40 E3
Peel Hall Gtr Man 34 B3
Pellon W Yorks 48 E3
Pelutho Cumb 68 B5
Pemberton Gtr Man 39 D8
Pen-gilfach Gwyn 15 B7
Pen-llyn Angl 26 C4
Pen-lôn Angl 14 B4
Pen-sarn Gwyn 6 C3
Pen-Ucha'r Plwyf Flints 31 E5
Pen-y-bont Llanerch Emrys Powys 10 D1
Pen-y-bryn Gwyn 7 E5
Pen-y-bryn Wrex 19 F6
Pen-y-cefn Flints 30 D4
Pen-y-coed Gwyn 7 E6
Pen-y-coed Powys 10 E1
Pen-y-coed Shrops 10 D2
Pen-y-felin Flints 31 F5
Pen-y-ffordd Flints 30 C4
Pen-y-garn Ceredig'n 2 F3
Pen-y-garnedd Angl 27 D7
Pen-y-graig Gwyn 4 B4
Pen-y-groeslon Gwyn 4 B4
Pen-y-maes Flints 31 D5
Pen-y-mynydd Flints 19 B7
Pen-y-Parc Flints 19 C6
Pen-y-stryt Denbs 18 D4
Penbodlas Gwyn 5 B5
Pencaenewydd Gwyn 14 F4
Pencarnisiog Angl 26 E4
Pencraig Angl 27 D6
Pencraig Powys 9 C5
Pendlebury Gtr Man 40 D4
Pendleton Gtr Man 41 E5
Pendleton Lancs 46 C4
Pendre Gwyn 2 C2
Penegoes Powys 3 C6
Pengorffwysfa Angl 27 A6
Penhosfeilw Angl 26 C1
Peniarth Gwyn 2 B3
Peniarth Powys 9 E8
Peniel Denbs 17 B8
Penisa'r-Waun Gwyn 15 B7
Penistone S Yorks 43 D6
Penketh Warrington 33 B7
Penkridge Staffs 13 F8
Penley Wrex 11 A5
Penllech Gwyn 4 B4
Penmachno Conwy 16 D3
Penmaen Rhos Conwy 29 D7
Penmaenan Conwy 28 D4
Penmaenmawr Conwy 28 D4
Penmaenpool Gwyn 7 E5
Penmon Angl 28 C2
Penmorfa Gwyn 15 F6
Penmynydd Angl 27 E7
Pennal Gwyn 2 C4
Pennal-isaf Gwyn 3 C5
Pennant Denbs 9 B5
Pennant Gwyn 8 D3
Pennant Powys 3 D8
Pennant-Melangell Powys 9 C5
Pennington Cumb 57 E6
Pennington Gtr Man 40 E2
Pennington Green Gtr Man 40 C1
Penny Bridge Cumb 57 D7
Penny Hill W Yorks 42 A3
Pennylands Lancs 39 C6
Penrhos Gwyn 5 B6
Penrhos-garnedd Gwyn 27 E8
Penrhyn Bay Conwy 29 C6
Penrhyndeudraeth Gwyn 6 A4
Penrhynside Conwy 29 C6
Penrith Cumb 71 E5
Penruddock Cumb 70 F3
Pensarn Conwy 29 D9
Pensby Mersey 31 C7
Penthryn Fechan Powys 10 E1
Pentir Gwyn 27 F8
Pentraeth Angl 27 D7
Pentre Flints 18 B5
Pentre Flints 31 F8
Pentre Powys 9 F8
Pentre Shrops 10 E4
Pentre Wrex 19 F6
Pentre Wrex 9 B7
Pentre-bach Gwyn 14 F3
Pentre Berw Angl 27 E6
Pentre-bont Conwy 16 D2
Pentre-cefn Shrops 10 C1
Pentre-celyn Denbs 18 D4
Pentre Cilgwyn Wrex 10 A1
Pentre-du Conwy 16 C3
Pentre-Ffwrndan Flints 31 E7
Pentre Gwynfryn Gwyn 6 C3
Pentre Halkyn Flints 31 E5
Pentre-Isaf Conwy 29 F7
Pentre Llanrhaeadr Denbs 18 B2
Pentre-llyn-cymmer Conwy 17 D7
Pentre-newydd Shrops 10 A2
Pentre Saron Denbs 17 B8
Pentre-uchaf Gwyn 5 A7
Pentredwr Denbs 18 E4
Pentrefelin Angl 27 A5
Pentrefelin Conwy 29 E6
Pentrefelin Denbs 18 F5
Pentrefelin Gwyn 6 A2
Pentrefelin Powys 9 D8
Pentrefoelas Conwy 17 D5
Pentre'r beirdd Powys 9 F8
Pentre'r Felin Conwy 29 F6
Pentre'r-gof Powys 9 F8
Pentrich Derby 25 D5
Penwortham Lane Lancs 45 E7
Penybont Ceredig'n 2 F3
Penybontfawr Powys 9 D6
Penycae Wrex 19 E6
Penycaerau Gwyn 4 C3
Penyffordd Flints 19 B7
Penyffridd Gwyn 15 C6
Penygarnedd Powys 9 D7
Penygroes Gwyn 14 D5
Penysarn Angl 27 A6
Peover Heath Ches 34 E2
Pershall Staffs 13 C6
Perthy Shrops 10 B4
Petre Bank Ches 35 C5
Petton Shrops 11 C5
Pewterspear Warrington 33 C7
Pica Cumb 62 B3
Pickley Green Gtr Man 40 D2
Pickmere Ches 33 D8
Pickstock Telford 12 D4
Pickup Bank Blackb'n 46 F3
Pickwood Scar W Yorks 48 F3
Picton Ches 32 E3
Picton Flints 30 C4
Pike Hill Lancs 47 D6
Pikehall Derby 24 C1
Pilley S Yorks 43 D8
Pilling Lancs 51 F7
Pilling Lane Lancs 51 F6
Pilsley Derby 25 B6
Pilsley Derby 36 E4
Pilsley Green Derby 25 B6
Pimbo Lancs 39 D6
Pimhole Gtr Man 41 B5
Pimlico Lancs 46 B3
Pincock Lancs 39 A8
Pinfold Lancs 38 B4
Pinsley Green Ches 20 E4
Pinxton Derby 25 C7
Pipe Gate Shrops 21 F7
Piper's Ash Ches 32 F3
Pismire Hill S Yorks 37 A7
Pistyll Gwyn 14 F2
Pitses Gtr Man 41 D7
Pitsmoor S Yorks 37 B7
Pitts Hill Stoke 22 D3
Plaistow Derby 25 C5
Plas Powys 9 E7
Plâs Berwyn Denbs 18 F4
Plas Canol Gwyn 6 E4
Plas Madoc Wrex 19 F6
Plas Nantyr Wrex 9 A8
Plas-yn-y-pentre Denbs 19 F6
Plasnewydd Gwyn 4 C4
Platt Bridge Gtr Man 39 D9
Platt Lane Shrops 11 A7
Platts Common S Yorks 43 D9
Pleasington Blackb'n 46 E1
Pleasley Derby 25 B7
Pleasleyhill Derby 25 B7
Pleckgate Blackb'n 46 D2
Pledwick W Yorks 43 A8
Plenmeller Northum 77 D7
Plumbland Cumb 69 D6
Plumbley S Yorks 37 C8
Plumgarths Cumb 58 B3
Plumley Ches 34 D1
Plumpton Cumb 70 D4
Plumpton Head Cumb 71 E5
Plumptonfoot Cumb 70 D4
Pobgreen Gtr Man 42 C2
Pogmoor S Yorks 43 C8
Poll Hill Mersey 31 C7
Ponsonby Cumb 62 E4
Pont Cyfyng Conwy 16 C2
Pont Cysyllte Wrex 19 F6
Pont-Faen Shrops 10 A2
Pont Hwfa Angl 26 C1
Pont Llogel Powys 9 E5
Pont-Rhythallt Gwyn 15 B6
Pont-rug Gwyn 15 B6
Pont-y-bodkin Flints 19 C6
Pont-y-pant Conwy 16 D2
Pontblyddyn Flints 19 B6
Pontfadog Wrex 10 A1
Pontllyfni Gwyn 14 D4
Pontrobert Powys 9 F7
Pool W Yorks 49 B6
Pool Quay Powys 10 F2
Poolend Staffs 22 C5
Pooley Bridge Cumb 64 B4
Poolford Staffs 22 C3
Poolsbrook Derby 37 E8
Poolstock Gtr Man 39 D8
Port Carlisle Cumb 78 D4
Port Dinorwic = Y Felinheli Gwyn 27 F7
Port e Vullen I/Man 80 B4
Port Erin I/Man 80 E1
Port St. Mary I/Man 80 E2
Port Sunlight Mersey 32 C1
Porth Colmon Gwyn 4 B3
Porth Dinllaen Gwyn 14 F1
Porth Tocyn Gwyn 5 C6
Porth-y-felin Angl 26 C1
Porth-y-waen Shrops 10 C2
Porthill Shrops 11 F6
Porthill Staffs 22 E3
Porthllechog Angl 27 A5
Porthmadog Gwyn 6 A3
Porthwgan Wrex 19 E8
Portico Mersey 32 A4
Portinscale Cumb 63 B7
Portobello W Yorks 43 A8
Portsmouth W Yorks 47 E7
Pott Shrigley Ches 35 D5
Potter Hill S Yorks 43 E8
Potternewton W Yorks 49 C8
Potters Brook Lancs 51 E8
Poulton Ches 19 C8
Poulton Mersey 31 A7
Poulton-le-Fylde Lancs 44 C4
Powfoot Dumf/Gal 74 C2
Powhill Cumb 74 E4
Pownall Park Ches 34 C3
Poynton Ches 35 C5
Poynton Telford 11 E8
Poynton Green Telford 11 E8
Pratthall Derby 37 E6
Prees Shrops 11 B8
Prees Green Shrops 11 B8
Prees Heath Shrops 11 A8
Prees Higher Heath Shrops 11 A8
Prees Lower Heath Shrops 11 B8
Prees Wood Shrops 11 B8
Preesall Lancs 51 F6
Preesall Moss Side Lancs 51 F6
Preesall Park Lancs 44 A4
Preesgweene Shrops 10 A2
Prenteg Gwyn 15 F7
Prenton Mersey 31 B8
Prescot Mersey 32 A4
Prescott Shrops 11 D5
Prestatyn Denbs 30 C3
Prestbury Ches 35 D5
Prestolee Gtr Man 40 C4
Preston Lancs 45 E7
Preston Shrops 11 F7
Preston Brockhurst Shrops 11 D7
Preston Brook Halton 33 C6
Preston Gubbals Shrops 11 E6
Preston on the Hill Halton 33 C6
Preston-under-Scar N Yorks 61 B7
Preston upon the Weald Moors Telford 12 E3
Prestwich Gtr Man 41 D5
Prestwood Staffs 23 F8
Priest Hutton Lancs 58 F4
Priestcliffe Derby 36 E2
Priesthaugh Scot Borders 78 B2
Priesthorpe W Yorks 48 C4
Priesthorpe W Yorks 49 C6
Priestley Green W Yorks 48 E4
Priestside Dumf/Gal 74 C2
Primrose Hill Lancs 38 C4
Prince Royd W Yorks 42 A4
Princes Park Mersey 32 B2
Prion Denbs 18 B2
Prior Rigg Cumb 76 C2
Prospect Cumb 68 C5
Puddinglake Ches 34 F1
Puddington Ches 31 E8
Pudsey W Yorks 47 E7
Pudsey W Yorks 49 D6
Pulford Ches 19 C8
Pwll-glas Denbs 18 D3
Pwlldefaid Gwyn 4 C3
Pwllheli Gwyn 5 A7
Pydew Conwy 29 D6
Pye Hill Notts 25 D6

Q

Quality Corner Cumb 62 B2
Quarmby W Yorks 42 A4
Quarndon Derby 24 F4
Quarndon Common Derby 24 F4
Quarrybank Ches 20 A4
Queen's Head Shrops 10 C3
Queen's Park Blackb'n 46 E2
Queens Park Ches 20 A1
Queensbury W Yorks 48 D3
Queensferry Flints 31 F8
Queenstown Blackp'l 44 C3
Queensville Staffs 13 D8
Quernmore Lancs 52 C2
Quernmore Lancs 52 D2
Quick Gtr Man 41 D8
Quick Edge Gtr Man 41 D8
Quina Brook Shrops 11 B7
Quixhill Staffs 23 F8

R

Raby Cumb 69 A6
Raby Mersey 31 D8
Rachub Gwyn 28 F2
Radcliffe Gtr Man 40 C4
Radmanthwaite Notts 25 B8
Radmoor Shrops 12 D2
Radmore Green Ches 20 D4
Rain Shore Gtr Man 41 A6
Rainford Mersey 39 D6
Rainford Junction Mersey 39 D6
Rainhill Mersey 32 A4
Rainhill Stoops Mersey 32 A5
Rainow Ches 35 D6
Rainowlow Ches 35 D6
Rainsough Gtr Man 41 D5
Raisbeck Cumb 65 E7
Raise Cumb 72 B2
Rake Head Lancs 47 F5
Rakes Dale Staffs 23 F7
Rakeway Staffs 23 F6
Rakewood Gtr Man 41 B7
Rampside Cumb 50 B3
Ramsbottom Gtr Man 41 A5
Ramsey I/Man 80 B4
Ramsgill N Yorks 55 A6
Ramshaw Durham 73 B7
Ramshorn Staffs 23 E7
Ranmoor S Yorks 37 B6
Rannerdale Cumb 63 C6
Ranton Staffs 13 D7
Ranton Green Staffs 13 D6
Rastrick W Yorks 48 F4
Rathmell N Yorks 53 D8
Ratten Row Cumb 70 B2
Ratten Row Cumb 70 C1
Ratten Row Lancs 45 B5
Raughton Cumb 70 B2
Raughton Head Cumb 70 B2
Ravenglass Cumb 56 A2
Ravenhead Mersey 39 F8
Ravenscliffe W Yorks 49 C5
Ravensdale I/Man 80 B3
Ravenseat N Yorks 66 F5
Ravensmoor Ches 21 D5
Ravensthorpe W Yorks 49 F6
Ravenstonedale Cumb 66 F2
Ravenstown Cumb 57 E8
Rawdon W Yorks 49 C6
Rawson Green Derby 25 E5
Rawtenstall Lancs 47 F5
Rawthorpe W Yorks 42 A5
Read Lancs 46 D4
Reagill Cumb 65 C7
Red Bull Ches 22 C2
Red Bull Staffs 12 B3
Red Dial Cumb 69 B8
Red Lumb Gtr Man 41 A5
Red Rock Gtr Man 39 C8
Red Scar Lancs 45 D8
Red Street Staffs 22 D2
Red Wharf Bay Angl 27 C7
Redbrook Wrex 20 F3
Redburn Northum 77 D8
Reddish Gtr Man 34 A4
Redhills Cumb 71 F5
Redmain Cumb 69 E5
Redmire N Yorks 61 B6
Rednal Shrops 10 C4
Redvales Gtr Man 40 C4
Reedley Lancs 47 C6
Reeds Holme Lancs 47 F5
Reeth N Yorks 61 A6
Regaby I/Man 80 B4
Renishaw Derby 37 D8
Renwick Cumb 71 C6
Reston Cumb 58 A3
Revidge Blackb'n 46 E2
Rhencullen I/Man 80 B3
Rhes-y-cae Flints 31 E5
Rhewl Denbs 18 B3
Rhewl Denbs 18 E4
Rhewl Shrops 10 B3

Thorncliff *Staffs* 23 C6
Thorncliffe *W Yorks* 43 B6
Thorner *W Yorks* 49 B9
Thornes *W Yorks* 43 A8
Thorngill *N Yorks* 61 C7
Thorngrafton *Northum* 77 C8
Thornham Fold *Gtr Man* 41 C6
Thornhill *Cumb* 62 E3
Thornhill *Derby* 36 E3
Thornhill *W Yorks* 43 A7
Thornhill Edge *W Yorks* 43 A7
Thornhill Lees *W Yorks* 43 A6
Thorns *W Yorks* 48 F5
Thorns Green *Ches* 34 C2
Thornsett *Derby* 35 B7
Thornship *Cumb* 65 D6
Thornthwaite *Cumb* 63 A7
Thornthwaite *N Yorks* 55 D7
Thornton *Lancs* 44 B3
Thornton *Mersey* 38 D3
Thornton *W Yorks* 48 D4
Thornton Hough *Mersey* 31 C8
Thornton in Craven *N Yorks* 54 F2
Thornton in Lonsdale *N Yorks* 59 F7
Thornton-le-Moors *Ches* 32 E3
Thornton Rust *N Yorks* 61 C5
Thorp *Gtr Man* 41 C7
Thorpe *Cumb* 64 A4
Thorpe *Derby* 23 D9
Thorpe *N Yorks* 54 C4
Thorpe Edge *W Yorks* 49 C5
Thorpe on the Hill *W Yorks* 49 E8
Threapland *Cumb* 69 D6
Threapland *N Yorks* 54 C3
Threapwood *Staffs* 23 F6
Threapwood *Wrex* 20 E1
Threlkeld *Cumb* 64 A1
Threshfield *N Yorks* 54 C3
Thrimby *Cumb* 65 B6
Thringarth *Durham* 66 B6
Thruscross *N Yorks* 55 D7
Thunder Bridge *W Yorks* 43 B7
Thurgoland *S Yorks* 43 D7
Thurlstone *S Yorks* 43 D6
Thurlwood *Ches* 22 C3
Thursby *Cumb* 70 A1
Thursden *Lancs* 47 C7
Thurstaston *Mersey* 31 C6
Thurston Clough *Gtr Man* 41 C8
Thurstonfield *Cumb* 75 E6
Thurstonland *W Yorks* 43 A8
Thwaite *Durham* 67 D8
Thwaite *N Yorks* 60 A3
Thwaite Head *Cumb* 57 B7
Thwaites *W Yorks* 48 B3
Thwaites Brow *W Yorks* 48 B3
Tibberton *Telford* 12 D3
Tibshelf *Derby* 25 B6
Tideswell *Derby* 36 D3
Tilley *Shrops* 11 C7
Tilley Green *Shrops* 11 C7
Tillington *Staffs* 13 D8
Tilstock *Shrops* 11 A7
Tilston *Ches* 20 D2
Tilstone Bank *Ches* 20 C4
Tilstone Fearnall *Ches* 20 B4
Timbersbrook *Ches* 22 B3
Timble *N Yorks* 55 E7
Timperley *Gtr Man* 34 B2
Tindale *Cumb* 76 E5
Tingley *W Yorks* 49 E7
Tinshill *W Yorks* 49 C7
Tinsley *S Yorks* 37 A8
Tintwistle *Derby* 42 E2
Tir-y-fron *Flints* 19 C6
Tirril *Cumb* 71 F5
Tissington *Derby* 24 D1
Tithe Barn Hillock *Mersey* 39 E8
Tithebarn *Staffs* 23 F7
Tittensor *Staffs* 13 A7
Tiverton *Ches* 20 B4
Tivoli *Cumb* 62 C2
Toadmoor *Derby* 25 D5
Tockholes *Blackb'n* 46 F2
Todhills *Cumb* 75 D7
Todmorden *W Yorks* 47 F7
Toll Bar *Mersey* 39 F6
Tonfanau *Gwyn* 2 C2
Tong *W Yorks* 49 D6
Tong Park *W Yorks* 48 C5
Tong Street *W Yorks* 49 D5
Tonge Fold *Gtr Man* 40 C3
Tonge Moor *Gtr Man* 40 B3
Tontine *Lancs* 39 D7
Toothill *W Yorks* 48 F4
Top Lock *Gtr Man* 39 C9
Top of Hebers *Gtr Man* 41 C6
Top o'th'Lane *Lancs* 45 F8
Topcliffe *W Yorks* 49 E7
Toppings *Gtr Man* 40 B3
Torkington *Gtr Man* 35 B5
Torpenhow *Cumb* 69 D7
Torrisholme *Lancs* 51 C8
Torver *Cumb* 57 B6
Tosside *N Yorks* 53 D7
Totley Bents *S Yorks* 37 C6
Totley Brook *S Yorks* 37 C6
Totley Rise *S Yorks* 37 C6
Totties *W Yorks* 42 C5
Tottington *Gtr Man* 40 B4
Tottlebank *Cumb* 57 D7
Tow House *Northum* 77 D8
Tower Hill *Ches* 35 D5
Tower Hill *Mersey* 38 D5
Town End *Cumb* 57 A8
Town End *Cumb* 57 C8
Town End *Cumb* 58 D2
Town End *Cumb* 59 D6
Town End *Cumb* 64 E1
Town End *Cumb* 64 F3
Town End *Cumb* 65 A5
Town End *Cumb* 65 A7
Town End *Derby* 36 D3
Town End *Mersey* 32 B4
Town End *W Yorks* 42 A3
Town Fields *Ches* 21 A5
Town Green *Gtr Man* 39 E8
Town Green *Lancs* 38 E5
Town Head *Cumb* 64 E1
Town Head *Cumb* 64 F3

Town Head *Cumb* 65 A6
Town Head *Cumb* 65 A7
Town Head *Cumb* 65 D7
Town Head *Cumb* 65 D8
Town Head *N Yorks* 53 B7
Town Head *N Yorks* 53 D8
Town Hill *N Yorks* 54 C4
Town Lane *Gtr Man* 40 D2
Town of Lowton *Gtr Man* 39 E9
Townend *Derby* 35 C8
Townfield *Durham* 73 B7
Towngate *Cumb* 71 B5
Townhead *Cumb* 68 D4
Townhead *Cumb* 71 D5
Townhead *Cumb* 71 E7
Townhead *Lancs* 53 E6
Townhead *S Yorks* 37 C6
Townhead *S Yorks* 42 D5
Townhead *Stoke* 22 E4
Townsend Fold *Lancs* 47 F5
Towyn *Conwy* 30 D1
Toxteth *Mersey* 32 B2
Trafford Park *Gtr Man* 40 E4
Tranmere *Mersey* 31 B8
Trawden *Lancs* 47 C7
Trawsfynydd *Gwyn* 7 A6
Tre-Ian *Flints* 18 A4
Tre-Mostyn *Flints* 30 D4
Tre Taliesin *Ceredig'n* 2 E4
Tre-wern *Powys* 9 C7
Treales *Lancs* 45 D5
Trearddur *Angl* 26 D2
Trederwen *Powys* 10 E2
Treeton *S Yorks* 37 B8
Tref-y-nant *Wrex* 19 F6
Trefaes *Gwyn* 4 B5
Trefdraeth *Angl* 27 E5
Treffanney *Powys* 9 E9
Treflach *Shrops* 10 C2
Trefnant *Denbs* 30 E2
Trefonen *Shrops* 10 C2
Trefor *Angl* 26 C4
Trefor *Angl* 27 D7
Trefor *Gwyn* 14 E3
Trefriw *Conwy* 16 B3
Tregaian *Angl* 27 D6
Tregarth *Gwyn* 28 F2
Tregeiriog *Wrex* 9 B8
Tregele *Angl* 26 A4
Trelawnyd *Flints* 30 D3
Trelogan *Flints* 30 C4
Tremadog *Gwyn* 15 F7
Tremeirchion *Denbs* 30 E3
Trench *Telford* 12 F3
Trent Vale *Stoke* 22 F3
Trentham *Staffs* 22 F3
Tre'r-ddol *Ceredig'n* 2 E4
Treuddyn *Flints* 19 C6
Trevalyn *Wrex* 19 C8
Trevor *Wrex* 19 F6
Trevor Uchaf *Denbs* 19 F5
Triangle *W Yorks* 48 F2
Trinity Fields *Staffs* 13 C8
Trofarth *Conwy* 29 E7
Tromode *I/Man* 80 D3
Trough Gate *Lancs* 47 F6
Troutbeck *Cumb* 64 F2
Troutbeck *Cumb* 64 F3
Troutbeck Bridge *Cumb* 64 F2
Troway *Derby* 37 D7
Troy *W Yorks* 49 C6
Trub *Gtr Man* 41 C6
Trubshaw *Staffs* 22 C3
Trunnah *Lancs* 44 B3
Tryfil *Angl* 27 C5
Tudweiliog *Gwyn* 4 A4
Tuebrook *Mersey* 32 A2
Tunnel End *W Yorks* 42 B2
Tunshill *Gtr Man* 41 B7
Tunstall *Lancs* 59 F6
Tunstall *Stoke* 22 D3
Tunstead *Gtr Man* 42 D2
Tunstead Milton *Derby* 35 C7
Tupton *Derby* 25 A5
Turf Hill *Gtr Man* 41 B7
Turn *Lancs* 41 A5
Turnditch *Derby* 24 E3
Turner Green *Lancs* 46 D1
Turnerheath *Ches* 35 D5
Turnhurst *Stoke* 22 D3
Turton Bottoms *Blackb'n* 40 A3
Twemlow Green *Ches* 34 F2
Twiss Green *Warrington* 40 E2
Twiston *Lancs* 47 B5
Two Dales *Derby* 24 B3
Two Mills *Ches* 32 E2
Tŷ-gwyn *Powys* 10 D2
Ty-mawr *Angl* 27 B6
Ty-mawr *Denbs* 30 D1
Ty-nant *Conwy* 17 F7
Ty-nant *Denbs* 18 E2
Tycrwyn *Powys* 9 E7
Tyddyn Dai *Angl* 27 A5
Tyddyn Llewely *Gwyn* 5 B7
Tyddyn Sieffre *Gwyn* 6 F4
Tyldesley *Gtr Man* 40 D2
Ty'n Coed *Angl* 27 D6
Tyn-y-ffridd *Powys* 9 B7
Ty'n-y-groes *Conwy* 29 E5
Ty'n-y-maes *Gwyn* 15 B8
Tyn-y-maes *Powys* 9 C7
Tyn-y-Pistyll *Conwy* 17 E7
Tyn-y-Rhos *Shrops* 10 A2
Tynygongl *Angl* 27 C6
Tytherington *Ches* 35 D5
Tywyn *Conwy* 29 D5
Tywyn *Gwyn* 2 C2

U

Undercliffe *W Yorks* 48 D5
Underdale *Shrops* 11 F7
Underwood *Notts* 25 D7
Union Mills *I/Man* 80 D3
Unstone *Derby* 37 D7
Unstone Green *Derby* 37 D7
Unsworth *Gtr Man* 41 C5
Unthank *Cumb* 70 B2
Unthank *Cumb* 70 D3
Unthank *Cumb* 71 C7
Unthank *Derby* 37 D6
Unthank End *Cumb* 70 D4
Up Holland *Lancs* 39 D7
Upper Armley *W Yorks* 49 D7
Upper Astley *Shrops* 11 E7
Upper Batley *W Yorks* 49 E6
Upper Bangor *Gwyn* 27 E9
Upper Battlefield *Shrops* 11 E7
Upper Birchwood *Derby* 25 D6
Upper Borth *Ceredig'n* 2 E3
Upper Cotton *Staffs* 23 E7
Upper Cumberworth *W Yorks* 43 C6
Upper Denby *W Yorks* 43 C6
Upper Denton *Cumb* 76 C5
Upper Elkstone *Staffs* 23 C7
Upper Ellastone *Staffs* 23 F8
Upper End *Derby* 35 D8
Upper Green *W Yorks* 49 E7
Upper Hackney *Derby* 24 B3
Upper Hartshay *Derby* 25 D5
Upper Heaton *W Yorks* 43 A5
Upper Hengoed *Shrops* 10 B2
Upper Hopton *W Yorks* 43 A5
Upper Hopton *W Yorks* 43 A5
Upper Hoyland *S Yorks* 43 D9
Upper Hulme *Staffs* 23 B6
Upper Marsh *W Yorks* 48 C2
Upper Midhope *S Yorks* 43 E6
Upper Moor Side *W Yorks* 49 D6
Upper Newbold *Derby* 37 E7
Upper Padley *Derby* 36 D4
Upper Tean *Staffs* 23 G6
Upper Threapwood *Ches* 20 E1
Upper Thurnham *Lancs* 51 E8
Upper Town *Derby* 24 D2
Upper Town *Durham* 73 D9
Upper Town *W Yorks* 48 D3
Upper Whiston *S Yorks* 37 B9
Upperby *Cumb* 75 F8
Uppermill *Gtr Man* 42 C1
Upperthong *W Yorks* 42 C4
Upperthorpe *Derby* 37 C9
Uppertown *Derby* 24 A4
Upton *Ches* 32 F3
Upton *Cumb* 70 D1
Upton *Halton* 32 B4
Upton *Mersey* 31 B7
Upton Heath *Ches* 32 F3
Upton Magna *Shrops* 11 F8
Upton Rocks *Halton* 32 C5
Urmston *Gtr Man* 40 F4
Utkinton *Ches* 20 B3
Utley *W Yorks* 48 B3
Uwchmynydd *Gwyn* 4 C2

V

Vale *W Yorks* 47 E7
Valeswood *Shrops* 10 D4
Valley *Angl* 26 D2
Vickerstown *Cumb* 50 B2
Victoria *S Yorks* 43 C5
Victoria Park *Gtr Man* 41 E6
Vivod *Denbs* 18 F4
Vulcan Village *Mersey* 39 F8

W

Waberthwaite *Cumb* 56 B3
Waddicar *Mersey* 38 E4
Waddington *Lancs* 46 B3
Wade Hall *Lancs* 45 F7
Wadshelf *Derby* 37 E6
Wadsley *S Yorks* 37 A6
Wadsley Bridge *S Yorks* 37 A7
Waen *Denbs* 17 B7
Waen *Denbs* 18 A3
Waen *Flints* 31 E5
Waen *Powys* 10 E1
Waen Aberwheeler *Denbs* 30 F3
Waen-dymarch *Flints* 31 E5
Waen Fach *Powys* 9 E9
Waen Goleugoed *Denbs* 30 E3
Waen-pentir *Gwyn* 15 A7
Waen-wen *Gwyn* 27 F8
Waggersley *Staffs* 13 A7
Waingroves *Derby* 25 E6
Wainstalls *W Yorks* 48 E2
Waitby *Cumb* 66 E3
Wakefield *W Yorks* 49 E8
Walby *Cumb* 76 D1
Walcot *Telford* 11 F8
Walden *N Yorks* 61 D6
Walden Head *N Yorks* 61 D5
Wales Bar *S Yorks* 37 C9
Walford *Shrops* 11 D5
Walford Heath *Shrops* 11 E5
Walgherton *Ches* 21 E6
Walk Mill *Lancs* 47 D6
Walkden *Gtr Man* 40 D3
Walker Fold *Lancs* 46 B2
Walkley *S Yorks* 37 B6
Wall End *Cumb* 57 D5
Wall Hill *Gtr Man* 41 C8
Wallasey *Mersey* 31 A7
Wallbank *Lancs* 41 A6
Wallsuches *Gtr Man* 40 B2
Walmer Bridge *Lancs* 45 F6
Walmersley *Gtr Man* 40 B4
Walshaw *Gtr Man* 40 B4
Walton *Cumb* 76 D3
Walton *Derby* 37 E7
Walton *Mersey* 38 E4
Walton *Staffs* 13 B7
Walton *Telford* 12 E1
Walton *W Yorks* 43 A9
Walton-le-Dale *Lancs* 45 E8

Walton on the Hill *Staffs* 13 D9
Walton Summit *Lancs* 45 E8
Walwen *Flints* 30 D4
Walwen *Flints* 31 D6
Wampool *Cumb* 74 F4
Warbreck *Blackp'l* 44 C3
Warburton *Ches* 33 B8
Warburton Green *Gtr Man* 34 B2
Warburton Park *Gtr Man* 33 A9
Warcop *Cumb* 66 C2
Ward Green *S Yorks* 43 D8
Ward Green Cross *Lancs* 46 C1
Wardle *Ches* 21 C5
Wardle *Gtr Man* 41 A7
Wardley *Derby* 36 E3
Wardsend *Ches* 35 C5
Wargrave *Mersey* 39 F8
Warhill *Gtr Man* 42 E1
Warland *W Yorks* 47 F7
Warley Town *W Yorks* 48 E3
Warmbrook *Derby* 24 D3
Warmingham *Ches* 21 B7
Warren *Ches* 34 E4
Warren *S Yorks* 43 E9
Warren Mountain *Flints* 19 B7
Warrington *Warrington* 33 B7
Warslow *Staffs* 23 C7
Warton *Lancs* 44 C5
Warton *Lancs* 52 A1
Warton Bank *Lancs* 44 C5
Warwick *Cumb* 76 E2
Warwick Bridge *Cumb* 76 E2
Wasdale Head *Cumb* 63 E6
Wash *Derby* 35 C8
Washerwall *Staffs* 22 E4
Washfold *N Yorks* 67 F9
Washpit *W Yorks* 42 C4
Waskerley *Durham* 73 B9
Watchgate *Cumb* 58 A4
Watchhill *Cumb* 69 C6
Watchhill *Dumf/Gal* 78 C4
Watendlath *Cumb* 63 C8
Water *Lancs* 47 E5
Water Swallows *Derby* 35 D8
Water Yeat *Cumb* 57 C6
Waterbeck *Dumf/Gal* 74 A4
Waterend *Cumb* 62 B5
Waterfall *Staffs* 23 D7
Waterfoot *Lancs* 47 F5
Waterhead *Cumb* 64 F2
Waterhouses *Derby* 23 D7
Waterloo *Blackb'n* 46 E2
Waterloo *Derby* 25 B6
Waterloo *Gtr Man* 41 D7
Waterloo *Mersey* 38 E4
Waterloo *Powys* 9 D8
Waterloo *Shrops* 11 B7
Waterloo Park *Mersey* 38 E4
Waterloo Port *Gwyn* 15 B5
Watermillock *Cumb* 64 B3
Water's Nook *Gtr Man* 40 C2
Waters Upton *Telford* 12 E2
Watersheddings *Gtr Man* 41 C7
Waterside *Blackb'n* 46 F3
Waterside *Cumb* 69 B7
Waterslack *Lancs* 58 E3
Waterthorpe *S Yorks* 37 C8
Wath *Cumb* 65 E8
Wath *N Yorks* 55 B6
Wath Brow *Cumb* 62 D3
Watnall *Notts* 25 E8
Waun *Gwyn* 15 B7
Waunfawr *Gwyn* 15 C6
Waverbridge *Cumb* 69 B7
Waverton *Ches* 20 B2
Waverton *Cumb* 69 B7
Wavertree *Mersey* 32 B2
Waymills *Shrops* 20 F4
Ways Green *Ches* 21 A6
Weardley *W Yorks* 49 B7
Wearhead *Durham* 72 D5
Weasdale *Cumb* 66 E1
Weaste *Gtr Man* 41 E5
Weaverham *Ches* 33 E7
Weeping Cross *Staffs* 13 D8
Weeton *Lancs* 44 C4
Weeton *N Yorks* 49 A7
Weeton Camp *Lancs* 44 C4
Weetwood *W Yorks* 49 C7
Weir *Lancs* 47 E6
Weirbrook *Shrops* 10 D4
Weld Bank *Lancs* 39 A8
Well Bank *Lancs* 46 F4
Well Green *Gtr Man* 34 B2
Welldale *Dumf/Gal* 74 C3
Wellhouse *W Yorks* 42 B3
Wellington *Cumb* 62 F4
Wellington *Telford* 12 F3
Wellington Hill *W Yorks* 49 C8
Wells Green *Ches* 21 D6
Welsh End *Shrops* 11 A7
Welsh Frankton *Shrops* 10 B4
Welshampton *Shrops* 11 A5
Welton *Cumb* 70 C2
Wem *Shrops* 11 C7
Wennington *Lancs* 52 A4
Wensley *Derby* 24 B3
Wensley *N Yorks* 61 C7
Wepre *Flints* 31 F7
Wereton *Staffs* 22 D1
Wern *Gwyn* 6 A2
Wern *Powys* 10 D2
Wern *Powys* 10 F2
Wern *Shrops* 10 B2
Wern-gerhynt *Powys* 3 C8
Wern-y-gaer *Flints* 31 F6
Werneth *Gtr Man* 41 D7
Werneth Low *Gtr Man* 35 A6
Werrington *Staffs* 22 E4
Wervin *Ches* 32 E3
Wescoe *Cumb* 63 A9
Wesham *Lancs* 44 C5
Wessington *Derby* 25 C5
West Bank *Halton* 32 C4
West Blackdene *Durham* 72 D5
West Bowling *W Yorks* 48 D5
West Bradford *Lancs* 46 B3
West Bretton *W Yorks* 43 B7
West Burton *N Yorks* 61 C6
West Curthwaite *Cumb* 70 B1
West Derby *Mersey* 32 A3
West Didsbury *Gtr Man* 34 A3
West End *Cumb* 75 E6
West End *Lancs* 46 D3

West End *Lancs* 51 C7
West End *N Yorks* 55 B6
West End *W Yorks* 49 C6
West End *W Yorks* 49 E5
West Felton *Shrops* 10 C3
West Gorton *Gtr Man* 41 F6
West Hall *Cumb* 76 C4
West Hallam *Derby* 25 F6
West Handley *Derby* 37 D7
West Kirby *Mersey* 31 B6
West Marton *N Yorks* 54 E1
West Morton *W Yorks* 48 B3
West Park *Mersey* 39 E6
West Park *W Yorks* 49 C7
West Royd *W Yorks* 48 C5
West Scholes *W Yorks* 48 D3
West Stonesdale *N Yorks* 67 F5
West Vale *W Yorks* 48 F3
West Witton *N Yorks* 61 D6
Westbrook *Warrington* 33 A6
Westby *Lancs* 44 D4
Westend Town *Northum* 77 C8
Western Bank *Cumb* 69 B7
Western Downs *Staffs* 13 D8
Western Point *Halton* 32 C4
Westfield *Cumb* 68 F2
Westfield *S Yorks* 37 C8
Westfield *W Yorks* 49 B5
Westfield *W Yorks* 49 F6
Westgate *Durham* 73 D6
Westhead *Lancs* 39 C5
Westhorpe *Derby* 37 D9
Westhoughton *Gtr Man* 40 C2
Westhouse *N Yorks* 59 F7
Westhouses *Derby* 25 C6
Westlands *Staffs* 22 F2
Westleigh *Gtr Man* 40 D1
Westleigh *Gtr Man* 40 D2
Westlinton *Cumb* 75 D7
Westmoor End *Cumb* 68 D5
Westnewton *Cumb* 69 C5
Weston *Ches* 21 D7
Weston *Ches* 34 E4
Weston *Halton* 32 C5
Weston *N Yorks* 55 F7
Weston *Shrops* 11 C8
Weston Coyney *Stoke* 22 F4
Weston Heath *Shrops* 11 C8
Weston Heath *Shrops* 13 F5
Weston Jones *Staffs* 12 D5
Weston Lullingfields *Shrops* 11 D5
Weston Rhyn *Shrops* 10 A2
Weston Underwood *Derby* 24 F3
Westvale *Mersey* 38 E5
Westville *Notts* 25 E8
Westward *Cumb* 69 B8
Westwick *Durham* 67 C9
Westwood *Notts* 25 D7
Westwood Park *Gtr Man* 40 E4
Westy *Warrington* 33 B7
Wetheral *Cumb* 76 E2
Wetheral Plain *Cumb* 76 E2
Wetley Rocks *Staffs* 22 E5
Wetreins Green *Ches* 20 D1
Wettenhall *Ches* 21 B5
Wetton *Staffs* 23 C8
Wetwood *Staffs* 13 B5
Whale *Cumb* 65 B5
Whaley Bridge *Derby* 35 C7
Whalley *Lancs* 46 C3
Whalley Banks *Lancs* 46 C3
Whalley Range *Gtr Man* 41 F5
Whalleys *Mersey* 39 C5
Wharf *N Yorks* 53 B7
Wharles *Lancs* 44 C5
Wharncliffe Side *S Yorks* 43 F7
Wharton *Ches* 33 F8
Wharton Green *Ches* 33 F7
Whasset *Cumb* 58 D4
Whatstandwell *Derby* 24 D4
Whaw *N Yorks* 67 F7
Wheatcroft *Derby* 25 C5
Wheatley *W Yorks* 48 E3
Wheatley Hill *W Yorks* 48 D3
Wheatley Lane *Lancs* 47 C5
Wheaton Aston *Staffs* 13 F6
Wheelock *Ches* 21 C8
Wheelock Heath *Ches* 21 C8
Wheelton *Lancs* 45 F9
Whelley *Gtr Man* 39 C8
Whelpo *Cumb* 69 D9
Whelprigg *Cumb* 59 D6
Whelston *Flints* 31 D6
Wheston *Derby* 36 D2
Whicham *Cumb* 56 D3
Whin Lane End *Lancs* 44 B4
Whinmoor *W Yorks* 49 C9
Whinny Heights *Blackb'n* 46 E2
Whins Wood *W Yorks* 48 C3
Whirley Grove *Ches* 34 D4
Whirlow *S Yorks* 37 C6
Whirlow Brook *S Yorks* 37 C6
Whisterfield *Ches* 34 D4
Whiston *Mersey* 32 A4
Whiston *S Yorks* 37 B9
Whiston *Staffs* 13 F7
Whiston *Staffs* 23 E6
Whiston Cross *Mersey* 32 A4
Whitbeck *Cumb* 56 D3
Whitby *Ches* 32 D2
Whitbyheath *Ches* 32 E2
Whitchurch *Shrops* 21 F5
Whitchurch Heath *Shrops* 21 F5
White Gate *Gtr Man* 41 D6
White Kirkley *Durham* 73 D8
White Lee *W Yorks* 49 E6
White Lund *Lancs* 51 C7
White Moor *Derby* 25 E5
White Moss *Cumb* 76 D2
White Stake *Lancs* 45 E7
Whitebirk *Blackb'n* 46 E3
Whitechapel *Lancs* 45 B8
Whiteclosegate *Cumb* 75 E8
Whitecote *W Yorks* 49 C6
Whitecross *Staffs* 13 D7
Whitefield *Gtr Man* 41 C5
Whitefield Lane End *Mersey* 32 B4
Whitegate *Ches* 33 F7
Whitehall *Lancs* 46 F2
Whitehaven *Cumb* 62 C2
Whitehaven *Shrops* 10 D2
Whitehough *Derby* 35 C7
Whiteley Green *Ches* 35 D5

Whitemoor *Nott'ham* 25 F8
Whitewell *Lancs* 52 F5
Whitewell Bottom *Lancs* 47 F5
Whitfield *Northum* 77 E8
Whitfield *Stoke* 22 D2
Whitford *Flints* 30 D4
Whitgreave *Staffs* 13 C7
Whitkirk *W Yorks* 49 D9
Whitle *Derby* 35 B6
Whitley *Gtr Man* 39 C8
Whitley Heath *Staffs* 13 C6
Whitley Lower *W Yorks* 43 A6
Whitley Reed *Ches* 33 C8
Whitmore *Staffs* 22 F2
Whitmore Heath *Staffs* 22 F1
Whitrigg *Cumb* 69 D7
Whitrigg *Cumb* 74 E4
Whittaker *Gtr Man* 41 A7
Whittington *Lancs* 59 E6
Whittington *Shrops* 10 B3
Whittington Moor *Derby* 37 E7
Whittle Hill *Gtr Man* 41 C5
Whittle-le-Woods *Lancs* 45 F8
Whittlestone Head *Blackb'n* 40 A3
Whitworth *Lancs* 41 A6
Whixall *Shrops* 11 B7
Wibsey *W Yorks* 48 D4
Widdop *W Yorks* 47 D7
Widnes *Halton* 32 C5
Wig *Powys* 9 F6
Wigan *Gtr Man* 39 C8
Wigglesworth *N Yorks* 53 D8
Wiggonby *Cumb* 69 A8
Wigton *Cumb* 69 B8
Wike *W Yorks* 49 B8
Wilberlee *W Yorks* 42 B3
Wilcott *Shrops* 11 E5
Wildboarclough *Ches* 35 F6
Wilderspool *Warrington* 33 B7
Wildwood *Staffs* 13 D8
Wilkesley *Ches* 21 F5
Willacy Lane End *Lancs* 45 C6
Willaston *Ches* 31 D8
Willaston *Ches* 21 C7
Willaston *Shrops* 12 A1
Williamthorpe *Derby* 25 A6
Willington Corner *Ches* 33 F5
Willoughbridge *Staffs* 21 F7
Willow Green *Ches* 33 D7
Willow Holme *Cumb* 75 E7
Willows *Gtr Man* 40 C3
Wilmslow *Ches* 34 C3
Wilmslow Park *Ches* 34 C4
Wilpshire *Lancs* 46 D2
Wilsden *W Yorks* 48 C3
Wilsill *N Yorks* 55 C7
Wilthorpe *S Yorks* 43 C8
Wilton *Cumb* 62 D3
Wincham *Ches* 33 D8
Wincle *Ches* 22 A5
Wincobank *S Yorks* 37 A7
Winder *Cumb* 62 C3
Windermere *Cumb* 58 A2
Windhill *W Yorks* 48 C5
Windle Mill *Ches* 34 F4
Windlehurst *Gtr Man* 35 B6
Windley *Derby* 24 E4
Windmill *Derby* 36 D3
Windmill Hill *Halton* 32 D3
Windy Arbor *Mersey* 32 B4
Windy Hill *Wrex* 19 D7
Windyharbour *Ches* 34 E3
Winewall *Lancs* 47 C7
Wingates *Gtr Man* 40 C2
Wingerworth *Derby* 37 E7
Wingfield Park *Derby* 25 D5
Winkhill *Staffs* 23 D7
Winksley *N Yorks* 55 B8
Winmarleigh *Lancs* 51 F8
Winnington *Ches* 33 E7
Winnothdale *Staffs* 23 F6
Winscales *Cumb* 62 A3
Winsford *Ches* 21 A6
Winsick *Derby* 37 F8
Winskill *Cumb* 71 E6
Winsley *N Yorks* 55 C8
Winstanley *Gtr Man* 39 D8
Winster *Cumb* 58 B2
Winster *Derby* 24 B2
Winterburn *N Yorks* 54 D2
Winterley *Ches* 21 C7
Winton *Cumb* 66 D3
Winton *Gtr Man* 40 E4
Winwick *Warrington* 33 A7
Winwick Quay *Warrington* 33 A6
Wirksworth *Derby* 24 D3
Wirksworth Moor *Derby* 24 D3
Wirswall *Ches* 20 F3
Wistanswick *Shrops* 12 C3
Wistaston *Ches* 21 D6
Wistaston Green *Ches* 21 D6
Wiswell *Lancs* 46 C3
Witherslack *Cumb* 58 D3
Withington *Gtr Man* 34 A4
Withington *Shrops* 11 F8
Withington Green *Ches* 34 E3
Withnell *Lancs* 46 F1
Withnell Fold *Lancs* 45 F9
Wixhill *Shrops* 11 C8
Wollaston *Shrops* 10 F3
Wolsingham *Durham* 73 D9
Wolstanton *Staffs* 22 E2
Wolstenholme *Gtr Man* 41 B6
Wolsty *Cumb* 68 A5
Wolverham *Ches* 32 D3
Wolverley *Shrops* 11 B6
Wood Eaton *Staffs* 13 E6
Wood End *Gtr Man* 41 B7
Wood Kirk *W Yorks* 49 E7
Wood Lane *Staffs* 22 D2
Wood Lanes *Ches* 35 C5
Wood Linkin *Derby* 25 E6
Wood Nook *W Yorks* 43 B8
Wood Road *Gtr Man* 40 B4
Woodale *N Yorks* 61 E6
Woodchurch *Mersey* 31 B7
Woodend *Ches* 35 B6
Woodend *Cumb* 56 A4
Woodend *Cumb* 62 D3
Woodend *Cumb* 69 F7
Woodend *Halton* 32 B4
Woodend *Notts* 25 C7
Woodford *Gtr Man* 34 C4
Woodgate Hill *Gtr Man* 41 B5

Woodhall *N Yorks* 61 B5
Woodhall Hills *W Yorks* 49 C6
Woodhey *Gtr Man* 40 A4
Woodhey *Mersey* 31 B8
Woodhey Green *Ches* 20 D4
Woodhouse *Cumb* 62 C2
Woodhouse *S Yorks* 37 B8
Woodhouse *W Yorks* 48 B3
Woodhouse *W Yorks* 49 D7
Woodhouse *W Yorks* 49 C7
Woodhouse Mill *S Yorks* 37 B8
Woodhouse Park *Gtr Man* 34 B3
Woodhouselees *Dumf/Gal* 75 A7
Woodhouses *Ches* 32 D5
Woodhouses *Cumb* 70 A1
Woodhouses *Gtr Man* 34 A2
Woodhouses *Gtr Man* 41 C6
Woodland *Cumb* 57 C5
Woodland *Durham* 67 A9
Woodlands *Dumf/Gal* 74 A1
Woodlands *W Yorks* 48 E8
Woodlane *Shrops* 13 C5
Woodlesford *W Yorks* 49 F9
Woodley *Gtr Man* 35 A5
Woodnook *Lancs* 46 E4
Woodplumpton *Lancs* 45 C7
Woodrow *Cumb* 69 B7
Woods End *Gtr Man* 40 E4
Woods Moor *Gtr Man* 35 B5
Woodseaves *Shrops* 12 B3
Woodseaves *Staffs* 13 C5
Woodsfold *Lancs* 45 C6
Woodside *Ches* 32 E5
Woodside *Cumb* 68 E3
Woodside *Derby* 37 E9
Woodside *W Yorks* 48 E4
Woodthorpe *Derby* 37 E9
Woodvale *Mersey* 38 B3
Woodwall Green *Staffs* 13 B5
Woodworth Green *Ches* 20 C4
Wooldale *W Yorks* 42 C5
Wooley *Northum* 72 A4
Woolfall Heath *Mersey* 32 A3
Woolfold *Gtr Man* 40 B4
Woolgreaves *W Yorks* 43 A8
Woolley *Derby* 25 B5
Woolley *W Yorks* 43 B8
Woolston *Shrops* 10 D3
Woolston *Warrington* 33 B7
Woolton *Mersey* 32 B3
Woore *Shrops* 21 F7
Wootton *Shrops* 10 C3
Wootton *Staffs* 23 E8
Workington *Cumb* 68 F2
Worleston *Ches* 21 C6
Wormhill *Derby* 36 E2
Worrall *S Yorks* 37 A6
Worsbrough *S Yorks* 43 D9
Worsbrough Bridge *S Yorks* 43 D9
Worsbrough Common *S Yorks* 43 C8
Worsley *Gtr Man* 40 D3
Worsley Hall *Gtr Man* 39 C8
Worsley Mesnes *Gtr Man* 39 D8
Worsthorne *Lancs* 47 D6
Worston *Lancs* 46 B4
Worthenbury *Wrex* 20 E1
Wortley *S Yorks* 43 E8
Wortley *W Yorks* 49 D7
Worton *N Yorks* 61 B5
Wray *Lancs* 52 B4
Wrayton *Lancs* 52 A4
Wrea Green *Lancs* 44 D5
Wreaks End *Cumb* 57 C5
Wreay *Cumb* 64 B3
Wreay *Cumb* 70 B3
Wrenbury *Ches* 20 E4
Wrenthorpe *W Yorks* 49 E8
Wrexham *Wrex* 19 D7
Wrexham Industrial Estate *Wrex* 19 E8
Wrightington Bar *Lancs* 39 B7
Wrinehill *Staffs* 21 E8
Wrockwardine *Telford* 12 F2
Wrose *W Yorks* 48 C5
Wyaston *Derby* 24 F1
Wybunbury *Ches* 21 E6
Wycoller *Lancs* 47 C7
Wyke *W Yorks* 48 E5
Wykey *Shrops* 10 D4
Wythburn *Cumb* 64 C1
Wythenshawe *Gtr Man* 34 B3
Wythop *Cumb* 69 F6

Y

Y Fali *Angl* 26 D2
Y Felinheli *Gwyn* 27 F7
Y Ffôr *Gwyn* 5 A7
Y-Ffrith *Denbs* 30 C2
Yanwath *Cumb* 71 F5
Yarlside *Cumb* 50 B3
Yarnfield *Staffs* 13 B7
Yarrow *Northum* 77 F7
Yatehouse Green *Ches* 33 F9
Yeadon *W Yorks* 49 C6
Yealand Conyers *Lancs* 58 F3
Yealand Redmayne *Lancs* 58 E4
Yealand Storrs *Lancs* 58 E3
Yearngill *Cumb* 69 C5
Yeaton *Shrops* 11 E5
Yeaveley *Derby* 24 F1
Ynys *Gwyn* 5 A7
Ynys *Gwyn* 6 A3
Ynys-hir *Ceredig'n* 2 D4
Ynys Tachwedd *Ceredig'n* 2 E3
Ynyslas *Ceredig'n* 2 E3
Ynysmaengwyn *Gwyn* 2 C2
Yockenthwaite *N Yorks* 60 E4
York *Lancs* 46 D3
Yorton *Shrops* 11 D7
Yorton Heath *Shrops* 11 D7
Youlgreave *Derby* 24 B2
Ysbyty Ifan *Conwy* 16 E4
Ysceifiog *Flints* 31 E5
Ysgeibion *Denbs* 18 C2
Ysgubor-y-coed *Ceredig'n* 2 D4